# DEWEY DECIMAL CLASSIFICATION:

*PRINCIPLES AND APPLICATION*

LOIS MAI CHAN

JOAN S. MITCHELL

# DEWEY DECIMAL CLASSIFICATION:

*PRINCIPLES*
*AND*
*APPLICATION*

THIRD EDITION

OCLC
OCLC Online Computer Library Center, Inc.
Dublin, Ohio
2003

Library of Congress Cataloging-in-Publication Data

Chan, Lois Mai
    Dewey decimal classification: principles and application / Lois Mai Chan, Joan S. Mitchell. -- 3rd ed.
        p.  cm.
    Rev. ed. of: Dewey Decimal Classification: a practical guide / Lois Mai Chan...[et al.]. 2nd ed. 1996.
    Includes bibliographical references and index.
    ISBN: 0910608-72-5 (alk. paper)
    1. Classification, Dewey decimal. I. Mitchell, Joan S. II. Title.
Z696.D7C48  2003
025.4'31—dc22                                  2003541780
                                                    CIP

OCLC Online Computer Library Center, Inc.
6565 Frantz Road
Dublin, OH 43017-3395 USA
www.oclc.org/dewey

The paper used in this publication meets the requirements of ANSI/NISO Z39.48-1992 (Permanence of Paper).

ISBN: 0-910608-72-5

 Recycled paper

# CONTENTS

## Chapter 4
## Subject Analysis and Classification of a Document

## Chapter 5
## Using the Manual

## Chapter 6
## Using the Relative Index

## Chapter 7
## Synthesis of Class Numbers or Practical Number Building

## Chapter 8
## Table 1: Standard Subdivisions

## Chapter 9
## Table 2: Geographic Areas, Historical Periods, Persons

## Chapter 10
## Use of Table 3 with Literature and Other Classes

## Chapter 11
## Table 4: Subdivisions of Individual Languages
## and Table 6: Languages

# PREFACE

*Dewey Decimal Classification: Principles and Application* introduces the reader to the principles underlying the Dewey Decimal Classification (DDC), and to the application of these principles in classifying and arranging collections of information resources. The two earlier editions of this work were published under the title *Dewey Decimal Classification: A Practical Guide.* The first draft of the first edition of this book began as a collaborative effort between Mohinder P. Satija and John P. Comaromi. After John Comaromi died in 1991, Lois Mai Chan completed the last four chapters and did the final rewriting and editing of the entire text. Chan and Joan S. Mitchell revised, updated, and expanded the second and third editions to reflect the changes in the corresponding editions of the DDC.

*Dewey Decimal Classification: Principles and Application* is aimed at both beginning classifiers and experienced Dewey users. It is designed to accompany *Dewey Decimal Classification and Relative Index,* Edition 22; all chapters and exercises have been updated to reflect this latest edition. Some background material that appeared in the Manual in previous editions of the DDC (prior to Edition 22) has been moved from the DDC proper to this book. Although the excerpts from the schedules, tables, Relative Index, and Manual are taken from the print version of Edition 22, the discussion and examples are relevant for users of the print and electronic versions.

The third edition begins with a brief history of the DDC, followed by a discussion of its structural principles, notation, and uses. Practical classification, which includes the analysis of subject content and assignment of class numbers, is also examined. The essential aim of this book is to explain how to apply the DDC schedules; that is, how to locate and assign appropriate class numbers, and synthesize class numbers. Because notational synthesis is at the heart of applying the DDC, a great deal of emphasis is placed on building numbers with notation from the schedules and tables.

The first three chapters cover the basic tenets of the Dewey Decimal Classification. Chapter 4 discusses subject analysis in general and assigning class numbers from the DDC in particular. Chapter 5 describes the Manual. Chapter 6 explains the structure of the Relative Index and its application. Beginning with Chapter 7, the process of number building is discussed in detail with step-by-step explanations illustrated with multiple examples. Chapter 7 explains and demonstrates number building with notation from the schedules. Chapters 8–12 cover the use of Tables 1–6. Chapter 13 contains examples and explanations for building complex numbers from multiple sources within the schedules and tables. Each of the chapters dealing with the practical application of the DDC includes exercises designed to reinforce the examples and explanations through practice. The answers are given in the appendix. For the convenience of users, the glossary includes the terms and definitions found in the glossary in volume 1 of Edition 22 plus additional terms used in this book.

The authors wish to acknowledge the following persons for reading the manuscript and making many invaluable suggestions on the text and exercises: Julianne Beall, Giles Martin, Winton E. Matthews, Jr., and Gregory R. New, assistant editors of the Dewey Decimal Classification; and Eliza B. Sproat, senior Dewey electronic products manager. The authors are also grateful to Judith Kramer Greene for editing the book; Theodora Hodges for proofreading the manuscript and preparing the index; Patricia Waldvogel Gayle and Cara Sparks for proofreading; and Libbie Crawford for overseeing production of the book.

## Chapter 1

# INTRODUCTION TO THE DEWEY DECIMAL CLASSIFICATION

## GENERAL INTRODUCTION

The objective of this chapter is to provide a general introduction to the Dewey Decimal Classification (DDC). It introduces the reader to the life of Melvil Dewey, who devised the Classification, and gives a brief account of the history of the DDC and its various editions. It also describes the overall plan of the Classification itself and explains the DDC notation.

Classification, defined as a logical system for the arrangement of knowledge, has played a vital role throughout the history of library and information services and management. Books and other library materials are arranged in a logical subject sequence in a library in order to facilitate browsing and retrieval. In online public access catalogs (OPACs), the classified approach has been found to be a fruitful method in meeting information needs.[1] Class numbers, besides indicating shelf order, are also useful access points to MARC records. Furthermore, classification has often been used as a tool for managing collections, for assisting in the creation of branch libraries, and for generating or arranging items in subject- or discipline-specific bibliographies.[2]

In the electronic environment, classification has been used increasingly as a means of organizing and accessing information.[3] With the rapid growth of networked resources, the enormous amount of information on the World Wide Web cried out for organization, and many web resource providers turned to classification for a solution. The early web categorization schemes resembled broad classification schemes, and most were lacking the rigorous hierarchical structure and careful conceptual organization found in established classification systems. Furthermore, many libraries, which began with a small set of electronic resources, adopted broad subject categorization when the size of their electronic resources became unwieldy.[4] Some of these subject schemes were developed from scratch by their home libraries; others used existing classification schemes. For example, the BUBL Information Service uses the DDC and CyberStacks uses the Library of Congress Classification (LCC).

---

[1] Karen Markey and Anh N. Demeyer, *Dewey Decimal Classification Online Project: Evaluation of a Library Schedule and Index Integrated into the Subject Searching Capabilities of an Online Catalog: Final Report to the Council on Library Resources* (Dublin, OH: OCLC Online Computer Library Center, 1986). Report No. OCLC/OPR/RR-86/1.

[2] Lois Mai Chan, "Exploiting LCSH, LCC, and DDC to Retrieve Networked Resources: Issues and Challenges," in *Proceedings of the Bicentennial Conference on Bibliographic Control for the New Millennium: Confronting the Challenges of Networked Resources and the Web, Washington, D.C., November 15–17, 2000,* sponsored by the Library of Congress Cataloging Directorate, edited by Ann M. Sandberg-Fox (Washington, DC: Library of Congress, Cataloging Distribution Service, 2001), pp. 159–78.

[3] Diane Vizine-Goetz, "Online Classification: Implications for Classifying and Document[-like Object] Retrieval," in *Knowledge Organization and Change: Proceedings of the Fourth International ISKO Conference, 15–18 July 1996, Washington, DC, USA,* organized by the Office of the Director for Public Service Collections, Library of Congress [and] the ISKO General Secretariat, and OCLC Forest Press, edited by Rebecca Green (Frankfurt/Main: Indeks Verlag, 1996), pp. 249–53.

[4] Thomas J. Waldhart, Joseph B. Miller, and Lois Mai Chan, "Provision of Local Assisted Access to Selected Internet Information Resources by ARL Academic Libraries," *Journal of Academic Librarianship* 26, no. 2 (2000): 100–109.

Over the years, in the United States and other countries, a number of general classification schemes have been devised, developed, and kept relatively up to date. Among these, the DDC is the most widely used, studied, and discussed classification system in the world.

The DDC was originally designed in 1873 for arranging the books and catalog of the library of Amherst College (Amherst, Massachusetts). It was published in 1876 for wider use in other libraries. The word "Dewey" in its current name is a reference to Melvil Dewey (1851–1931), who devised the Classification. The second word, "Decimal," refers to the base-ten notation that is used to denote and relate subjects. It employs Arabic numerals treated like decimal fractions, hence the name of the classification: Dewey Decimal Classification.

## MELVIL DEWEY

Dewey's full name was originally Melville Louis Kossuth Dewey; he was born on December 10, 1851 (the tenth day of the tenth month, according to the early Roman republican calendar), an apt birthday for the creator of a *decimal* classification. His family was poor and resided in a small town in upper New York State. Later, in accordance with his quest for economy in every sphere of life, he cut short his given name to Melvil, dropped his middle names and, for a brief period of time, even spelled his family name as Dui. He invented his system when he was twenty-one and was working as a student-assistant in the library of Amherst College in Amherst, Massachusetts.

Most of the classification schemes used in Dewey's day consisted of broad categories with the books in each category numbered sequentially as they were acquired. The category marks and numbers represented fixed places on library shelves—an arrangement that is now known as a "fixed location system." Thus, whenever a library's collection or a category within its collection grew beyond the space allotted to it, all the books had to be reclassified—at considerable expense. Dewey asked himself: Why not classify a book once and for all? Why not give a book a notation that is true from shelf to shelf, from range to range, and from building to building? With these questions in mind he set out to seek a solution. He studied writers on library economy (which in those days meant the administration and management of the services of libraries), and visited many libraries.[5] In retrospect, Dewey recounted his thoughts in an essay published in 1920, using his characteristic phonetic spelling:

> In visiting over 50 libraries, I was astounded to find the lack of efficiency, and waste of time and money in constant recataloging and reclassifying made necessary by the almost universally used fixt system where a book was numberd according to the particular room, tier, and shelf where it chanced to stand on that day, insted of by class, division and section to which it belonged yesterday, today and forever. Then there was the extravagant duplication of work in examining a new book for classification and cataloging by each of a 1000 libraries insted of doing this once for all at some central point.[6]

---

[5] "Preface," in Melvil Dewey, *A Classification and Subject Index for Cataloguing and Arranging the Books and Pamphlets of a Library* (Amherst, MA: Printed by the Case, Lockwood & Brainard Co., 1876). Reprinted as *Dewey Decimal Classification, Centennial 1876–1976*, by Forest Press Division, Lake Placid Education Foundation (Kingsport, TN: Kingsport Press, 1976), p. 3.

[6] Melvil Dewey, "Decimal Classification Beginnings," *Library Journal* 45 (Feb. 15, 1920): 151.

Dewey thought about the problem night and day. Then, as the story goes, one morning in May 1873, when he was sitting in the Amherst Chapel attending to religious obligations, an idea flashed across his mind that put the problem to rest:

> After months of study, one Sunday during a long sermon by Pres. Stearns, while I lookt stedfastly at him without hearing a word, my mind absorbed in the vital problem, the solution flasht over me so that I jumpt in my seat and came very near shouting "Eureka"! It was to get absolute simplicity by using the simplest known symbols, the arabic numerals as decimals, with the ordinary significance of nought, to number a classification of all human knowledge in print; . . .[7]

In other words, Dewey decided to use decimal numbers to denote the *subjects* of books, rejecting ordinal integers that represented positions in space (e.g., 1, 2, 3, 4, . . . representing the first, second, third, and fourth books acquired by a library in a particular category). Dewey's invention of *relative* location made it possible for growth without having to renumber books because he numbered books according to their intellectual content, not according to their physical location—the latter changes, the former never does.

For the intellectual base for his system, Dewey divided the world of knowledge into ten main classes, each class into ten divisions, and each division into ten sections, and on and on until a point was reached where further branching would produce subjects of such specificity that no works were likely to be written upon them. The universe of knowledge was thus mapped in a hierarchy from the broadest subjects to the narrowest. For notation, or the numbering system used in a classification, Dewey employed Arabic numerals 0 to 9 on each level of the hierarchy. For example, 3 represents social sciences, 34 represents law, 341 law of nations, 3416 law of war, and so forth. Each additional digit represents the subject in greater detail. Note that each number behaves like a decimal fraction that provides linear order for the subjects of the entire library—that is, the numbers above are actually .3, .34, .341, .3416. It was a simple and revolutionary idea.

On May 8, 1873, Dewey submitted the plan to the library committee of Amherst College and obtained approval to apply his idea in organizing both the library collection and the classified subject catalog. His work created a revolution in library science and set in motion a new era of librarianship. Melvil Dewey is deservedly called the father of modern librarianship.

Throughout his career, Dewey focused his energy and intellect on transforming librarianship from a vocation to a modern profession. He helped establish the American Library Association (ALA) in 1876; he was secretary of ALA from 1876 to 1890 and president during the 1890/1891 and 1892/1893 terms. He co-founded and edited *Library Journal*. He was a promoter of library standardization and formed a company to market library supplies, a company that eventually became the Library Bureau. He was also a pioneer in library education. In 1883, Dewey became the librarian of Columbia College (now Columbia University) in New York City, and while there he founded the first ever library school in the United States, which opened on January 1, 1887. Two years later, because of policy disagreements with Columbia's trustees about the school, Dewey was forced to leave Columbia.[8] Soon afterwards, in December 1889, he became the director of

---

[7] Dewey, "Decimal Classification Beginnings," p. 152.

[8] John P. Comaromi, *The Eighteen Editions of the Dewey Decimal Classification* (Albany, NY: Forest Press, 1976), p. 2.

the New York State Library at Albany, retiring from that position in 1906. His range of knowledge and work was wide and varied. Besides librarianship, he also took keen interest in coeducation, metrics, and simplified spelling; in everything he did, he was a reformer and crusader who inspired others to join in his work.

Dewey died from a stroke on December 16, 1931. He remains unsurpassed in librarianship for his ingenuity and versatility, for his vision, and for bringing grand library projects to successful conclusion and fruition. Today, however, Dewey is most widely known for the classification system that bears his name.

## HISTORY OF THE DEWEY DECIMAL CLASSIFICATION

The Dewey system, published anonymously in 1876 in Amherst, Massachusetts, was entitled *A Classification and Subject Index for Cataloguing and Arranging the Books and Pamphlets of a Library*. It was a pamphlet of forty-four pages, and, as its name implies, was designed primarily as a practical scheme for arranging library books. The Dewey Decimal Classification, the system that began with that pamphlet, still serves this function in tens of thousands of libraries throughout the world more than a century after its first publication. In addition, as noted earlier, it is also used as a tool for knowledge management in the electronic environment.

The second edition of the Classification (thoroughly revised and enormously expanded) was published in 1885. In many respects, the second edition may be considered one of the most important editions because it established the forms and policies that were to remain in force for the next sixty-five years.

Another major event in the history of the Dewey Decimal Classification occurred in the late 1890s. The newly founded (September 1895) International Institute of Bibliography, later called the International Federation for Information and Documentation, requested and received permission from Dewey to translate and adapt the DDC to serve as the organizational base for preparing a universal bibliography. The European effort eventually resulted in a considerably modified classification now called the Universal Decimal Classification. It was first published in 1905 in French, but since then has appeared in several dozen languages and in various levels of development: full, medium, and abridged. It is widely used in Europe, Africa, and South America.

Until his death in 1931, Dewey worked with his editors (Walter S. Biscoe, Evelyn May Seymour, and Dorkas Fellows), overseeing their efforts in expanding and developing the Classification. The 13th edition (1932), published the year after Dewey's death, was designated the Memorial Edition, and was the first edition to bear his name in the title.

The 14th edition (1942) was much enlarged and somewhat unwieldy. It was criticized by many librarians who asserted that most of its growth was disproportionate and imbalanced.[9] To rectify this lopsided growth, the 15th edition, known as the "Standard Edition," displayed all fields of knowledge evenly but in skeletal detail, a reduction which made it one-tenth the intellectual (numerical) size of its predecessor. This meant that only libraries of 200,000 volumes or fewer could be served by it. As a result, the Standard Edition was an almost complete failure and, ironically, was not accepted by the profession that had called for it and that had participated in its planning.

---

[9] Comaromi, *Eighteen Editions*, pp. 359–60, 374.

The very survival of the system was now at stake. The 16th edition (1958) was produced with support from the Library of Congress under the able editorial direction of Benjamin A. Custer. Custer gave the Classification a new lease on life by modernizing it and establishing a diplomatic balance between tradition and change. Edition 17 (1965) was revolutionary in many respects, including its emphasis on subject relationships and on classification by discipline, a new area table, and especially its new index. The index represented a drastic reduction from that of Edition 16, containing far fewer entries and many more cross references. However, the index was severely criticized for these changes,[10] and was eventually replaced at no cost by a new one based on the Edition 16 pattern.

With Edition 18 (1971), the first edition to be produced in three volumes, the DDC made a giant step towards a faceted approach. Five new tables were added, providing increased possibilities for number building. Edition 19 (1979) was the last edition published under the direction of Custer. Edition 20 (1989), in four volumes, was supervised by John P. Comaromi, who was editor from 1980 to 1991. Edition 20 was the first to be produced by an online editorial support system. The database created by this system could be used to produce future editions and a variety of products. Edition 21 was begun under the editorial direction of John P. Comaromi. After his death in 1991, Joan S. Mitchell assumed the position of editor and completed the edition. Edition 21 was published in 1996, and Edition 22 in 2003, both under Mitchell's direction. Edition 22 was the first edition of the DDC produced wholly in the context of the web environment. In this environment, the DDC can be updated continuously, and the updates can be communicated regularly to DDC users. The web has also facilitated timely cooperation with DDC's international user base.

Edition 22 contains many new numbers and topics. These range from new geographic provisions, e.g., the updating of administrative regions in Quebec, to new numbers for emerging topics in fields such as computer science and engineering, sociology, medicine, and history. Many new built-number entries and additional terms have been added to the Relative Index to cover sought topics and provide a wider base of entry vocabulary.

Two changes in Edition 22 are particularly worthy of note: the removal of Table 7 and the streamlining of the Manual. These changes were motivated by a desire to promote classifier efficiency. Details of these changes will be given in later chapters of this book.

## Development of the Classification

There are two aspects of working with a classification system: one is to provide appropriate class numbers for the classification of books and other materials; the other is to ensure that its schedules reflect the current state of knowledge. The former is known as "applying" the system. The latter process is referred to as "developing" the system. While both processes are important, this chapter will focus on developing the system. Such work entails both ongoing revision and major revision, as when a whole main class or major subclass is reworked. Revising Dewey is a lengthy, systematic, and democratic process that pays heed to user needs and new advances in classification and knowledge.

The development of the Dewey Decimal Classification, which is owned by OCLC Online Computer Library Center, Inc., is carried out in the Dewey editorial office at the Library of

---

[10] Frances Hinton [Review of the Dewey Decimal Classification], *Library Resources & Technical Services* 10 (Summer 1966): 393–402.

Congress in Washington, D.C. The Dewey editorial office is physically located in the Decimal Classification Division, which is also the home of the Dewey subject specialists. The subject specialists apply DDC numbers to cataloging records distributed by the Library of Congress. They have done this continuously since 1930, and, in recent years have applied over 110,000 numbers annually to works catalogued by the Library of Congress. The Dewey editors are therefore in close contact with the people who use the DDC on a daily basis. By working closely with the subject specialists, the editors can detect trends in the current literature early on and incorporate these trends into the schedules and tables.

The DDC is revised and developed by the editor and four assistant editors on an ongoing basis. The process of developing a schedule includes researching the subject area; discussing problems and potential changes with the classification specialists; looking at the published literature and other forms of information resources for literary warrant; and conferring with subject experts. The editors must also consider the ripple effect of revisions on the classification system as a whole and the impact of proposed changes on users. The editors depend on the Library of Congress online catalog and OCLC's WorldCat for guidance on literary warrant and use of the Classification. Terminology for captions and indexing terms is gleaned from the current literature, *Library of Congress Subject Headings (LCSH)*, thesauri, and reference sources. The resulting draft schedule is reviewed by the editors and then sent to the Decimal Classification Editorial Policy Committee (EPC) for review and recommended action.

The EPC is a ten-member international board whose main function is to advise the editors on matters relating to changes, innovations, and the general development of the Classification. EPC is the advocate group for DDC users; its members represent national, public, special, and academic libraries, and schools of library and information science. Current EPC members come from Australia, Canada, the United Kingdom, and the United States.

The development and review process is more elaborate for a major revision. EPC evaluates the initial draft for outside review. Various review committees and individual experts then study the draft and submit formal reports to the EPC. The comments of the review committees are considered carefully and may result in a revised draft for further review by the EPC.

## Publication of the DDC

**Formats**: Until 1993, the DDC was published in a print format only. Since then, it has been issued in electronic forms as well.

**Versions:** Over its history, the DDC has appeared in two versions, full and abridged. The current full edition, Edition 22, was published in 2003. Abridged Edition 14 is planned for publication in 2004. Although abridged editions are intended for small libraries that are unlikely to grow significantly, an abridged edition can easily accommodate collections of up to 20,000 volumes.

**Electronic products:** Beginning in 1993, the DDC became available in a DOS version called Electronic Dewey. The entire schedules, tables, Relative Index, and Manual of DDC 20 were stored on a CD-ROM. Electronic Dewey also included up to five frequently used Library of Congress subject headings linked to each DDC number and a sample bibliographic record for the most frequently occurring subject heading.

Dewey for Windows, a Microsoft Windows®-based version of Electronic Dewey, was released at the same time as the publication of Edition 21. Dewey for Windows was based on the Edition 21 database and included the same features as the DOS version along with several enhancements. From 1996 through 2001, Dewey for Windows was issued annually. In addition to statistically mapped Library of Congress subject headings, Dewey for Windows included selected LC subject headings mapped to DDC numbers in the major revised schedules in Edition 21.

WebDewey, released by OCLC in June 2000 as part of its Cooperative Online Resource Catalog (CORC) service, was first introduced as a web-based version of Edition 21. In January 2002, OCLC made WebDewey more widely available. WebDewey is currently available through "OCLC Connexion," the OCLC cataloging environment. OCLC also released Abridged WebDewey, a web-based version of Abridged Edition 13, in January 2002. These services, which replace Electronic Dewey and Dewey for Windows, are available to libraries via annual subscription for single-user or site licenses. Edition 22 was integrated into WebDewey in June 2003, and Abridged Edition 14 was integrated into Abridged WebDewey in December 2003. WebDewey features include:

- thousands of Relative Index terms and built numbers not available in the print version of the DDC;
- Library of Congress subject headings that have been statistically mapped to Dewey numbers from records in WorldCat or intellectually mapped by the DDC editors;
- 35,000 of the over 50,000 LC subject headings found in the OCLC publication, *People, Places & Things*;[11]
- selected mappings from Medical Subject Headings (MeSH);
- links from mapped LC subject headings to the LCSH authority records;
- quarterly database updates incorporating the latest changes to the DDC, plus LCSH mappings, index terms, and built numbers.

Abridged WebDewey is a web-based version of an enhanced database based on the latest abridged edition of the DDC. Similar to WebDewey, Abridged WebDewey features include:

- LC subject headings that have been intellectually mapped to Dewey captions and index terms by the DDC editors, including many from the OCLC publication, *Subject Headings for Children*;[12]
- links from mapped LC subject headings to the LCSH authority records; and
- mappings between abridged Dewey numbers and subject headings from the latest edition of H.W. Wilson's *Sears List of Subject Headings*;[13]
- quarterly database updates incorporating the latest changes to the DDC that also impact the abridged edition, LCSH mappings, *Sears* mappings, index terms, and built numbers.

---

[11] *People, Places & Things: A List of Popular Library of Congress Subject Headings with Dewey Numbers* (Dublin, OH: Forest Press, 2001).

[12] Lois Winkel, ed., *Subject Headings for Children: A List of Subject Headings Used by the Library of Congress with Abridged Dewey Numbers Added*, 2nd ed., numbers verified by Winton E. Matthews, Jr. (Albany, NY: Forest Press, 1998).

[13] Minnie Earl Sears, *Sears List of Subject Headings*, 18th ed., edited by Joseph Miller (New York: H.W. Wilson Co., 2004).

**Updates**: The Dewey Decimal Classification is kept up-to-date between editions through its online services, WebDewey and Abridged WebDewey. Selected changes to the DDC are also noted on a webpage (http://www.oclc.org/dewey/updates/) entitled *Updates to the Dewey Decimal Classification,* which lists selected new and changed entries, LCSH/DDC: numbers of current interest, discussion papers, tips, and other news relating to the Classification.

## Use of the DDC

Currently, the Dewey Decimal Classification is the most widely used library classification system in the world. More than 135 countries have adopted it, and it has been translated into over 30 languages. Translations of the latest full and abridged editions of the DDC are completed, planned, or underway in Arabic, Chinese, French, German, Greek, Hebrew, Icelandic, Italian, Korean, Norwegian, Russian, Spanish, and Vietnamese. In the United States, approximately 95% of all public and school libraries, 25% of all college and university libraries, and 20% of all special libraries use the DDC. In addition, as noted earlier, Dewey is used for other purposes, e.g., as a browsing and navigating mechanism for resources on the World Wide Web.

## BASIC PLAN OF THE CLASSIFICATION

The DDC is a universal scheme that treats knowledge as a whole, dividing it into ten main classes that are denoted by Arabic numerals used as decimal fractions. When Dewey made his decisions on the nature and order of classes, he viewed the world of knowledge as being divided into four realms: generalia, the realm of reason, the realm of the imagination (literature), and the realm of memory. This structure reflected the influence of two librarians, William T. Harris and Edward W. Johnston.[14] Dewey divided his classification into ten main classes:

| | |
|---|---|
| 0 | [General works] |
| 1 | Philosophy |
| 2 | Theology |
| 3 | Sociology |
| 4 | Philology |
| 5 | Natural Science |
| 6 | Useful Arts |
| 7 | Fine Arts |
| 8 | Literature |
| 9 | History |

Over the years, the DDC has evolved into a modern classification scheme, constantly striving to accommodate new knowledge and to find new ways of aligning knowledge. It has gradually incorporated many of the emerging theories of classification. Nevertheless, three basic principles, evident from the very beginning of the Classification, remain in force today:

(1) Division by discipline. In the DDC, basic classes are organized first by disciplines or fields of study. The main classes shown above correspond to the academic disciplines in Dewey's day; some of these disciplines have now be-

---

[14] Comaromi, *Eighteen Editions*, pp. 21–22.

come broader areas of study, each in turn comprising various disciplines. Nevertheless, the principle that the parts of the DDC are arranged first by discipline and then by subject still holds and remains the most basic principle of the Classification.

(2)  Structural hierarchy. The DDC organizes knowledge first by discipline then by subject in a hierarchical structure progressing from the general to the specific. Certain notes regarding the nature of a class hold true for all of its subordinate classes.

(3)  Notational hierarchy. The DDC notation reflects the hierarchical structure of the scheme. Within a particular hierarchy, coordinate topics are usually represented by notation with the same number of digits. Broader topics are usually represented by one fewer digit in the notational hierarchy, and narrower topics are usually represented with one more digit in the notational hierarchy. Details regarding notation follow.

## NOTATION (NUMBERING SYSTEM)

The Dewey Decimal Classification is basically a number-building machine that provides both intellectual order and physical location in one step. The engine of the DDC is notation. Notation may be defined as a systematic series of shorthand symbols used to denote classes and their subdivisions, and to reveal relationships among subjects. It mechanizes the arrangement of books in a library or of records in an electronic database. Brevity is implied in notation, but is not its main concern. The primary role of notation is to make the system work by revealing the classification conceptually and visibly

As mentioned earlier, to denote subjects Dewey decided to use a pure and simple notation: Arabic numerals treated like decimal fractions. Its notation is the DDC's most characteristic feature, and remains Dewey's most revolutionary contribution to the development of library classification. It is very powerful, as it reveals the coordination and subordination of subjects—intellectually and on the shelf—and can be expanded without disturbing topics already classed. Before one learns to use the Classification, it is important to understand the nature of its notation.

How decimal notation indicates subject hierarchy and relationships can be seen in considering the three subjects denoted by 8, 81, and 9, respectively. In decimal notation, 81 is subordinate to (that is, is a subtopic under) 8 while 9 is a new topic on the same level as 8. If there were topics at 82, 83, and so on, they would be coordinate with 81.

In the DDC, a digit stands for a main class; for example, 5 stands for the sciences. Strictly and mathematically speaking, the numbers denoting the main classes are decimal numbers and should have been written as .0 Computers, information & general works, .4 Language, .5 Science, and so on. The .5 is extended, like a decimal fraction, to indicate the subdivisions of the sciences; that is .59 stands for animals, .599 stands for mammals, .5996 stands for ungulates, .59963 stands for even-toed ungulates, .599633 stands for pigs, and .5996332 stands for wild boars.

To simplify the ordinal value of the decimal fractions as Dewey uses them, and for ease of arrangement, there is a convention that no number in the DDC shall have fewer than three digits. If any number has fewer than three significant digits, additional zeros are added to the right or to the left of the significant digits to make up a three-digit number, for example, 001, 010, 100.

For brevity, simplicity of notation, and ease of reading, a decimal point is placed after the third digit in the full DDC number; hence, 599.6, 599.63, etc. The *decimal point*, or *dot*, is not a decimal point in the mathematical sense. It is a psychological pause to break the monotony of numerical digits and to ease the transcription and copying of the class number. Also, psychologists believe that 324.13 is more easily remembered than 32413. The decimal point assists the eye and the memory. A DDC class number should never end in a 0 anywhere to the right of the decimal point, because an ending zero in this case carries no significance.

In summary, a DDC class number has three attributes:

(1)   the digits are treated as decimal fractions;
(2)   every number consists of at least three digits, e.g., 5 is written as 500, 53 as 530;
(3)   a decimal point is inserted between the third and the fourth digits, e.g., 324.3, 362.14, 386.24, when a class number extends beyond three digits.

The ten main classes in the DDC are now denoted as:

| | |
|---|---|
| 000 | Computer science, information & general works |
| 100 | Philosophy & psychology |
| 200 | Religion |
| 300 | Social sciences |
| 400 | Language |
| 500 | Science |
| 600 | Technology |
| 700 | Arts & recreation |
| 800 | Literature |
| 900 | History & geography |

This is called the *first summary* of the DDC schedules. For the beginner it is the first practical step in learning the system. More details on the main classes in the DDC appear in chapter 4 of this book.

## SUMMARY

Classification is a device to organize knowledge in a logical fashion. The Dewey Decimal Classification was conceived in 1873 and published in 1876 by Melvil Dewey (1851–1931), considered to be the father of modern librarianship. The continually revised Classification is now in its twenty-second edition, and is issued in print and electronic forms. The DDC uses decimal fractions to denote the ten main classes from 0 Computer science, information & general works to 9 History & geography. Decimal fractions can be expanded infinitely to accommodate new subjects; in addition they are universally understood, and reveal the intellectual hierarchy of the subjects they represent.

**Chapter 2**

# ORGANIZATION OF THE DEWEY DECIMAL CLASSIFICATION, EDITION 22

## STRUCTURE OF THE PRINT EDITION

The current edition of the Dewey Decimal Classification is the 22nd in the series that began in 1876. Its bibliographic details follow:

> Dewey, Melvil. *Dewey Decimal Classification and Relative Index* / devised by Melvil Dewey. Edition 22 / edited by Joan S. Mitchell, Julianne Beall, Giles Martin, Winton E. Matthews, Jr., and Gregory R. New. 4 volumes. Dublin, OH: OCLC Online Computer Library Center, Inc., 2003. ISBN 0-910608-70-9

From the 1st edition (1876) through the 15th revised edition (1952), the DDC was published in one volume. The 16th (1958) and the 17th (1965) editions were issued in two volumes, the second being devoted primarily to the index (called the Relative Index). The 18th (1971) and the 19th (1979) editions were issued in three volumes. Since the 20th edition (1989), the print edition has been issued in four volumes.

The parts of the DDC and their locations in the four-volume set of Edition 22 are:

> Volume 1: Prefatory material, New Features, Introduction, Glossary, Index to the Introduction and Glossary, Manual, Tables 1–6, Relocations and Discontinuations, Reused Numbers
> Volume 2: Summaries; Schedules: 000–599
> Volume 3: Schedules: 600–999
> Volume 4: Relative Index

## VOLUME 1: INTRODUCTION, GLOSSARY, MANUAL, TABLES, LISTS OF CHANGES

### Prefatory Material and New Features

Volume 1 begins with a foreword by the chair of the Decimal Classification Editorial Policy Committee (EPC). EPC is a ten-member international advisory board whose main function is to advise the editors and OCLC on changes, innovations, and the general development of the DDC. The foreword describes the committee's work as well as features and policies of Edition 22; it is followed by the preface and acknowledgments. The next section, "New Features in Edition 22," describes the major changes in the edition and includes lists of selected new and expanded numbers in the tables and schedules.

### Introduction

Basic instructions on the use of the DDC are found in the next part of the front matter: "The Introduction to the Dewey Decimal Classification." The introduction outlines the nature and structure of the DDC, and explains the rules that govern how to apply the DDC. The introduction offers guidance on determining the subject of a work (subject analysis), which is the first step in the classification process. It also instructs classifiers on how to locate, within the DDC framework, the class number that best fits the subject. Once the correct class number is found, the introduction provides further guidance on the process of building (synthesizing) a number either from the schedules or from any of the tables. This process is important because it allows classifiers to represent more specifically the subject content of the work at hand.

Although written in a clear, simple style, the ideas presented in the introduction can be difficult to grasp; therefore, the text is divided into small sections to facilitate comprehension. Time spent studying the introduction will be repaid many times over in mastering the application of Dewey. The instructions in the introduction are explained with ample illustrations in the remaining chapters in this book.

## Glossary

The introduction is followed by the glossary, which has provided useful assistance since its first appearance in Edition 18. It defines and explains the various technical terms used in the application of Dewey. An index to the introduction and glossary follows the glossary.

## Manual

The Manual follows the introduction and glossary. The Manual gives advice on classifying in difficult areas. It is arranged by Dewey numbers for quick access. References from the schedules and tables direct the classifier to the Manual for additional information about a specific number, range of numbers, or choice among numbers. The Manual is explained in greater detail in chapter 5.

## Tables

The rest of volume 1 is devoted to the six numbered tables of notation that can be added to class numbers to provide greater specificity. The tables provide the means of representing complex subjects. They are never used alone, but are required at times to specify aspects of a subject not expressed in the main numbers in the schedules. The tables are:

| | | |
|---|---|---|
| Table 1 | | Standard Subdivisions |
| Table 2 | | Geographic Areas, Historical Periods, Persons |
| Table 3 | | Subdivisions for the Arts, for Individual Literatures, for Specific Literary Forms |
| | T3A | Subdivisions for Works by or about Individual Authors |
| | T3B | Subdivisions for Works by or about More than One Author |
| | T3C | Notation to Be Added Where Instructed in Table 3B, 700.4, 791.4, 808–809 |
| Table 4 | | Subdivisions of Individual Languages and Language Families |
| Table 5 | | Ethnic and National Groups |
| Table 6 | | Languages |

An earlier table (Table 7 Groups of Persons) has been deleted in Edition 22 and replaced by direct use of notation already available in the schedules and in notation 08 from Table 1.

Use of Tables 1–6 will be discussed in detail in chapters 8–12, with many examples of their application.

## Lists of Changes

The next segment of volume 1, "Relocations and Discontinuations," is meant for classifiers who want to track changes from Edition 21 to Edition 22. This list is followed by "Reused Numbers," a short list of numbers (other than those resulting from the replacement of Table 7) whose meanings have changed completely from those in the previous edition. The "Comparative and Equivalence Tables" found in previous editions were not needed in Edition 22, since this edition does not contain any complete or extensive revisions.

## VOLUMES 2–3: SCHEDULES

The schedules consist of a long sequence of DDC numbers with captions describing the class each number represents, and notes explaining the use of the class. The schedules are located in two volumes: volume 2, containing 000–599; volume 3, containing 600–999. The schedules form the core of the Classification. To use them correctly and efficiently, it is necessary to know their typographical devices, and to understand the various constraints regarding the headings and the instructions accompanying them.

## Summaries

Volume 2 begins with the three summaries (outlines) of the Dewey Decimal Classification. The summaries are important in understanding the overall structure of the DDC, and are therefore an important learning tool.

The *first summary* contains the ten main classes, providing a broad overview of the DDC:

|     |     |
| --- | --- |
| 000 | Computer science, information & general works |
| 100 | Philosophy & psychology |
| 200 | Religion |
| 300 | Social sciences |
| 400 | Language |
| 500 | Science |
| 600 | Technology |
| 700 | Arts & recreation |
| 800 | Literature |
| 900 | History & geography |

The *second summary* displays one hundred divisions, ten for each main class; it appears on page 14. The *third summary* shows the ten parts into which the hundred divisions are divided, resulting in a thousand sections.

The summaries give Dewey numbers and their accompanying captions. The captions have been edited to make browsing easier, and so may not match the complete headings found in the schedules.

Taken together, the three summaries provide, in varying detail, an overview of the intellectual and notational structure of the DDC system. Necessarily brief, however, they do not always reveal the full substance of what the numbers represent. To understand the breadth of each number and caption, one must consult, and study, the schedules.

# Second Summary
## *The Hundred Divisions*

| | | | | |
|---|---|---|---|---|
| 000 | Computer science, knowledge & systems | | 500 | Science |
| 010 | Bibliographies | | 510 | Mathematics |
| 020 | Library & information sciences | | 520 | Astronomy |
| 030 | Encyclopedias & books of facts | | 530 | Physics |
| 040 | [Unassigned] | | 540 | Chemistry |
| 050 | Magazines, journals & serials | | 550 | Earth sciences & geology |
| 060 | Associations, organizations & museums | | 560 | Fossils & prehistoric life |
| 070 | News media, journalism & publishing | | 570 | Life sciences; biology |
| 080 | Quotations | | 580 | Plants (Botany) |
| 090 | Manuscripts & rare books | | 590 | Animals (Zoology) |
| | | | | |
| 100 | Philosophy | | 600 | Technology |
| 110 | Metaphysics | | 610 | Medicine & health |
| 120 | Epistemology | | 620 | Engineering |
| 130 | Parapsychology & occultism | | 630 | Agriculture |
| 140 | Philosophical schools of thought | | 640 | Home & family management |
| 150 | Psychology | | 650 | Management & public relations |
| 160 | Logic | | 660 | Chemical engineering |
| 170 | Ethics | | 670 | Manufacturing |
| 180 | Ancient, medieval & eastern philosophy | | 680 | Manufacture for specific uses |
| 190 | Modern western philosophy | | 690 | Building & construction |
| | | | | |
| 200 | Religion | | 700 | Arts |
| 210 | Philosophy & theory of religion | | 710 | Landscaping & area planning |
| 220 | The Bible | | 720 | Architecture |
| 230 | Christianity & Christian theology | | 730 | Sculpture, ceramics & metalwork |
| 240 | Christian practice & observance | | 740 | Drawing & decorative arts |
| 250 | Christian pastoral practice & religious orders | | 750 | Painting |
| 260 | Christian organization, social work & worship | | 760 | Graphic arts |
| 270 | History of Christianity | | 770 | Photography & computer art |
| 280 | Christian denominations | | 780 | Music |
| 290 | Other religions | | 790 | Sports, games & entertainment |
| | | | | |
| 300 | Social sciences, sociology & anthropology | | 800 | Literature, rhetoric & criticism |
| 310 | Statistics | | 810 | American literature in English |
| 320 | Political science | | 820 | English & Old English literatures |
| 330 | Economics | | 830 | German & related literatures |
| 340 | Law | | 840 | French & related literatures |
| 350 | Public administration & military science | | 850 | Italian, Romanian & related literatures |
| 360 | Social problems & social services | | 860 | Spanish & Portuguese literatures |
| 370 | Education | | 870 | Latin & Italic literatures |
| 380 | Commerce, communications & transportation | | 880 | Classical & modern Greek literatures |
| 390 | Customs, etiquette & folklore | | 890 | Other literatures |
| | | | | |
| 400 | Language | | 900 | History |
| 410 | Linguistics | | 910 | Geography & travel |
| 420 | English & Old English languages | | 920 | Biography & genealogy |
| 430 | German & related languages | | 930 | History of ancient world (to ca. 499) |
| 440 | French & related languages | | 940 | History of Europe |
| 450 | Italian, Romanian & related languages | | 950 | History of Asia |
| 460 | Spanish & Portuguese languages | | 960 | History of Africa |
| 470 | Latin & Italic languages | | 970 | History of North America |
| 480 | Classical & modern Greek languages | | 980 | History of South America |
| 490 | Other languages | | 990 | History of other areas |

*Consult schedules for complete and exact headings*

## Structure of a Schedule Page

Basically, each page of the schedules consists of a sequence of entries. An entry in the schedules is a self-contained unit consisting of a number or span of numbers, a heading, and often one or more notes. For example, p. 963 of volume 2, which appears on page 16, has entries ranging from 516.373 to 518.26.

There are nearly 27,000 entries printed in the schedules. The total number of available schedule numbers is far greater than that figure, since numbers may be extended by various number-building procedures; these will be discussed in later chapters. In addition, there are nearly 9,000 entries in the six tables in volume 1. Table notation may be added to most schedule numbers, thus producing an almost infinite set of class numbers.

Each page consists of two columns:

(1)   Number column: the column of class numbers printed vertically on the left-hand side of the schedule page;

(2)   Heading and notes column: the column to the right of the number column. The heading is a word or phrase that describes the meaning of the number on the left.

The columns and their corresponding headings are printed in varying type sizes depending upon their positions in the hierarchy. Type size decreases the lower one goes in the notational hierarchy. For example, note the type sizes of the following numbers and their headings in volume 2:

| Number | Heading | Type size |
|--------|---------|-----------|
| **341** | **Law of nations** | **12 point bold** |
| **341.2** | **The world community** | **10 point bold** |
| 341.23 | United Nations | 10 point light |

When a number is expanded beyond the decimal point, the three digits for the section are only given once on a page, in the number column when the section number changes, or in page headers when listings under a section number continue over several pages.

## Hierarchy

Hierarchy means the sequence of subjects in their successive subordination. Hierarchy in DDC is expressed through structure and notation. Structural hierarchy means that each topic, other than those represented by the main classes, is subordinate to and part of the broader topics above it. Logically, whatever is true of a general topic is true of all of its subordinate topics, a principle referred to as "hierarchical force."

Notational hierarchy is expressed by length of notation. Numbers at any given level are usually subordinate to a class whose notation is one digit shorter; coordinate with a class whose notation has the same number of significant digits; and superordinate to a class with numbers one or more digits longer. In the printed schedules, the notational hierarchy, or increasing specificity of subjects, is repre-

| | | |
|---|---|---|
| .373 | | Riemannian geometry |
| | | Including Sasakian geometry |
| .374 | | Minkowski geometry |
| | | Including Einstein geometry |
| .375 | | Finsler geometry |
| .376 | | Cartan geometry |

**.4**      **Affine geometry**

> Class affine differential geometry in 516.36

**.5**      **Projective geometry**

> Class projective differential geometry in 516.36

**.6**      **Abstract descriptive geometry**

> *See also 604.2015166 for descriptive geometry in technical drawing*

**.9**      **Non-Euclidean geometries**

> Including Bolyai, elliptic, Gauss, hyperbolic, inversive, Lobachevski geometries; imbeddings of non-Euclidean spaces in other geometries
>
> Class a specific type of non-Euclidean geometry with the type, e.g., non-Euclidean analytic geometries 516.3

**[517]**      **[Unassigned]**

> Most recently used in Edition 17

**518**      **Numerical analysis [*formerly* 515]**

> Class here applied numerical analysis [*formerly* 519.4], numerical calculations, numerical mathematics
>
> Class approximations and expansions in 511.4
>
> *For numerical statistical mathematics, see 519.5*

**.1**      **Algorithms [*formerly* 511.8]**

**.2**      **Specific numerical methods**

> Class specific numerical methods applied to a particular field in 518.4–518.6

.23      Graphic methods

> Including nomography [*formerly* 511.5]

.25      Finite element analysis

> Class here finite strip method, finite volume method

.26      Iterative methods

sented by a shift of indention of the verbal heading to the right, and by the addition of a meaningful digit to the number in the left column.

For example:

| | |
|---|---|
| 600 | Technology (Applied sciences) |
| 610 | Medicine and health |
| 613 | Personal health and safety |
| 613.7 | Physical fitness |
| 613.71 | Exercise and sports activities |
| 613.717 | Running and walking |

In the example shown, each heading, except Technology, is subordinated to the immediately superordinate heading. Note the lengthening of the digit chain in the number column and the shift in typographical indention to the right in the corresponding headings. In the schedules under 613.717, there are two entries at the same indention:

| | |
|---|---|
| 613.717 | Running and walking |
| 613.717 2 | Running |
| 613.717 6 | Walking |

The numbers assigned individually to running (613.7172) and to walking (613.7176) are coordinate numbers; they are at the same level of the notational and structural hierarchies.

Sometimes it is not possible to express structural hierarchy through notation. When this is the case, special devices are used to indicate relationships among topics. Among these are centered entries, see-reference notes, and dual headings. A dual heading is used when a subordinate topic is the major part of the subject; the subject as a whole and the subordinate topic as a whole share the same number. For example:

| | |
|---|---|
| 599.9 | Hominidae Homo sapiens |

Centered entries are explained later in this chapter; see-reference notes are introduced in chapter 3.

## Sequence of Numbers

The entire schedules have been arranged in a single numerical sequence from 000 to 999; therefore, it should not be difficult to locate a desired class number. For the convenience of users and for rapid location, the section numbers, i.e., three-digit figures, are always printed on the top corners of each page.

## VOLUME 4: RELATIVE INDEX

Volume 4 consists of the Relative Index, the index to the Dewey Decimal Classification. It is more powerful than a simple alphabetical index, and is considered one of Melvil Dewey's most important and enduring contributions to library classification.

The Relative Index arranges subject terms alphabetically, and links the terms to the discipline in which they appear in the schedules. It is called "relative" because it relates subjects to disciplines. In the schedules, subjects are distributed among disciplines; in the Relative Index, however, subjects are arranged alphabetically. Under each subject, names of disciplines and terms implying disciplines (e.g., "area planning" implying "Civic art" in the following example), are subarranged alphabetically:

| | |
|---|---|
| Airports | 387.736 |
| architecture | 725.39 |
| area planning | 711.78 |
| construction | 690.539 |
| engineering | 629.136 |
| institutional housekeeping | 647.963 9 |
| law | 343.097 7 |
| military engineering | 623.66 |
| public administration | 354.79 |
| transportation services | 387.736 |
| *see also* Aircraft | |

As a topic, airports may appear elsewhere in the schedules other than under the numbers listed in the Relative Index. There may be a song about airports, or a movie, or a poem, or a short story, or a bibliography, or a social service number for protecting people at airports. But the Relative Index cannot list them all. In such cases, the classifier must first determine the context or discipline in which the topic of airports is treated in the work and then examine the schedules for the most appropriate number. For example, for a short story with airports as a theme, the correct number would be found in the main class for literature.

Since the Relative Index is a key to the schedules, a full chapter (chapter 6) will be devoted to a discussion of its importance, complexity, and use.

## READING THE SCHEDULES

As noted earlier, the full meaning of a DDC number depends on its position in the hierarchy to which it belongs. Thus, in many cases, a particular caption can only be understood within the context of its superordinate numbers. For example:

341.231    Functions and activities

If this entry were taken in isolation, the classifier would not understand whose functions and activities were being discussed. But if this entry is read in conjunction with (or in the context of) its immediately superordinate heading (i.e., the heading found at 341.23 United Nations), then its meaning becomes clear—it is the functions and activities of the United Nations. If perused still further in the context of its superordinate number twice removed, the meaning of this entry becomes the Law of nations (341) of the functions and activities of the United Nations.

The prime justification for a brief heading is that it is a straightforward and convenient way to avoid repetition and clutter on the schedule page. However, the advantage of economy on the printed page can sometimes be a disadvantage online if the user views an entry in isolation without its superordinate numbers. The electronic version overcomes this difficulty by offering a display option that includes hierarchies.

## DDC NUMBERS IN THE SCHEDULES

As explained in chapter 1, all digits in a DDC number are treated as decimal fractions, with the decimal point serving as a psychological pause between the third and fourth digits. In the print version, if a class number extends beyond six digits, the remaining digits are printed in groups of three, with a space between each group. For example:

> 341.026 5      Multilateral treaties
>
> 621.381 542 2    Video display components

This space has exactly the same purpose as that of the decimal point, namely to make it easier to copy and remember class numbers. The spaces have no meaning beyond this, and should not be confused with the segmentation of numbers provided in Library of Congress cataloging to show the logical breaks in numbers.

### Numbers in Square Brackets

At various levels in the schedules and tables, there are many class numbers that are enclosed in square brackets. For example:

> [309]       [Unassigned]
>
> 515[.624]    Numerical integration

Any number enclosed in square brackets is not valid, and should not be used. There are five kinds of bracketed numbers:

(1)   Three-digit numbers never assigned any content in the scheme: Such numbers have always been vacant. For example:

> [009]     [Never assigned]

The number of such entries is decreasing, as gaps are used to accommodate new topics or fields of study.

(2)   Currently unassigned three-digit numbers: Some bracketed numbers, which were once valid, have remained vacant since a previous edition. Such numbers carry the heading [Unassigned] and a note stating when the number was last used. For example:

> [007]     [Unassigned]
>           Most recently used in Edition 16
>
> [426]     [Unassigned]
>           Most recently used in Edition 18

The number of such temporarily vacant numbers varies from edition to edition; they result from revision of the DDC.

(3)   Vacated numbers: These bracketed numbers have been vacated for the current edition; that is, their contents have been shifted to other numbers. As a matter of policy, such numbers are not immediately reused in order to minimize confusion and inconvenience to users. The shifting of a topic or a heading from a number to another number is called a *relocation*. There is always a note that

tells the location to which the contents of the number have been moved. When numbers are vacated, the meaning or topic represented by the vacated number usually remains somewhere in the scheme. Examples:

[619]     Experimental medicine
              Relocated to 616.027

652[.5]   Word processing
              Relocated to 005.52

(4)   Discontinued numbers: These bracketed numbers are numbers from the previous edition that are no longer used because the concept represented by the number has been moved to a more general number in the same hierarchy, or has been dropped entirely. For example:

615[.882]   Folk medicine
                   Number discontinued; class in 615.88

(5)   Hook numbers:  Hook numbers are numbers that have no meaning in themselves, but are used to introduce specific examples of a topic. Hook numbers have headings that begin with "Miscellaneous," "Other," or "Specific"; and they do not contain add notes, including notes, or class-here notes. Hook numbers are not bracketed, but standard subdivisions are bracketed directly following the hook number. For example:

652.302     Specific levels of skill

[.302 01–.302 09]  Standard subdivisions
                   Do not use; class in 652.3001–652.3009

## Numbers in Parentheses

The DDC lists standard notation for English-language users. At certain places in the schedules, options are provided for users whose needs are not met by the standard notation. Options are a means of accommodating cultural differences, and provide a mechanism for emphasizing topics of local importance. For example, in order to give prominence to the religion, literature, or language of a particular country, libraries may insert letters in the notation or use briefer notation (e.g., as indicated under 290 Other religions).

In the schedules, optional numbers are enclosed in parentheses. These numbers may be used by individual libraries if preferred. They are not part of the standard notation. Examples:

(330.159)   Socialist and related schools
                   (Optional number; prefer 335)

(819)          American literatures in English not requiring local emphsis
                   (Optional number and subdivisions; prefer 810–818 for
                   all American literatures in English. Other options are
                   described under 810–890)

# CENTERED ENTRIES

In the schedules there are often headings denoted not by one number but by a span of numbers identified by the symbol > in the number column. For example:

> 250–280     Christian church

> 616.1–616.8  Diseases of specific systems and organs

These spans and their corresponding headings are called centered entries. The entry is called "centered" because the span of numbers is printed in the center of the page rather than in the number column on the left side of the page. A centered entry is used to indicate and relate structurally a span of numbers. As a span, these numbers form a single concept for which there is no specific hierarchical notation available.

Usually, a broad subject that has subdivisions is represented by a single number. In the case of centered entries, however, such a subject is covered by a span of coordinate numbers. This device shortens the notation for each of the subdivisions by one digit, but results in the loss of hierarchy in the notation.

Centered entries occur at all levels of hierarchy, and hundreds of them can be found in the DDC schedules and tables.

Not all spans of numbers, however, are centered entries; some spans are given either to show the position of standard subdivisions or to save space when the same instruction applies to a series of numbers. For example:

697.000 1–.000 9     Standard subdivisions

809.1–.7     Literature in specific forms
                Add to base number 809 the numbers following 808.8 in
                808.81–808.87, e.g., history, description, critical
                appraisal of poetry 809.1 . . .

In such cases the span is given in the number column.

# SUMMARY

Edition 22 of the DDC consists of four volumes. Volume 1 contains prefatory and introductory materials, the Manual, the six tables, and lists of changes from Edition 21 to Edition 22. Volumes 2 and 3 contain the schedules, which form the core of the system, with entries arranged in one sequence of decimal fraction numbers from 000 to 999. Volume 4 contains the Relative Index. Every entry in the schedules is to be read in the context of its superordinate headings. Class numbers given in square brackets are not to be used, and those in parentheses are optional. A centered entry uses a span of numbers to represent a single concept for which there is no specific hierarchical notation available.

## Chapter 3

# STRUCTURE AND ORGANIZATION
## OF THE SCHEDULES:
## NOTES AND INSTRUCTIONS

## INTRODUCTION

The previous chapter introduced Edition 22 of the Dewey Decimal Classification, noting the contents of its four volumes and concluding with information about the composition of a schedule page and its entries, particularly numbers and captions. This chapter concentrates on another aspect of schedule entries, the notes found under many numbers. Such notes have various functions. Some explain the contents of a class or subset of a class; some explain apparent peculiarities in a number, some refer to other numbers, and still others refer to the Manual when extensive information is required. The most important notes are those that tell how to build or synthesize numbers. DDC notes can be grouped by function: the various categories of notes and the terms for the notes that fall into them are listed and discussed below.

## NOTES THAT DESCRIBE WHAT IS FOUND IN A CLASS

In many cases, the caption accompanying a class number is not sufficient for identifying what is included in the number. Notes are provided to clarify the meaning of the caption, to delineate the scope of the number, or to indicate topics included in the number that are not clearly stated in the caption. With the exception of including notes, notes that describe what is in a class have hierarchical force (see chapter 2 for a discussion of hierarchical force).

### Definition Notes

*Definition notes* are used when: (a) a term in the heading is broader or more limited in meaning than is commonly accepted; (b) a term has multiple or ambiguous meanings in *Webster's Third New International Dictionary of the English Language* and other general unabridged dictionaries; or (c) a term is new to the language. For example:

    321.03    Empires
                Systems in which a group of nations are governed by a
                single sovereign power

    634.99    Agroforestry
                Forestry in combination with other farming

### Scope Notes

*Scope notes* limit the heading to the characteristics listed in the note. For example:

    579.16    Miscellaneous nontaxonomic kinds of organisms
                Not provided for elsewhere

    662.666   Rocket fuels (Rocket propellants)
                Liquid and solid

The first example instructs the classifier to use 579.16 for nontaxonomic kinds of organisms for which provision has not been made elsewhere in the same schedule. In the second example, only liquid and solid rocket fuels are allowed at number 662.666; gas propellants would not be classed at this number.

Some scope notes expand rather than contract the contents of a number. For example:

> 171   Ethical systems
>> Regardless of time or place

> 782.1  Dramatic vocal forms     Operas
>> Regardless of type of voice or vocal group

## Number-built Notes

*Number-built notes* identify and explain the source of built (synthesized) numbers listed in the schedules and tables. Built (synthesized) numbers are occasionally included in the schedules or tables to provide additional information or to indicate exceptions to regular add instructions. For example:

> 433       Dictionaries of standard German
>> Number built according to instructions under 430.1–438

> 571.92    Plant diseases
>> Number built according to instructions under 571–572
>> *For diseases of domestic plants, see 632.3*

In the first example, 433, a built number, is listed in the schedule to provide an explicit listing for a three-digit number. In the second case, the built number 571.92 is listed to accommodate a see-reference to the treatment of diseases of domestic plants.

## Former-heading Notes

*Former-heading notes* are supplied when the heading associated with a class number has been revised from one edition to the next to such a degree that the new heading bears little or no resemblance to the former heading, even though the meaning of the number has remained substantially the same. For example:

> 615.88    Traditional remedies
>> Former heading: Empirical and historical remedies

## Variant-name and Former-name Notes

*Variant-name notes*, which contain synonyms or near-synonyms of the caption, also help indicate what is found in a class. For example:

> 305.235   Young people twelve to twenty
>> Variant names: adolescents, teenagers, young adults, youth

Earlier names of geographic areas in the same number are given in *former-name notes*. The following example is from Table 2:

> —714 471  City of Québec
>> Former name: Quebec Urban Community

## Class-here Notes

*Class-here notes* list major topics that are included in a class. These topics may be broader or narrower than the heading, overlap it, or define another way of looking at essentially the same material.[1]  For example:

> 576.5   Genetics
>            Class here heredity. . .

The note means that heredity, though not strictly speaking genetics, is to be classed with genetics at 576.5.  Two more examples:

> 006.32       Neural nets (Neural networks)
>                   Class here connectionism, neural computers

> 372.357     Nature study
>                   Class here environmental studies

Class-here notes are also used to indicate that interdisciplinary and comprehensive works[2] on the topic in question are classed in the number under which the note appears. For example:

> 305.231     Child development
>                   Class here interdisciplinary works on child development

> 368.82       Burglary, robbery, theft insurance
>                   Class here comprehensive works on crime insurance

## Including Notes

*Including notes* identify topics that are in "standing room" in the number where the note is found.  Including notes list topics that are considered part of the class, but which are less extensive in scope than the concept represented by the class.  Standing-room numbers provide a location for topics with relatively few works written about them, but whose literature may grow in the future, at which time they may be assigned their own number.[3]  For example:

> 372.35       [Elementary education in] Science and technology
>                   Including metric system

The note conveys the sense that, logically speaking, metric system may not seem to be a part of the entry.  At the same time, the subject metric system is not fully developed in elementary education, because the literature on the topic is not substantial enough to justify its having its own class number.  Therefore, for the time being, the subject of elementary education in the metric system is classed at 372.35.

---

[1] Topics in class-here notes are said to *approximate the whole* of a class.  That means that class numbers for such topics may be extended by means of number building; number building will be discussed in later chapters.

[2] In Dewey, the term *interdisciplinary work* refers to a work that treats a subject from the perspective of more than one discipline, and the term *comprehensive work* refers to a work that treats a subject from various points of view within a single discipline.

[3] Standard subdivisions cannot be added to topics in standing room, nor are other number-building techniques allowed for these topics.

To take another example:

> 340.55     Medieval European law
> Including feudal law, medieval Roman law

Whether or not one considers feudal law or medieval Roman law to be medieval European law, they are to be classed at this number. "At" is used to convey the message that no additional notation can be added to 340.55 for works on feudal law and medieval Roman law; such works are assigned 340.55 and no more. For works on medieval European law in general, however, 340.55 may have additional notation appended to it.

In Edition 21, including notes replaced the following types of notes found in earlier editions: contains notes (for major components of the number that do not have their own subdivisions), example notes (examples of an abstract category), and common-name notes (common English names for scientific taxonomic terms).

Entries in the taxonomic schedules may have two including notes. The first including note contains the scientific taxonomic names above the level of family; the second contains the common and genus names. For example:

> 584.38     Iridales
> Including Burmanniaceae
>
> Including blackberry lily, crocuses, freesias, gladiolus (sword lilies), saffron, tigerflowers

Including notes are also used to indicate where interdisciplinary or comprehensive works on a topic are classed. For example:

> 583.48     Betulales
> Including alders, filberts (hazelnuts), hornbeams; comprehensive works on ironwoods

Unlike class-here notes, interdisciplinary or comprehensive works mentioned in including notes are considered to be in standing room. If the literature on ironwoods were to grow in the future, a number would be developed for comprehensive works on these trees.

## NOTES THAT DESCRIBE WHAT IS FOUND IN OTHER CLASSES

Several types of notes alert users to topics outside of the scope of the number in question. These include *class-elsewhere notes, see references,* and *see-also references.* Each of these notes has hierarchical force.

### Class-elsewhere Notes

*Class-elsewhere notes* are in direct contrast to class-here notes and including notes: they lead to topics not located at the number in which the note is located. Class-elsewhere notes give the location of interrelated topics or distinguish among numbers in the same notational hierarchy. They are used to show preference order among topics, to lead to broader or narrower topics in the same notational hierarchy, to override the first-of-two rule,[4] or to lead to the comprehensive or interdisciplinary number for the topic. A

---

[4] The first-of-two rule is discussed in chapter 4.

class elsewhere note takes the form of "Class . . . in . . ." There are several kinds of "class . . . in . . ." notes. The simplest is straightforward:

> 551.21    Volcanoes
> Class volcanic thermal waters and gases in 551.23;
> class petrology of volcanic rocks in 552.2

In this example, the class-elsewhere note instructs the classifier to prefer the number for thermal waters and gases (551.23) over the number for volcanoes (551.21) when classifying on a work about volcanic thermal waters and gases.

Another kind of "class . . . in . . ." note scatters the topic to several numbers. In this circumstance, all that can be given is an example of the scattering. Here are two examples:

> 353.463    Public investigations and inquiries
> Class legislative oversight hearings on administrative
> matters with the subject in public administration, e.g.,
> on administration of social welfare 353.5

> 613.711    Fitness training for sports
> Class a specific kind of fitness training with the kind,
> e.g. weight lifting 613.713 . . .

## "CLASS COMPREHENSIVE WORKS IN . . ." TYPE

A special type of "class . . . in . . ." note, the *comprehensive-works note*, is used for topics that fall in several classes in the same discipline. For example:

> 551.3    Surface and exogenous processes and their agents
> Class comprehensive works on landforms in 551.41;
> class comprehensive works on sedimentology in 552.5

Comprehensive-works notes are also used for topics listed under a centered entry. Centered entries are signaled by an arrow > at the left margin. The comprehensive-works note assigns a single class number for a work that covers all the topics in the centered-entry span. For example:

> >  307.1–307.3    Specific aspects of communities
> Class comprehensive works in 307

That is to say, if there were a work on communities that encompassed planning and development (307.1), movement of people (307.2), and the structure of communities (307.3), it would be classed in 307.

Every centered entry contains a note that tells users where to class comprehensive works on the topics in the span. This note is needed because no work is ever assigned a span of numbers. For example:

> >  172–179    Applied ethics (Social ethics)
> Class comprehensive works in 170

> >  250–280    Christian church
> Class comprehensive works in 260

In other words, a comprehensive work on the Christian church is classed in 260, with Christian social and ecclesiastical theology.

## "CLASS INTERDISCIPLINARY WORKS IN . . ." TYPE

A similar note with broader coverage than the comprehensive-works note is the *interdisciplinary-works note*. Such notes are used when topics fall in two or more disciplines. Substance abuse, for instance, may fall in ethics, religion, law, social welfare, and medicine, to name only a few of the places for which there is explicit provision for the topic in the schedules. In the example below, there is a reference from the medicine number (613.8) to the interdisciplinary number in social welfare (362.29):

> 613.8      Substance abuse (Drug abuse)
> > Class interdisciplinary works on substance abuse in 362.29

For each "class . . . in . . . " note, there is usually a reciprocal class-here note (or including note) in the entry to which the class-elsewhere note refers:

> 362.29      Substance abuse
> > Class here drug abuse; interdisciplinary works on
> > substance abuse, addiction, habituation, intoxication

An important consideration in using the interdisciplinary number is that the work must contain significant material on the discipline in which the interdisciplinary number is found.

## SEE REFERENCES

*See references* lead from a stated or implied comprehensive number for a concept to the component (subordinate) parts of the concept. See references take the form "For . . . see . . ." and appear in italics. For example:

> 004.16      Microcomputers
> > Class here laptop, notebook, palmtop, pen, personal,
> > pocket, portable, wearable computers; workstations;
> > comprehensive works on minicomputers and micro
> > computers
> > *For minicomputers, see 004.14*

004.16 is the *stated* comprehensive number for minicomputers and microcomputers, and the see reference leads to the component part, minicomputers, in another number. An example of the use of a see reference with an *implied* comprehensive number follows:

> 001.42      Research methods
> > Class here scientific method
> > *For historical, descriptive, experimental methods,*
> > *see 001.43*

See references may also lead from the interdisciplinary number for a concept to treatment of the concept in other disciplines. For example:

> 181.45      Yoga
> > Class here interdisciplinary works on the practice of
> > yoga and yoga as a philosophical school
> > *For yoga as a religious and spiritual discipline,*
> > *see 204.36; for Hindu yoga as a religious and*
> > *spiritual discipline, see 294.5436; for hatha yoga,*
> > *physical yoga, see 613.7046*

See references are also used to lead from comprehensive or interdisciplinary works in including notes to treatment of the topic in a different location. For example:

> 613.943 5   Mechanical methods of birth control
> > Including intrauterine devices, comprehensive works
> > on condoms
> > > *For use of condoms for disease prevention, see 613.95*

Another type of see reference, a *scatter see reference,* is used to lead to component parts of the topic scattered throughout all or part of the Classification. The note includes an example of one of the scattered parts. For instance:

> 579.82      Minor divisions of algae
> > Class here . . . comprehensive works on flagellates . . .
> > > *For a specific kind of flagellate, see the kind, e.g.,*
> > > *Zoomastigophorea 579.42 . . .*

## See-also References

*See-also references* point to topics that are tangentially related to the topic where the note is given. See-also references appear in italics and follow see references in the same entry. For example:

> 306.872     Husband-wife relationship
> > *See also 613.96 for sexual techniques*
>
> 780.266     Sound recordings of music
> > *See also 781.49 for recording of music*

## NOTES THAT EXPLAIN CHANGES OR IRREGULARITIES

Four types of notes explain changes from earlier editions or irregularities in the schedules or tables resulting from special provisions. These are revision notes, discontinued notes, relocation notes, and do-not-use notes.

## Revision Notes

*Revision notes* alert users to major changes that have occurred in a schedule since the previous edition. They are especially helpful to classifiers who have used earlier Dewey editions. Revision notes introduce *complete* or *extensive* revision of a division or section in a particular edition of the DDC. There are no complete or extensive revisions of major areas in Edition 22; however, examples can be found in earlier editions. In Edition 21, complete revision notes are given under the headings for Table 2 —47 Eastern Europe     Russia, 350 Public administration and military science, and 570 Life sciences Biology. For example:

> 350      Public administration and military science
> > Except for military science (355–359), this schedule is new
> > and has been prepared with little or no reference to previous
> > editions. Most numbers have been reused with new meanings
> >
> > A comparative table giving both old and new numbers for a
> > substantial list of topics and equivalence tables showing the
> > numbers in the old and new schedules appear in volume 1 in
> > this edition

In Edition 21, extensive revision notes are given under the headings for 370 Education, 560 Paleontology Paleozoology, 580 Plants, and 590 Animals in Edition 21. For example:

>370 Education
>>This schedule is extensively revised, 370.1, 370.7, 375–377, and 378.14–378.19 in particular departing from earlier editions
>>A comparative table . . .

## Discontinued Notes

*Discontinued notes* identify numbers in which all or part of the contents have been moved to a broader number in the same hierarchy, or have been dropped entirely. Discontinued notes take several forms:

>513[.54] Octal system (Base 8 system)
>>Number discontinued; class in 513.5

>331.257 22 Compressed workweek
>>Use of this number for comprehensive works on workweek discontinued; class in 331.257

>649.4 Child health care
>>Use of this number for clothing discontinued because without meaning in context

In the first example, the note explains that the complete contents of the number have been moved to a broader number in the same hierarchy. In this case, the number was discontinued because the topic does not have a sufficient literature. Any literature on the topic will henceforth be found at the listed superordinate number. In the second example, comprehensive works on the workweek have been discontinued to the number for hours of work 331.257, because the workweek approximates the whole of the meaning of the broader number. In contrast, a compressed workweek is only one aspect of the hours of work. In the third example, the topic of clothing has been dropped entirely because it was without meaning in the context of child health care.

## Relocation Notes

*Relocation notes* indicate that all or part of the contents of a number in the previous edition have been moved to a different number in the current edition. For example:

>174[.24] Questions of life and death
>>Relocated to 179.7

>321 Systems of governments and states
>>Comprehensive works on heads of state and administration relocated to 352.23

Sometimes topics are relocated because of dual provision, that is, the inadvertent provision of more than one place in the DDC for the same aspect of a subject. For example, in DDC 21, self-help groups were located at both 374.22 Groups in adult education and 361.4 Group work. This has been corrected in Edition 22:

> 374.22    Groups in adult education
>           Self-help groups relocated to 361.4

The relocation eliminates the dual provision for this topic.

Certain topics are relocated throughout part or all of the Classification. These are called scatter relocations. For example:

> [545]     Quantitative analysis
>           . . . specific quantitative techniques relocated to the
>           technique in 543, e.g., volumetric analysis 543.24

Thus, quantitative techniques used in analytical chemistry have been relocated ("scattered") to the specific technique throughout 543.

## FORMERLY NOTES

When a topic has been relocated to a specific number or span, a *formerly note* that indicates where the topic used to be located is given at the new location. The formerly note is part of the caption or part of a class-here or including note. It is given in the form of [*formerly* . . .] or, in the case of a dual provision, [*formerly also* . . .]. Formerly notes are printed in italics and followed by the former number. For example, the formerly notes corresponding to the relocation notes in 174.24, 321, and 374.22 are as follows:

> 179.7     Respect and disrespect for human life
>           Including questions of life or death in medical ethics
>           [*formerly* 174.24] . . .
>
> 352.23    Chief executives
>           Class here comprehensive works on heads of state
>           [*formerly* 321] . . .
>
> 361.4     Group work
>           Including self-help groups [*formerly also* 374.22] . . .

Formerly notes cannot be provided for relocations scattered throughout part or all of the Classification ("scatter relocations").

## Do-not-use Notes

*Do-not-use notes* instruct the classifier not to use all or part of the regular standard subdivision notation or an add table provision under a particular class number, but instead to use special provisions or the standard subdivision notation at a broader number. For example:

> 629[.1340287]   Testing and measurement [of aircraft components]
>                 Do not use; class in 629.1345

The note conveys the information that the regular standard subdivision notation for testing and measurement (0287) is not used with 629.134 to represent testing and measurement of aircraft components; material on that topic is to be classed in 629.1345, the number for tests and measurements of aircraft in general.

## SEE-MANUAL NOTES

Many numbers in the schedules and tables carry references to specific passages in the Manual. The references appear in the form of a note beginning with the phrase "*See Manual at . . . ,*" and appear in italics. For example:

> 303.376     Censorship
> *See Manual at 363.31 vs. 303.376, 791.4*
>
> 904         Collected accounts of events
> *See Manual at 900: Historic events vs. nonhistoric events*

A see-Manual reference may lead to a full note on the topic, a portion of a note on a topic, the discussion of several numbers, or other situations. A detailed discussion of the Manual is provided in chapter 5.

## NUMBER-BUILDING NOTES

The DDC began as an enumerative scheme that listed ready-made numbers for subjects. Starting with the second edition, the DDC has increasingly made provisions for number building, also referred to as notational synthesis. Number building is the process of making a given number appropriately more specific by adding notation from the tables or other parts of the schedules.

To a certain extent, the system is still partly enumerative: it does not allow all possible combinations, and it continues to provide ready-made numbers for many complex subjects in the schedules. Nevertheless, over the years, it has incorporated many elements of a faceted classification scheme. Each new edition of the DDC has included more facilities for number building. Several of the major revisions in recent editions feature notational synthesis as a basic feature of the schedule, e.g., 780 Music, 351–354 Public administration, 570 Life sciences     Biology.

A facet is a characteristic belonging to a class of works. For instance, in the DDC, literature has four facets: (1) Language, e.g., Russian; (2) Literary form, e.g., fiction; (3) Period, e.g., Victorian; and (4) Theme and feature, e.g., realism. In number building, these facets are combined ("synthesized") to reflect the content of the work being classified.

In Edition 22, almost every number in the schedules can be further extended by notation either from one or more of the tables or from the schedules themselves. The two methods discussed below explain most of the notational synthesis in the scheme.

### Adding Standard Subdivisions from Table 1

Any number from Table 1 Standard Subdivisions can be added[5] to any number in the schedules for a topic that equals or approximates the whole of the class unless there is a specific instruction to the contrary. Occasionally there are instructions that standard subdivisions cannot be added. For instance, standard subdivisions are not to be added for topics in standing room. Nor can they be added when their significance would be redundant. For example, a number meaning history from Table 1 should not be added to a class number that already implies history.

---

[5] In number building in the DDC, "to add" means "to append" or "to attach to," rather than "to add" in the arithmetic sense.

## STANDARD-SUBDIVISIONS-ARE-ADDED NOTES

*Standard-subdivisions-are-added* notes are provided under multiterm headings to indicate whether a standard subdivision may be added to one or all of the terms in the heading.[6] For example:

> 636.73 Working and herding dogs
> Standard subdivisions are added for working and herding dogs together, for working dogs alone

# Adding Notation from Tables 2–6 or from the Schedules

Adding a number from Tables 2–6 or notation derived from the schedules to any other number in the schedules can be done only when instructed to do so in the schedules or tables. The instruction for this kind of synthesis or number building is given in a note that usually takes the form of "Add to base number . . . the number following. . . ." Proper understanding and implementation of such number-building notes, or *add notes*, are central to the synthesis of class numbers in the DDC.

Add notes can be further divided into two broad categories, individual add instructions and collective instructions.

## INDIVIDUAL ADD INSTRUCTIONS

An individual add note that appears under a specific entry is intended solely for that entry. For example:

> 340.524–.529 Law of traditional societies in modern world
> Add to base number 340.52 notation 4–9 from Table 2, e.g., traditional law of the Sahara 340.5266

Each add note includes one or more examples, as shown above.

## COLLECTIVE INSTRUCTIONS

In the print version of the DDC, sometimes an add instruction applies to a series of numbers occurring on a single page or on a number of pages of the schedules. In such a case, all the entries to which the instruction applies are marked with an asterisk (*) or some other symbol, and at the foot of each page containing such entries there is a footnote giving the location of the appropriate add instruction. The footnote applies to all the numbers marked by the symbol. This is done to avoid repetition of add notes in each entry. An example of such a collective add note can be seen in the development under 495 in volume 2, where 495.1, 495.6, 495.7, 495.8, and 495.9191 have been marked with asterisks:

> 495.1 *Chinese
> .6 *Japanese
> .7 *Korean
> .8 *Burmese
> .919 1 *Lao

---

[6] For further discussion of adding standard subdivisions, see chapter 8.

At the bottom of the page, a footnote provides the add instruction:

*Add to base number as instructed under 420–490

The note means that all of the asterisked numbers can be further extended, if desired, according to the instructions given under the centered entry at 420–490:

> 420–490     Specific languages
Except for modifications shown under specific
entries, add to base number for each language
identified by * notation 01–8 from Table 4, e.g.,
grammar of Japanese 495.65 . . .

Add notes are the backbone of the number-building equipment of the DDC. Moreover, they are a major factor in the correct use of Dewey. For this reason, the majority of the following chapters in this book will be devoted to number building and the various kinds of add notes.

## ORDER AND IMPORTANCE OF NOTES

Notes in the schedules generally appear in the following order: revision, former-heading, definition, number-built, standard-subdivisions-are-added, variant-name, scope, including, class-here, arrange, add (including subdivisions-are-added), build, preference,[7] discontinued, relocation, class-elsewhere, see-reference, see-also-reference, see-Manual, and option notes.

Many entries have more than one note. In such cases no one note inhibits another. The DDC schedules abound with numerous definition, scope, including, class-here, and class-elsewhere notes, and see references. These notes help immensely in the correct classifying of a document. They also help achieve uniformity in the interpretation of entries and therefore promote consistency in the application of the DDC in all libraries in all countries. The notes in the schedules and tables are essential, therefore, in helping explain the positions, boundaries, and scope of various subjects.

## SUMMARY

An entry in the DDC, especially one that is frequently used, may contain various notes that help interpret the scope and meaning of the class number. Definition and scope notes formally define, illustrate, or explain the scope of the entry and its various topics. Variant-name, class-here, and including notes list the topics classed in a given class number. Class-elsewhere notes and references direct users to a better or more specific class number for a related topic. Revision, discontinued, relocation, and do-not-use notes alert users to changes or special applications. Such notes are of great importance and are possibly the only way to avoid the problem of the lack of consensus on the boundaries of different subjects. Central to the process of synthesis of numbers or number building are the various add notes that have increased the capacity of the DDC to classify more and more subjects in ever greater detail.

---

[7] Preference notes are introduced in chapter 4.

## Chapter 4
# SUBJECT ANALYSIS AND CLASSIFICATION OF A DOCUMENT

## INTRODUCTION

The objectives of this chapter are to explain: first, how to determine the specific subject of a document; second, how to separate the subject proper from other aspects of the work such as the author's viewpoint, the form of presentation, and the physical medium or form; and, third, how to assign to a document the appropriate class number by following the hierarchical pathway mapped in the schedules.

The work of practical library classification, in its essence, is to find the appropriate place for a document in the overall scheme of the classification system, and to assign the appropriate notation from the classification schedules to the document. Therefore, the work of classification requires knowledge of both the contents of the document being classified and the structure and mechanism of the classification system.

The layout of the Dewey Decimal Classification (DDC) system, especially of the schedules, was explained in the first three chapters. This chapter sets forth the process of subject analysis of documents and the assignment of appropriate class numbers.

The work of subject analysis is of paramount importance in bibliography and library science. Though many people approach a library collection or other information resources by way of an author or title, the basis for their particular interest is almost always a subject. This is true even in recreational reading. The smallest error at the subject analysis stage of classification can defeat the purpose of classification, because works classed in inappropriate places are lost to readers. Those who browse a collection will not find them, and those who use the subject catalog as a starting point often pass over records with class numbers that do not reflect their topic. Thus, in subject analysis, care and circumspection must be constant companions.

## ANALYZING THE SUBJECT CONTENT OF A DOCUMENT

The first step in classification is to determine the subject content of a document. The classifier often begins with the title and other preliminary material. In the case of a book, such preliminary material includes the author's preface, table of contents, and the bibliography, if any. Accompanying material such as the packaging of a sound recording may also be of help. For an electronic resource, helpful material also includes the abstract or description of the resource. As a last resort, the classifier may need to consult subject experts.

In analyzing the subject content of a document, the classifier first determines the subject proper. Other aspects to be considered are the author's viewpoint, the form of presentation, and the physical medium in which the document appears. Some documents treat two or more topics and/or one or more aspects of a topic. In subject analysis, these individual topics and aspects must be identified.

### Titles and Subtitles

The title of a work and its subtitle (if it has one) must be read carefully. A subtitle immediately follows the title proper; it is also called the secondary or explanatory title.

A subtitle normally elucidates or clarifies the theme of the work. For example, in *Winston Churchill: A Life,* the subtitle explains that the work is a biography. In a majority of cases the title and the subtitle of a work, taken together, sufficiently reveal the subject of the work. The subtitle is often the more revealing of the two. Authors seek to seize attention by the title proper; they intend to inform with the subtitle. Here are a few examples in support of this assertion:

(1)  Returning to Eden: animal rights and human responsibilities
(2)  The image of eternity: roots of time in the physical world
(3)  Winning: the psychology of competition
(4)  A story of Christian activism: the history of the National Baptist Convention, U.S.A., Inc.
(5)  Beyond the Milky Way: hallucinatory imagery of the Tukano Indians
(6)  Small finds: ancient Javanese gold
(7)  Secret city: photographs from the USSR
(8)  The monster with a thousand faces: guises of the vampire in myth and literature
(9)  Matthias: a novel
(10) The Arctic Grail: the quest for the North West Passage and the North Pole, 1818–1909

## FANCIFUL OR CATCHY TITLES

If the title of the work is fanciful or otherwise ambiguous, it will probably not reveal the subject of the work. Note the following titles:

(1)  The eagle and the dragon
(2)  Silicon idol
(3)  Tiger's milk
(4)  Asian drama
(5)  Third wave
(6)  Asking for trouble

The actual subjects of these works, as gathered from their subtitles or elsewhere, are:

(1)  Foreign relations between the United States and China
(2)  A work on computer chips
(3)  A book on housewives and their routines
(4)  Economic conditions of Third World countries
(5)  A futuristic look into the coming society
(6)  Memoirs of a vice chancellor of an Indian university

These examples show that, to classify well, the classifier has to look beyond titles.

## INCOMPLETE TITLES

Some titles seem to be incomplete, at least from the classifier's point of view. For example, a work entitled *Shakespeare* could be a biography, a critical appraisal, or a collection of Shakespeare's works. A work entitled *Canada* does not reveal the aspect of Canada portrayed; it could be a treatise, a travel guide, or an atlas.

On the other hand, a title may seem to be complete in itself but is incomplete from the classifier's perspective. For example, a book entitled *Reign of Henry VII* will have to be read in the context of the history of England, even though England does not figure in the title. Such incomplete titles will often require the classifier to seek assistance elsewhere in the work.

## TITLE WORDS NOT USEFUL TO CLASSIFIERS

Some title words are not helpful to classifiers even though they are indicative of subject content; other title words have nothing to do with content. For example, a book entitled *Rudiments of Economics* will get the main class number for economics (330) because in 330 there are no provisions for the level at which a work treats the subject. Rudimentary, elementary, intermediate, and advanced are terms often used in titles, but they are no help in classification unless the relevant schedules make these distinctions. For example, Edition 19 of the DDC contained separate numbers for elementary, intermediate, and advanced algebra in 512.9042–.9044; in Edition 20, these were discontinued to 512.9 Foundations of algebra. On the other hand, Edition 22 contains separate entries for elementary, intermediate, and advanced levels of accounting at 657.042–.046.

An example of a work with title words that do not indicate content is *A Memorable and Rewarding Journey to Nepal*. Whatever the author thinks of his or her subject, the subject still is only a journey to Nepal. The rest of the words in the title are superfluous with regard to classification, however important and true they may be to the author. Remember: classification is based on the subject of the work, not on its title.

## CLEAR BUT UNFAMILIAR TITLE WORDS

Some titles may be crystal clear to those who understand the subject, but to a classifier who knows little about the subject, their meaning would doubtless be lost. Such titles are usually scientific, technical, or esoteric. For example:

(1)  Introduction to compression neuropathy
(2)  Fundamentals of tribology
(3)  Fundamentals of acoustics
(4)  An analysis of the Zend Avesta

The first two contain technical terms: the first deals with the cause of carpal tunnel syndrome, the second with friction; the third title may be either the physics or technology of sound, and the last deals with the holy scriptures of the Parsees. To a layperson or a novice classifier these terms may not be familiar. But then sometimes even nontechnical and nonesoteric terms may not be well known. Take the following:

(1)  Nuremberg Trials
(2)  War of the Roses
(3)  Third Reich
(4)  The Great Depression
(5)  Crimean War
(6)  Whistled languages

These titles are neither fanciful nor obscure. They are all apt, yet their meanings may not be altogether familiar to the classifier. For unfamiliar terms, an appropriate encyclopedia or dictionary must be consulted. For this reason, some libraries maintain a reference collection in their cataloging departments.

## PARALLEL TERMINOLOGY

The title of a work may be clear and complete, yet it may contain a term for a concept that differs from the terminology in the schedules. For example, a work on the Japanese Diet, like a work on the U.S. Congress, will get the number for legislative bodies. In Nepal such a body is called the Rashtriya Panchyat. These concepts have terminology that differs from country to country. In such cases the terminology in the title must be interpreted by the classifier to conform to the standard terminology used in the DDC schedules.

## LITERARY TITLES

In the DDC, as in most library classifications, literary works are not classified by subject. In Class 800 (Literature) in the DDC, classification of literature is determined by the language, form, and period in which it was written. For example, Thomas Hardy's novels, say, *A Pair of Blue Eyes* and *Far from the Madding Crowd*, will get the same class number, i.e., the number for English novels written in the Victorian period, to which Thomas Hardy belongs. The class numbers for the two novels, as well as other novels by Hardy or by other Victorian authors for that matter, would share the same number, because the number means Victorian novel, and not specifically Thomas Hardy.

## Other Subject Indicators Found in the Work Itself

In many works the title alone does not reveal subject content. Therefore, classifiers should never classify by title alone, however clear and unambiguous a title may seem. Titles may be incomplete or deceptive or may not reveal anything beyond the typographer's art. Whatever the case, the true subject of the work must always be verified from other parts of the work.

After the title and subtitle, the classifier should look for information that summarizes the purpose and theme of the work. In most cases this can be found on the left inside flap of a book's jacket (dust cover), on the back cover in the case of a paperback, on the container of a nonprint item, in the abstract of a report or article, or on the homepage of a web site. The preface or introduction should be read in order to learn about the author's intent and final thoughts. A preface or introduction written by someone other than the author often indicates the subject of the work and suggests the place of the work in the development of scholarship on the subject. The table of contents displays the structure of the work and lists major topics treated in the work; chapter titles often show aspects or subtopics and so help clarify content. The bibliography, the subject index, and the series to which the work belongs, if any, may also provide useful clues in determining the subject of the work.

## Outside Sources

If the sources described above are inadequate and some doubts remain that subject content has been satisfactorily identified, reviews of the work may be helpful. As a last resort, subject experts may be consulted.

## Determining the Discipline for a Work

Because classification with the DDC is first by discipline and then by subject, the classifier must also determine the discipline, or field of study, of the work being classified. This is not always a simple process, since any subject may be treated from the standpoint of one or more disciplines. For example, the subject iron is scattered in the DDC among several disciplines, including metallurgy, building materials, mining, and inorganic chemistry. Thus, in order to place a work about iron properly, the classifier must determine which discipline is the best fit for the work in hand. Guidance for selecting the correct discipline is provided below in the discussion about assigning class numbers from the schedules.

## Analysis of Works with Complex Subjects

Often a particular work treats two or more subjects or a single subject with two or more facets, or aspects. DDC notation, however, does not always provide a single class number for these multitopical or multifaceted works. To complicate matters further, because class numbers have been closely tied to shelf location in American libraries, each item is usually assigned only one class number even though two or more numbers may apply. Therefore, when it is necessary to choose among competing class numbers, it is extremely important to analyze and understand the composition of the subjects being treated in the work in hand. Complex subjects are discussed further below and in chapter 13.

### MULTITOPICAL WORKS

A work may treat two or more subjects either separately or in relation to one another. The two or more subjects may belong to the same discipline or may be from different disciplines. For example, a history of France and Germany may treat the two countries separately or focus on the relationship between them, and the book entitled *Crime and the American Press* treats two subjects in relation to one another.

### MULTIFACETED WORKS

A work may treat a subject with two or more facets. For example, a book about crimes in nineteenth-century France contains the main subject crimes with two facets: time and space (or place).

### INTERDISCIPLINARY WORKS

A work may treat a subject from the point of view of more than one discipline. Such works are called *interdisciplinary works*. For example, a work about the social and psychological development of the child, in which the subject "child" is treated from the points of view of both sociology and psychology, is an interdisciplinary work.

## Analysis of the "Nonsubject" Aspects of a Work

In library classification the process of subject analysis of a work does not end with the determination of subject and discipline. We still have to know several other things about the work. These "nonsubject" aspects include the author's viewpoint, the form of presentation, and the physical medium of the document.

### AUTHOR'S VIEWPOINT

Any core subject can be presented from various viewpoints. For example:

Theory of economics
History of economics
Research in economics

The subject of all three works is clearly "economics." However, the Dewey system goes further. It includes provisions that enable the classifier to express the fact that a work is theoretical or historical or a summary of the latest advances in research. That is because its base class number can be extended by notation that indicates these viewpoints. This procedure will be addressed further when we take up Table 1 Standard Subdivisions in chapter 8.

## FORM OF PRESENTATION

A document can be presented in many forms: it can be a bibliography, a periodical, a dictionary, or the proceedings of a conference on a specific subject. For example:

> A bibliography of economics
> A periodical on economics
> A dictionary of economics
> Proceedings of an international conference on economics held in 1996

Other forms include: statistical tables, handbooks, compilations of abbreviations, illustrations, directories, exhibits, and so on. The following examples illustrate subjects that include the author's viewpoint and/or the form of presentation:

(1)  A pictorial history of England
(2)  Formulas in electrical engineering
(3)  Research in cataloging
(4)  A handbook of data processing in banking
(5)  A commission report on the relations of the U.S. President and the U.S. Congress

Separating the elements, we have:

|     | *Subject* | *Form* | *Viewpoint* |
|-----|-----------|--------|-------------|
| (1) | England | pictures | history |
| (2) | Electrical engineering | formulas | |
| (3) | Cataloging | | research |
| (4) | Banking | handbook | data processing |
| (5) | Relations of President/Congress | report | |

The notation for most of these forms and viewpoints is found in Table 1, which will be discussed in chapter 8.

## PHYSICAL MEDIUM OR FORM

With the advances in information technology and publishing, we have seen documents arrive in various physical formats. A document can be a printed book, a microfiche, or a microfilm. It can be in the form of a video recording, an audiotape, a computer disk, a compact disc (CD-ROM), a computer file, or an Internet or web resource. It is possible to indicate in the DDC number some of these physical forms (again by way of standard subdivisions in Table 1). However, more often than not, information about the physical form of a document is not revealed in the class number, but is carried elsewhere in the cataloging record.

# ASSIGNING CLASS NUMBERS FROM THE SCHEDULES

As noted above, subject analysis of a document is not dependent on the classification system being used: the subject must first be determined whether one is using the Library of Congress scheme, the Colon Classification, or the DDC. In practice, nevertheless, when classifying with the DDC, it is necessary to do subject analysis within the context of the disciplinary structure Dewey provides. For this reason, knowledge of the structure and intellectual basis of the DDC is a prerequisite. We begin with the underlying structure of the Classification and the order of the main classes and divisions. The historical basis of the structure of the main classes and divisions in the DDC was presented in chapter 1 of this book. The following is a description of the basic structure of the DDC as it stands now:

### 000 Computer science, information & general works

The 000 class is the most general class and is used for works not limited to any one specific discipline, e.g., encyclopedias, newspapers, general periodicals. Two categories of works fall in this class:

(1) Works in umbrella or tool disciplines, that is, disciplines relating to or applied to many other disciplines, e.g., systems analysis and computer science (003–006), bibliography (010 and 090), library and information sciences (020), museology (069), journalism and publishing (070).

(2) Multidisciplinary works, e.g., general encyclopedias (030), general periodicals (050), works on general organizations (060), general collections (080).

Thus, in addition to general subjects, the 000 class is also used for certain specialized disciplines that deal with knowledge and information, e.g., computer science, library and information science, journalism. Each of the other main classes (100–900) comprises a major discipline or group of related disciplines.

### 100 Philosophy & psychology

Class 100 covers philosophy (which is the most general field and the field that provides system and logic for all other fields), parapsychology and occultism, and psychology.

### 200 Religion

Class 200 is devoted to religion and theology (the science of the absolute). Both philosophy and religion deal with the ultimate nature of existence and relationships, but religion treats these topics within the context of revelation, deity, and worship.

### 300 Social sciences

Class 300 covers the social sciences, which include:

Sociology and anthropology (301–307): The study of the processes, interactions, groups, culture, and cultural institutions that give form and purpose to every society. Part of the subject matter of sociology is found in 390 Customs, etiquette, folklore.

Statistics (310): The raw data, in numerical form, for the study of human society. Statistics as a discipline is classed in 519.5.

Political science (320): The study of the distribution and uses of power within a society. In order to maintain internal peace and safety from external threat, societies devise political processes and institutions such as the state and government. An extension of political science is found in 351–354 Public administration.

Economics (330): The production and allotment of scarce goods and services. Part of the subject is found in 380 Commerce, communications, transportation.

Law (340): Law is one of the chief instruments of social control, consisting of the whole body of customs, practices, and rules that are recognized in a society as binding, and are promulgated or enforced by a central authority.

Public administration and military science (350): Class 350 covers the maintenance of order through the executive branch of government and public administration, and the administration of the defense forces of society.

Social problems and services (360): No matter how well power is distributed, laws written, and societies governed, problems occur. They are treated here.

Education (370): The introduction of individuals to the order and intellectual products of society.

Commerce, communications, transportation (380): Commerce is the distribution of goods and services, and is a part of the discipline of economics. Transportation, an activity that adds to the value of goods moved, is also a part of the discipline of economics. Both communications and transportation have been developed primarily in response to commercial needs and practices, e.g., trade, banking, accounting.

Customs, etiquette, folklore (390): An extension of anthropology and sociology. Melvil Dewey considered customs to be the culmination of social activity and classed them in 390, just before language.

## 400 Language

Class 400 covers language, society's way of recording itself. It comprises linguistics, language in general, and specific languages. It does not include literature, which is arranged by language and found in 800.

## 500 Science

Class 500 is devoted to the natural sciences and mathematics. The natural sciences (520–590) describe and attempt to explain the world in which we live. They describe the laws of nature and move from inorganic phenomena on a large scale (astronomy) to organic life on an advanced scale (zoology). The natural sciences are preceded by mathematics (510), and are followed by technology (600) and the fine arts (700).

The schedule for the life sciences (560–590) received a major overhaul in Edition 21, and Edition 22 follows the same organizational pattern. The reversal of preference from organism to process is the most significant change of the revision. The processes include physiology, pathology, biochemistry, and related subjects. Anatomy and morphology are placed in this sequence because they are basic to an understanding of how all internal biological processes work. While preference between organism and process was reversed for internal biological processes and structures developed in 571–575, preference for organism was retained in other subjects in biology. The distinction is based upon the recognition of fundamental differences between the literature on the biology of processes and the literature on the biology of whole organisms. The first requires study of parts of the organisms to find out how the various processes work; the second requires study of whole organisms or taxonomic groups and their relationships to each other and the environment. Furthermore, the first is studied primarily in laboratories, where the literature usually focuses on experimental research; the second is studied primarily in the field, where the literature usually focuses on descriptive research. In the first, the process studied in one organism is usually seen as typical of all living organisms (or as typical of a large class of organisms such as animals, vertebrates, or mammals), e.g., cell division, blood circulation, immune reactions. In the second, topics are usually seen as typical only of the specific type of organism being studied, e.g., snail shells, reproductive behavior of sticklebacks, weaverbird nests.

### 600 Technology

Class 600 consists of the utilization of the sciences to harness and manipulate the natural world and its resources for the benefits of humankind. Many topics can be discussed from either a technological or a social point of view. If a work discusses how to make, operate, maintain, or repair something, it is normally classed in technology. If, on the other hand, it discusses the social implications of a technological operation, it falls in the social sciences, e.g., the economic importance of lumbering 338.17498, not 634.98.

### 700 Arts & recreation

Class 700 covers the arts: art in general, fine and decorative arts, music, and the performing arts. Recreation, including sports and games, is classed in 790. The original heading for 790 was Amusements.

### 800 Literature

Class 800 covers literature: rhetoric, prose, poetry, drama, and so forth. The exception is folk literature, which is classed with customs in 398.

Works classed in 800 are products of the imagination. This does not mean that they are not true. A young woman reading Amy Tan's *The Joy Luck Club* was asked by an acquaintance what she was reading. When she told him, the acquaintance remarked that he did not read fiction, he only read the truth. The reader responded, "But this is the truth." Many works of poetry, drama, and fiction, and many essays, speeches, and letters, are true in an analogous sense also. Nevertheless, although many literary works may have a strong subject focus, they are still works of the imagination, not factual reporting or exposition. A work of the imagination is classed in 800 even if it contains a lot of subject information. Thus, a novel by Tom Wolfe about the corruption of Wall Street finance (*The Bonfire of the Vanities*) is classed in American literature, not in financial economics or in crime; similarly, Shakespeare's *King Henry V* goes in English drama, not in English history.

On the other hand, works other than those of the imagination are classed under their appropriate subjects, even though they are written in what is usually considered a literary form. A dialogue by Plato is classed in philosophy; a poem on the circulation of the blood is classed in medicine. A child's counting book may be classed in the provision for arithmetic in 510 Mathematics. No one is claiming that the question "What is literature?" is easy to answer.

**900 History & geography**

Class 900 is devoted to history and geography. When a work is a story of events that have transpired or an account of existing conditions in a particular place or region, it is classed in 900. A history of a specific subject is classed with the subject.

The foregoing discussion has tried to show the basic structure of the DDC and the distinction among classes. It is usually fairly easy to grasp the subject, but grasp of the proper class or discipline is not so readily accomplished. A classifier can acquire the knowledge of where to begin looking for a topic in the DDC by studying the ten main classes, the hundred divisions, and the one thousand sections. The more the classifier knows about them, the more efficient he or she will become.

## Searching for the Right Class Number

The schedules themselves must always be consulted in order to arrive at the correct class number. The schedules consist of a long list of numbers for all subjects and their subdivisions arranged in logical order. There are two ways to enter the schedules. One is through the Relative Index. It is a quick method, but it does not help in understanding the structure of Dewey. The other method is to trace the class number by following the hierarchical ladder down each meaningful rung until the number that best fits the topic is found. This is the better approach, and the one that is more effective for learning the DDC structure. In some cases, however, consulting the Relative Index can help a classifier get "a foot in" the schedules.

## CLASSIFICATION BY DISCIPLINE

It should be constantly kept in mind that the DDC is a classification divided first by discipline. Disciplines may be found in main classes, divisions, or sections. The ten main classes in Dewey represent the broadest areas of study. These classes have two zeros to the right, e.g., 400 Language. Divisions are the next level down; they have one zero to the right, e.g., 410 Linguistics. Next come the sections, e.g., 411 Writing systems, 412 Etymology, etc. Further subdivisions are occasionally referred to as subsections (four digits) or subsubsections (five digits). To classify properly from the DDC schedules, therefore, one proceeds from the broad to the narrow, from the general to the specific, from the main class to the division to the section, and so on. Some examples follow.

### Example 1

Take the title *Married Women in the Labor Force*. To begin to classify the work, one must first understand that its subject falls in main class 300 Social sciences, and more narrowly in division 330 Economics. The classifier's general knowledge of the Relative Index will help with these choices. At this point, the classifier may either scan the sections of 330 in the third summary or go directly to 300 in the schedules, where the sections and subsections of 330 Economics, including 331 Labor economics, are listed. Under 331, the number 331.4 for Women workers is found. This is the right place to be, even though it is somewhat broader than the topic of the book in hand (that is, not all women who work are married). For that reason, the search does not end here. Scanning the subdivisions of 331.4, the classifier finds 331.43 Married women. This is the appropriate number for the book being classified. Here the search ends. The classifier assigns this number to the catalog record. The proper number has been arrived at by narrowing the area of search at each stage where the ten roads diverged to different destinations. Visually, the entire path can be shown by the following structured diagram (Figure 4.1).

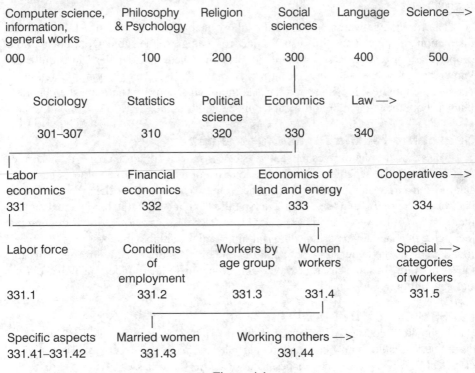

**UNIVERSE OF KNOWLEDGE**

| Computer science, information, general works | Philosophy & Psychology | Religion | Social sciences | Language | Science —> |
|---|---|---|---|---|---|
| 000 | 100 | 200 | 300 | 400 | 500 |

| | Sociology | Statistics | Political science | Economics | Law —> |
|---|---|---|---|---|---|
| | 301–307 | 310 | 320 | 330 | 340 |

| Labor economics | Financial economics | Economics of land and energy | Cooperatives —> |
|---|---|---|---|
| 331 | 332 | 333 | 334 |

| Labor force | Conditions of employment | Workers by age group | Women workers | Special —> categories of workers |
|---|---|---|---|---|
| 331.1 | 331.2 | 331.3 | 331.4 | 331.5 |

| Specific aspects | Married women | Working mothers —> |
|---|---|---|
| 331.41–331.42 | 331.43 | 331.44 |

Figure 4.1

**Example 2**

Here is another title: *Lower House of Parliament.* The classifier should know immediately that the work belongs in political science, and after a little experience with the DDC, the classifier should know that 320 is political science. The third summary leads to the proper section: 328 The legislative process (the work of parliaments). Under 328 in the schedules, the classifier learns that 328.3 Specific topics of legislative bodies is an available class, and it happens to have its own summary, which provides the number 323.32 for lower houses of legislatures—a perfect match. The search is ended. Its linear course is charted in the following example:

| | |
|---|---|
| 300 | Social sciences |
| 320 | Political science |
| 328 | The legislative process |
| 328.3 | Specific topics of legislative bodies |
| 328.32 | Lower houses |

To repeat, the first two rungs of the ladder may be reached from memory, and perhaps the third from experience. Then the classifier shifts to the schedules and moves from general to specific, narrowing the area of search at every rung of the hierarchical ladder, often with the assistance of a summary.

**Example 3**

The last title is *Anatomy of the Large Intestine*, a work about the human large intestine. Knowledge of the structure of these disciplines may not help in this case. All creatures on the planet, except human beings, have their anatomy and physiology classed in 571 Physiology and related subjects, and properly so. Human beings are a special case. When the DDC was first devised, human anatomy and physiology were placed with the useful arts (medicine, specifically) in order to be part of the technology needed most often by students of these subjects. At that time, a century ago, it was physicians more than any other class of scholars who studied anatomy and physiology. That is why human anatomy is found in medicine instead of in division 570 Life sciences Biology. Since medicine is a reasonable location for human anatomy, it has not been moved to biology. Equally reasonable is the location of the anatomy, physiology, and pathology (illnesses) of farm animals in veterinary medicine in the technology number for farming. Needless to say, in classifying one has to know that human anatomy is located in technology, not in biology where all other anatomies (save for farm animals) are found. Thus, by way of the Relative Index or through the summaries, the classifier finds 611 Human anatomy, cytology, histology. The summary there reveals that 611.3 is the number for digestive tract organs. At 611.3, the classifier sees that the intestine has been given the number 611.34, and the large intestine 611.347. Here the search ends with another perfect match of title and class. In the real world things do not always work out so nicely, of course. The route the classifier followed is traced below:

| | | |
|---|---|---|
| 600 | Technology (Applies science) | |
| 610 | Medicine and health | |
| 611 | | Human anatomy, cytology, histology |
| 611.3 | | Digestive tract organs |
| 611.34 | | Intestine |
| 611.347 | | Large intestine |

## Denoting Nonsubject Aspects

If the subject of a work has been presented from a specific viewpoint (e.g., theoretical or historical) or in a recognized form (e.g., a periodical or dictionary), at the first opportunity the classifier should separate the viewpoint and form from the subject proper. Both viewpoint and form are nonsubject characteristics of the document. After the number for the subject is found, the number for the viewpoint or form (from Table 1 Standard Subdivisions) can be added to it. For example, the word *"Dictionary"* in the title *A Dictionary of Photocopying Technology* is simply the form of presentation of the subject. The first step is to determine the class number for the subject proper—Photocopying—in the usual way. In this case, the class number is 686.4. The next step is to add to 686.4 the number for dictionaries (—3) found in Table 1. Then the two numbers are joined, with the standard subdivision number coming last, to arrive at 686.403. (For a detailed discussion of Table 1, see chapter 8.)

Often a subject is studied in the context of a geographic area; the area number to be attached to the subject number is usually taken from Table 2, where area numbers are listed. (For a detailed discussion of Table 2, see chapter 9.)

In the majority of cases the number arrived at through the structural ladder is a broad one. At that number there may be instructions in the form of add notes (discussed in chapter 3) that allow the classifier to extend the number by another number taken either from the schedules or any of the tables. There are six tables:

| | | |
|---|---|---|
| Table 1 | | Standard Subdivisions |
| Table 2 | | Geographic Areas, Historical Periods, Persons |
| Table 3 | | Subdivisions for the Arts, for Individual Literatures, for Specific Literary Forms |
| | T3A | Subdivisions for Works by or about Individual Authors |
| | T3B | Subdivisions for Works by or about More than One Author |
| | T3C | Notation to Be Added Where Instructed in Table 3B, 700.4, 791.4, 808–809 |
| Table 4 | | Subdivisions of Individual Languages and Language Families |
| Table 5 | | Ethnic and National Groups |
| Table 6 | | Languages |

These tables will be discussed at length in chapters 8–12.

## COMPLEX SUBJECTS

What is written above is, in fact, an over-simplified view of practical classification. The reality is that subject analysis is not so simple—even for the experienced classifier. A document may pose unique and unimagined problems. Sometimes a work embodies a composite subject or it may be an agglomeration of seemingly unrelated subjects. Moreover, even though subject analysis has been done correctly, too often there is not a class number that fits the topic nicely; the final class arrived at is often three sizes too large or three sizes too small. In such cases, the classifier has to put the topic in the class that is too large. Interdisciplinary notes help overcome the problem of multidisciplinary subjects.

### Number Building

When encountering a document with a complex subject the first thing to do is to look in the schedules for a ready-made number. Failing that, one must determine whether a number can be built or synthesized, either by following add instructions or by extending the schedule number for the main subject with notation from the tables. In number building, *citation order*, i.e., the order or sequence of facets appearing in a class number, is an important consideration. For the sake of consistency, facets applicable to a particular class should be arranged in the same order in all built numbers. It does not matter whether the class number has been extended from the schedules or tables; what matters is consistency of order. Citation order is discussed in detail in later chapters (note, in particular, chapter 7).

Number building begins with a base number to which another number is added. There are four sources of additional notation from which to build numbers: (A) Table 1 Standard Subdivisions; (B) Tables 2–6; (C) other parts of the schedules; and (D) add tables in the schedules. With the exception of standard subdivisions from Table 1, all other elements may be added only upon instructions in the schedules or tables. Because number building is an essential procedure in the application of the DDC, it is discussed in depth in the following chapters in this book.

## Choosing Appropriate Numbers

In spite of in-depth enumeration and provisions for synthesis of multitopical subjects, there are still cases where it is not possible to provide a co-extensive number (i.e, a number that covers all facets of the subject) for the content of a particular work. Many works treat different subjects separately or in relation to one another. Others treat a subject from different perspectives or cover one or more facets of a subject. The DDC does not always provide ready-made numbers or allow synthesis for all the facets covered in the work being classified. For example, take the title *Treatment of Heart Disease According to Homeopathy*. In the DDC, there is a separate number for homeopathy (615.532) and another for diseases of the heart (616.12), but it is not possible to combine the two. We may specify treatment, but will have to choose one base number and ignore the other aspect. Take another example, *Classification in Public Libraries*. Separate DDC numbers exist for library classification (025.42) and for public libraries (027.4), but there is no provision for combining them. One reason for such problems is that Dewey is still a partially enumerative classification rather than a totally faceted system aimed at complete subject analysis of documents, particularly documents on minute or very specialized topics.

In those cases where a co-extensive number for a complex work can neither be found in the schedules nor built from the tables or schedules, the classifier must choose one subject or one facet/aspect and ignore any other or others. The question then is which to ignore and which to consider. The guidelines for classifying such works appear in sections 5.7–5.10 of the introduction to Edition 22 and are summarized below.[1]

### TWO OR MORE SUBJECTS TREATED SEPARATELY

Many works treat two or more subjects. These subjects may belong in different disciplines or come from the same discipline. In general, the discipline, subject, or aspect given the fullest treatment is preferred. If treatment is equal among the subjects or aspects, the classifier should follow the general guidelines on number choice given in the introduction to Edition 22 unless specific instructions in the schedules indicate otherwise. Specific instructions appearing in the schedules or tables override those given in the introduction.

### Two Subjects

When two subjects falling in the same discipline are treated separately in the work and there is no class number covering both subjects, the number for the subject given fuller treatment in the work is chosen. When the subjects are treated equally, the number coming first in the numerical sequence is chosen. This is called the *first-of-two rule*. For example, a work on trumpets (788.92) and bugles (788.95) is classed in 788.92. A work on the fine arts and literature is classed in 700 (Arts) rather than in 800 (Literature), and a work on the English language and English literature is classed in 420 (English language) rather than in 820 (English literature).

---

[1] Melvil Dewey, *Dewey Decimal Classification and Relative Index*, Edition 22, edited by Joan S. Mitchell, Julianne Beall, Giles Martin, Winton E. Matthews, Jr., and Gregory R. New (Dublin, OH: OCLC, 2003), v. 1, pp. xliii–xlv.

However, this rule does not apply when there is a specific instruction in the schedules to class a work in the second number. Nor does it apply when the two subjects constitute the major subdivisions of a broader (i.e., more general) number. In this case, the broader number is chosen.

### Three or More Subjects

When a work deals with three or more subjects that are all subdivisions of a broader subject, the next broader number that includes them all is chosen. This is called the *rule-of-three*. For example, a work on Chinese, Japanese, and Korean languages is classed in 495 Languages of East and Southeast Asia even though the number 495 also covers other Asian languages such as Tibetan, Burmese, and Tai.

## TWO OR MORE SUBJECTS TREATED IN RELATION TO ONE ANOTHER

When a work covers two or more subjects treated in relation to one another, the number expressing this relationship, if available, is chosen. For example, a work on church and state is classed in 322.1 (the number in political science for church and state); a work on religion in public schools is classed in 379.28 (the number in education for the place of religion in public schools).

If there is no class number expressing the relationship, the choice depends on the nature of the relationship. A work treating two or more interrelated subjects is classed with the subject that is being acted upon. For example, a work on Shakespeare's influence on Keats is classed with the number for Keats. This is called the *rule of application*, and it takes precedence over all other rules.

## INTERDISCIPLINARY WORKS

If the work treats a subject from the point of view of two or more disciplines, the interdisciplinary number, if provided, is chosen. To be a candidate for application of the interdisciplinary number, the work must contain significant material on the discipline in which the interdisciplinary number is found. The interdisciplinary number may be indicated in the schedules by a note, and it appears opposite the first unindented term in the Relative Index. For example:

| | |
|---|---|
| Community-school relations | 306.432 |
| education | 371.19 |
| higher education | 378.103 |
| sociology | 306.432 |

As a result, a work on community-school relations that focuses on sociological and educational benefits would be classed in 306.432, the interdisciplinary number in sociology for community-school relations. However, if the work focuses just on the mechanics of setting up a community-school partnership to improve higher education, it would be classed in 378.103, the number in higher education for community-school relations.

If a subject is not given an interdisciplinary number, the class number in the discipline given the fullest treatment in the work is chosen. When the work involves many disciplines, numbers in 000 Computer science, information & general works are also possibilities.

Any other situation follows the rules for multitopical works.

## WORKS TREATING TWO OR MORE ASPECTS OF A SUBJECT

For works that treat two or more aspects of a subject, a ready-made number, if available, is used. If such a number is not available, the classifier should determine whether a number covering all the facets can be built. If not, a choice must be made between two or more numbers each covering some but not all of the aspects. The following sections discuss the guidelines for choosing numbers.

### Order of Preference

In choosing among different potential class numbers for the same work, certain aspects are preferred over others. Decision making in such situations depends upon many factors. First of all, between two or more aspects or characteristics of a subject (such as age, area, gender, historical periods, national origin), the one emphasized by the author may be considered foremost. If there is no such emphasis, then the general (and common sense) rule is that the most specific aspect is to be chosen. To be sure, to determine which is the most specific aspect is not always easy. To help resolve such situations certain guidance has been provided in the introduction to Edition 22.

In the DDC, *preference order* is officially defined as:

> The order indicating which one of two or more numbers is to be chosen when different characteristics of a subject cannot be shown in full by number building. A note (sometimes containing a table of preference) indicates which characteristic is to be selected for works covering more than one characteristic. When a notation can be synthesized to show two or more characteristics, it is a matter of citation order.[2]

In the schedules and tables, there are *tables of preference* (previously called tables of precedence) or *preference notes* where appropriate, as well as certain other general rules for choosing among numbers for two or more aspects.

### Table of Preference

A table of preference establishes the priority of one topic or aspect over another or others in a multitopical or multifaceted subject. Chapter 8 contains a discussion of the table of preference in Table 1 Standard Subdivisions. Such tables also appear throughout the schedules. For example, the following table of preference is found under 155.42–155.45 [Child psychology by] Specific groupings:

| | |
|---|---|
| Exceptional children . . . | 155.45 |
| Children by status, type, relationships | 155.44 |
| Children in specific age groups | 155.42 |
| Children by sex | 155.43 |

This table of preference must be observed in cases of complex subjects involving two or more aspects in a given title. For example, take the title *Psychology of Exceptional Sibling Children*. This complex subject can be broken into the following viable components:

| | |
|---|---|
| Psychology of sibling children | 155.443 |
| Psychology of exceptional children | 155.45 |

---

[2] Dewey, *Dewey Decimal Classification*, Edition 22, v. 1, p. lxxi.

Since, according to the table of preference above, 155.45 Exceptional children is to be preferred over 155.44 or its subdivisions, the class number will be 155.45. Similarly, according to the same table of preference, for a work on the psychology of preschool girls, the number 155.423 Psychology of children three to five is chosen over the number 155.433 Psychology of girls.

Another example of a table of preference is found under 658.401–658.409 Specific executive management activities:

| | |
|---|---|
| Personal aspects of executive management | 658.409 |
| Management of executive personnel | 658.407 |
| Internal organization | 658.402 |
| Managing change | 658.406 |
| Negotiation, conflict management, crisis management, contracting out | 658.405 |
| Planning, policy making, control, quality management | 658.401 |
| Decision making and information management | 658.403 |
| Social responsibility of executive management | 658.408 |
| Project management | 658.404 |

When one applies the above table, the results are:

(1) Decision making and information management for internal organization
658.402 not 658.403

(2) Policy making for project management
658.4012 not 658.404

Examples of many more such tables throughout the schedules can be cited. In addition there are preference notes with the same effect.

## Preference Notes
Instead of being in tabulated form, the order of preference of topics may be given as a general instruction to use either an earlier or later number in a specific schedule. Examples of such instructions are given below.

### USING EARLIER NUMBER
In some situations, the classifier is instructed to use the earlier number. For example:

> 331.3–331.6    Labor force by personal characteristics

Unless other instructions are given, class a subject with aspects in two or more subdivisions of 331.1–331.6 in the number coming first, e.g., young North American native women 331.34408997 (*not* 331.408997 or 331.6997)

In application:

Immigrant women labor
331.4    Women workers; not 331.62 Immigrants and aliens or its subdivisions

Middle-aged migrant workers
331.394  Middle-aged workers; not 331.544 Migrant and casual workers

## USING LAST NUMBER

More frequently, there are instructions to use the last number. For example, under 365 Penal and related institutions, the instruction reads:

> Unless other instructions are given, class a subject with aspects in two or more subdivisions of 365 in the number coming last, e.g., maximum security prisons for women 365.43 (*not* 365.33)

Therefore for:

> Maximum security military prisons
> 365.48     Military prison and prison camps, not 365.33 Institutions
>                  by degree of security

> Reform of halfway houses for juveniles
> 365.7     Reform of penal institutions, not 365.42 Institutions for
>                 juveniles

Under 395 Etiquette (Manners), a similar note appears with an instruction to use the class number coming last in 395. For example:

> Etiquette for wedding invitations
> 395.4     Social correspondence; not 395.22 [Etiquette for]
>                 Engagements and weddings

> Table manners for children
> 395.54     Table manners; not 395.122 [Etiquette for] Children

## General Guidelines for Preference

When no specific instructions are provided under a particular class, there are general guidelines for determining the order of preference. These guidelines are given in sections 5.7–5.10 of the introduction in volume 1 of the DDC[3] and are summarized below:

### BY THE NUMBER OF ZEROS IN A CLASS NUMBER

A general guideline, called the *rule of zero*, instructs the classifier to choose the number with the fewest zeros at the same position if a comparison can be made. In other words, at the same point of a hierarchy (e.g., the same main number or division), a subdivision without a zero is to be preferred over a subdivision with a zero; and similarly, a subdivision with one zero is to be preferred over a subdivision with two zeros. For example:

> Qualification of teachers in private schools
> 371.12     Professional qualifications of teachers; not 371.02 Private
>                 schools

> Manufacture of metal outdoor furniture
> 684.18     Outdoor furniture; not 684.105 Metal furniture

> Architecture of wooden ceilings
> 721.7     Ceiling; not 721.0448 Wood

---

[3] Dewey, *Dewey Decimal Classification*, Edition 22, v. 1, pp. xliii–xlv.

The rationale behind such a policy is that, generally, in a particular hierarchy in the DDC, subdivisions with a zero or two zeros are used for subdivisions applicable to the topic as a whole, whereas subdivisions without a zero represent specific subtopics.

## PREFERRING CONCRETE OVER ABSTRACT

When no specific guidance is provided in the schedules or tables and the rule of zero does not apply, there is the *table of last resort*:

(1)   Kinds of things
(2)   Parts of things
(3)   Materials from which things, kinds, or parts are made
(4)   Properties of things, kinds, parts, or materials
(5)   Processes within things, kinds, parts, or materials
(6)   Operations upon things, kinds, parts, or materials
(7)   Instrumentalities for performing such operations

This table is based on the principle of preferring the kind of thing over the part; the concrete over the abstract; thing/material over the process; and process over the agent.

The table of last resort should be used with caution. Do not apply this table if it appears to disregard the author's intention and emphasis. For example, if the author's emphasis in a work is clearly on process over thing or material, then the general order of preference should be reversed.

## SOURCES OF READY-MADE NUMBERS

In addition to the inside and outside sources of knowledge about the subject of a work, there are sources for ready-made class numbers for specific titles. These include:

(1)   Cataloging copy prepared by central or cooperative cataloging agencies or libraries such as the British Library and the Library of Congress (the home of the Decimal Classification Division, where the Dewey editorial office is also located);

(2)   Cataloging copy prepared by libraries sharing cataloging information found in union catalogs maintained by bibliographic utilities such as OCLC and RLG;

(3)   Cataloging-in-Publication (CIP) data given on the verso of the title pages of books whose publishers are enrolled in the CIP program at the Library of Congress or British Library; and

(4)   National bibliographies, such as the Australian National Bibliography, the British National Bibliography, and the Indian National Bibliography.

Some of these sources, including many of the national bibliographies, appear in print form. Many appear in electronic form. For instance, MARC bibliographic records prepared by the Library of Congress form a part of OCLC's WorldCat. They are also available through the online catalog of the Library of Congress, which can be found on the Library's web site (http://catalog.loc.gov/).

## SUMMARY

The work of practical classification involves two operations: determining the subject of a work and determining the disciplinary context in the DDC for that subject. The first operation involves the careful subject analysis of the document being classified. The subject of the work is what the author focuses upon, what he or she describes. This can be learned from the title and subtitle, with assistance from the book jacket or container, homepage, preface, table of contents, bibliography, and subject index. The title alone is never a sufficient indication of what a work is about, however simple and clear it may appear to be. It is also important to differentiate the author's viewpoint, the form of presentation, and the physical medium or form of the document from the subject proper.

The second operation, once the subject is properly analyzed, is to find the appropriate number to represent the subject. This process of classification begins by determining the main class, the division, and the section for the subject. This could be called "disciplinary analysis." When this has been done, classifiers should scan the subsections through levels of increasing specificity until they arrive at the appropriate number. They should proceed from general to specific, narrowing their search at every juncture. The various summaries can assist them by enabling a rapid transit down the hierarchical chain.

A number may also be further extended by adding another number either from the schedules or from any of the tables. But it must be remembered that Dewey is still not an exhaustive classification, and the class number whether found ready-made or extended by any device may still not cover all the aspects of the subject. In cases where a single number does not cover all topics or aspects a choice must be made among two or more available numbers. The choices in these cases are made according to the order of preference given in tables of preference, preference notes, or instructions in the introduction to the DDC.

In order to facilitate classification by the DDC and to render the operation more cost-effective, classifiers may consult various sources for ready-made numbers assigned by cataloging agencies or other libraries. Cataloging information, including class numbers, is available in electronic form as well as in print form, such as on the verso of the title pages of books.

## EXERCISES

Exercise 1:

Identify the class numbers for the following subjects:

(1) Aves: a zoological study

(2) Human heart diseases

(3) Nursing interventions for patients with meningitis

(4) 20th-century sculpture

(5) Reign of Elizabeth I of England

Exercise 2:

Classify the following subjects by using the appropriate table of preference:

(1) Preparing lunches for schools

(2) Deportation for political offenses

(3) Decorative lighting for weddings

(4) Miniature portrait paintings of women

(5) Compensation of working mothers

Exercise 3:

Identify the class numbers for the following subjects:

(1) Educational services in adult women prisons

(2) Retired immigrant labor

(3) Economics of production efficiency in agriculture

(4) Public safety programs about the transportation of radioactive materials

Exercise 4:

Identify the class numbers for the following subjects:

(1) Curricula in elementary schools

(2) Color printing by photomechanical techniques

(3) Manufacture of metallic chairs

(4) Atomic weight of curium (chemical element)

(5) Breeding of Oriental horses

(6) Diseases of arrowroot (starch crop)

## Chapter 5

# USING THE MANUAL

## INTRODUCTION

The Manual for the Dewey Decimal Classification gives advice on classifying in difficult areas, and provides guidance on choosing among related numbers.

The Manual was first published as part of the DDC in volume 4 of Edition 20. Its direct predecessor was *Manual on the Use of the Dewey Decimal Classification: Edition 19*,[1] which was published separately three years after the publication of Edition 19. The Edition 19 Manual was intended as a pragmatic guide to the Classification for practicing classifiers and students. It is arranged by Dewey number, and contains notes of varying lengths. "New Features in Edition 20" described the relationship between the Edition 19 Manual and the Edition 20 integrated Manual as follows:

> The Manual represents the core of a much larger body of notes first introduced in the separately published 1982 *Manual on the Use of the Dewey Decimal Classification: Edition 19*. . .The briefer notes of the 1982 Manual, and those that need to be used frequently, have been incorporated in the Schedules and Tables.[2]

In Edition 21, the Manual was greatly expanded. For Edition 22, the editors reviewed the appropriateness, length, and style of Manual notes with an eye toward streamlining the Manual to promote efficiency in classification. Information easily accommodated in notes in the tables and schedules has been transferred from the Manual, and redundant information already present in the schedules and tables has been eliminated. Basic instructions on the use of the Dewey Decimal Classification are consolidated in the introduction to Edition 22, and background information on schedules and tables is now located in this book. The remaining Manual entries have been rewritten in a consistent style to promote quick understanding and efficient use. The schedules, tables, and Relative Index contain references to the remaining Manual notes. In Edition 22, the Manual is located in volume 1, directly preceding the tables.

## SCOPE OF THE MANUAL

The Manual is not an exhaustive guide to the DDC. It is a selective guide that includes assistance on choosing among numbers and detailed instructions on the use of complicated schedules (e.g., Table 3, 004–006, 780, 800). Information is placed in the Manual when it cannot be succinctly represented within the framework of notes in the schedules and tables.

---

[1] John P. Comaromi and Margaret J. Warren, *Manual on the Use of the Dewey Decimal Classification: Edition 19* (Albany, NY: Forest Press, 1982).

[2] Melvil Dewey, *Dewey Decimal Classification and Relative Index*, Edition 20, edited by John P. Comaromi, Julianne Beall, Winton E. Matthews, Jr., and Gregory R. New (Albany, NY: OCLC Forest Press, 1989), v. 1, p. xix.

The Manual contains three kinds of notes:

(1) Notes on problems common to more than one number
(2) Notes on problems involving only one number (or a number and its subdivisions)
(3) Notes on differentiating numbers

## NOTES ON PROBLEMS COMMON TO MORE THAN ONE NUMBER

The Manual contains explanations of problems common to more than one number. The issues addressed may occur in a span of numbers (linked by "–") or a group of related numbers (linked by "and"). For example, the following Manual note offers advice on the classification of works by individual philosophers:

> 180–190
> Historical, geographic, persons treatment of philosophy
>
> Class single works by individual philosophers with the topic in philosophy. If there is no focus on a specific topic, class a work expressing primarily the philosopher's own viewpoint with the collected works of the philosopher in 180–190, e.g., use 193 for a general work by Hegel, such as *Phenomenology of Spirit*.
>
> Class a work by an individual philosopher that is primarily a discussion of other philosophers' writings with the other philosophers' writings. For example, use 190 for a work by a western philosopher that is mostly a criticism of contemporary philosophers.
>
> Use 100 for a work by an individual that takes a broad look at many questions in philosophy and does not seek to argue for the individual's own viewpoint.

The treatment of a production recorded in a different medium from the original production is explained succinctly in the Manual note at 791.437 and 791.447, 791.457, 792.9:

> 791.437 and 791.447, 791.457, 792.9
> Films, radio programs, television programs, stage productions
>
> A production recorded in a different medium than the original production is classed with the recording, not with the production, e.g., a staged opera recorded for television 791.4572 (a television program), *not* 792.542 (a staged opera).

For a classifier who occasionally uses these numbers, the note in the example above provides a welcome explanation of the treatment of such productions. For the classifier who uses the 790 Recreational and performing arts schedule on a regular basis, reading this note once will be sufficient.

Similarly:

>T1—081 and T1—082, T1—08351, T1—08352, T1—08421, T1—08422
>Men and women, Males twelve to twenty and females twelve to twenty,
>Young men and young women
>
>Use subdivisions for men and women only if the works explicitly
>emphasize the sex of the people treated . . .

The Manual note in the example above focuses on a single topic, identification of the sexes. Since this topic applies to the use of several standard subdivisions, it is explained more efficiently in the Manual as opposed to being listed under each applicable subdivision in Table 1.

General information notes involving a span of numbers will be discussed in the next section.

## NOTES ON PROBLEMS INVOLVING ONLY ONE NUMBER

A second kind of note, on problems involving only one number or a number and its logical subdivisions, is used to explain certain aspects of a schedule that cannot be explained within the regular framework of notes in the schedules and tables. Such a note may be needed due to the length of the explanation, the nature of the problem, and/or the frequency of use of the information. This type of note is also used for general information about a schedule.

For example, the Manual note for 220.92 describes the treatment of biography of individual persons in the Bible in 220 and its subdivisions:

>220.92
>Biography of individual persons in Bible
>
>Class a comprehensive biography of a Biblical person with the book
>or books with which the person is most closely associated, usually
>the historical part of the Bible in which the person's life is narrated,
>e.g., Solomon, King of Israel, in 1st Kings 222.53092. Solomon's
>association with 223 Poetic books is weaker. However, some
>Biblical persons are more closely associated with nonhistorical
>books, e.g., class Isaiah and Timothy with the books that bear their
>names, 224.1092 and 227.83092, respectively. Although they
>appear briefly in historical narratives, their lives are not narrated in
>full there. Use 225.92 for the apostles John, Peter, and Paul, since
>each is associated with a number of books in the New Testament, but
>use 226.092 for the other apostles, associated primarily with Gospels
>and Acts.

The Manual note for 221 Optional numbers for books of Old Testament (Tanakh) focuses on optional numbers for books of Tanakh. The note includes an alphabetic index to preferred and optional numbers for each book, followed by an optional schedule (222–224).

## General Information Notes

The general information (or general instructions) note, which may be located at a single number, a number and its subdivisions, or a span of numbers, is very important. General information notes should be read carefully by all users of the DDC, and referred to later as necessary.

Examples of general notes are the Manual notes on Table 3, Table 3A, Table 3B, and Table 5. Each contains detailed instructions on the use of the table in question, illustrated by sample titles with accompanying DDC numbers. The Manual notes on Table 3A and Table 3B also include flow charts that lead the classifier through each decision point in the table. The information previously presented in the general information note for Table 1 has been moved to the introduction to Edition 22 and is repeated in this book.

Several highly faceted schedules for which revisions were introduced in Edition 20 and Edition 21 continue to have lengthy Manual notes. These include 004–006, 352–354, 579–590, and 780. The Manual notes for these schedules contain detailed instructions on their use and, in some cases, several examples.

General information notes are not limited to main table numbers or main class and division numbers in the schedules. Subdivisions of classes with general information notes may have their own notes. The Manual note for Table 3B —1 Preference order for poetry, for instance, contains information on preference order illustrated by sample titles with DDC numbers. Even though there is a major Manual note for 780 Music, 782 Vocal music has its own Manual note complete with a flow chart.

### NOTES ON MAJOR REVISIONS

Major revisions in each edition of the DDC are introduced and explained by an extensive Manual note. The Manual note addresses the history and reasons for the revision, outlines the basic structure of the revised schedule, and gives detailed examples on its use with sample titles as illustrations. Since Edition 22 does not contain any major revisions, there are no examples of this type of note in the current edition. In Edition 21, two such revisions had major Manual notes: 351 Public administration and 560–590 Life sciences. Information from the notes on the major revisions in Edition 21 has been incorporated into the Edition 22 introduction, schedules, and tables, and is also included in this book. Notes that fit the other categories have remained.

### NOTES DIFFERENTIATING AMONG NUMBERS

A third kind of note is the note differentiating among numbers, the "versus" note. This is the most common type of note found in the Manual. The numbers may be within the same discipline or in different disciplines. In each case, the "if-in-doubt" number is specified. Two examples follow:

> 549 vs. 548
>
> Mineralogy vs. Crystallography
>
> Use 549 for the crystallography of specific minerals unless the minerals are used to study or explain a topic in 548, e.g., quartz, feldspar, and related crystals 549.68, but a study of isomorphism using quartz, feldspar, and related crystals 548.3. If in doubt, prefer 549.

004.6 vs. 621.382, 621.3981
Digital communications

Use 004.6 for works on digital communications that do not emphasize engineering, including works dealing with telecommunications and data communications engineering plus interfacing and communications in computer science.

Use 621.382 for works on digital telecommunications, or digital aspects of both telecommunications and data communications, that emphasize engineering. Use 621.3981 for works on computer data communications that emphasize engineering.

If in doubt, prefer in the following order: 004.6, 621.382, 621.3981.

## ORGANIZATION OF THE MANUAL

To facilitate its use, the Manual is arranged in the numerical order of the tables and schedules. Notes on the tables precede notes on the schedules. Each Manual note is listed at the preferred or "if-in-doubt" number. For classes with more than one note, the notes are usually arranged in the order listed under "Scope of the Manual" earlier in this chapter. Within each sequence, the broader span comes before the narrower span or individual numbers. A "vs." note always appears last. For example, the sequence of notes beginning with 004 is as follows:

004–006
004–006 vs. 621.39
004 vs. 005

The numbers are accompanied by their corresponding headings from the tables and schedules. The headings appear in boldface type on the line following the numbers. For example:

300 vs. 600
**Social sciences vs. Technology**

If the focus of the Manual note can be summarized in a single phrase, that heading is used in lieu of the headings. For example:

324 vs. 320.5, 320.9, 909, 930–990
**Political movements**

Subheadings are used to divide lengthy notes into sections. In several places, sections in notes are divided into subsections. The headings for subsections appear centered in italics. For example, the Manual note for 780 Music includes the following section and subsection:

**Examples**
*Works about music*

See-also references link related Manual notes within the Manual. See-also references may be from the full Manual note, or a paragraph or section of the note, to another Manual note (or section thereof). Each reference is listed in italics at the end of the paragraph, section, or note to which it applies. For example, the following reference appears at the end of the "Musicians" section of the Manual note for 780.92 Musicians and composers:

> See also 781.6 for discussion of musicians associated with traditions of music other than classical.

## SEE-MANUAL REFERENCES

*See-Manual references* in the schedules and tables refer the classifier to the entries in the Manual. The reference may be to a full note, several notes, and/or a section of a note. For example, the following see-Manual references to two Manual notes appear in the centered entry 571–575 Internal biological processes and structures:

> See Manual at 571–575 vs. 630; also at 579–590 vs. 571–575

In the entry for 904 Collected accounts of events, there is a reference to a section of a Manual note:

> See Manual at 900: Historic events vs. nonhistoric events

See-Manual references appear in the Relative Index under the appropriate index terms for the Manual note or section of the note (see the discussion in chapter 6).

## SUMMARY

The Manual provides practical advice on selected areas of the Dewey Decimal Classification. It gives guidance on choosing among numbers for the same topic, and detailed instructions on using complicated schedules.

## Chapter 6

# USING THE RELATIVE INDEX

## INTRODUCTION

An index is ordinarily an alphabetically arranged list of concepts occurring in a particular work. The index to the DDC is called the *Relative Index*. It has been a major part of each edition since the first (1876). It is, of course, primarily an adjunct or aid in the use of the schedules, which contain the core of the DDC. Nevertheless, for the DDC, it has always been a feature that transcends the normal usefulness of a good back-of-the-book index. The Relative Index is considered by many to be one of Melvil Dewey's paramount and enduring contributions to library classification and indexing.

## NEED AND IMPORTANCE OF THE RELATIVE INDEX

All terms found in the schedules and in the tables have been arranged logically in whole/part and genus/species relations, in other words, in a systematic order that proceeds from the general to the specific. Such arrangements are designed to mirror the structure of knowledge and its evolution. To locate a desired subject in the schedules, one needs at least a preliminary knowledge of its position in the universe of knowledge. But, as was stated earlier, it is very difficult, if not impossible, for any person, however learned, to have even a preliminary knowledge of all the subjects in the universe of knowledge. Therefore, at one time or another everyone who uses the DDC has to use the Relative Index, the key to the schedules. There are several reasons why.

### Limited Knowledge of the Classifier

A classifier at times may not always be familiar with the subject of the work being classified. At other times, the classifier may understand the subject but may not be aware of its location in the overall system. Take, for example, the subject of birthday cards: one may not even be able to guess where its primary class might fall. Some classes, such as engineering, are so crammed with topics that it is no easy matter to locate the desired subject by paging through the engineering schedule.

In some cases, through no fault of the classifier, the hierarchical trail leads to false ends or blind alleys. More determined efforts only incur increased frustration. At such times the Relative Index provides a road to the desired subject.

### Location of Some Subjects in the DDC

In addition, in the DDC itself the positions of some subjects are neither logical nor in accord with current scholarly consensus. Although many of the misplacements in the original plan of 1876 have been rectified in later editions, some remain to this day. In later developments of the system some new subjects had to be placed in locations outside of the preferred notational hierarchy because there were no vacant numbers available at logical places. Again, in these situations, the Relative Index can guide the classifier to the appropriate numbers.

## VALUE OF THE RELATIVE INDEX

There are different views on the use of the Relative Index. One group believes in using the schedules, i.e., the systematic hierarchical ladder, as much as possible. For them, the Relative Index should be used minimally and only in hours of difficulty. They believe that the more classifiers rely on the index, the more slowly they will learn the structure of the DDC.

Another view gives prime importance to the Relative Index, even going so far as to suggest that it be consulted every time one assigns a number. For those who hold this view, the Relative Index is the door through which one must pass before entering the house of Dewey numbers. Those who perhaps have too much faith in alphabetical arrangement, and who do not care to take the time to learn the logical approach that the schedules provide, subscribe to this view.

The most reasonable view is that classifiers should use the Relative Index as needed.

Whatever one thinks of the Relative Index and its use, it must be borne in mind that it is an integral part of the system and has always been so. This much is clear from the title: *Dewey Decimal Classification and Relative Index*. Therefore, the index should not be taken as merely an adjunct or a convenient key to the schedules. It complements the schedules by providing an independent approach to the classified structure they embody. Furthermore, the index goes beyond the straightforward alphabetical indexing of terms; through a helpful indexing technique, terms are also listed according to the disciplines in which they appear.

## NOMENCLATURE: RELATIVE INDEX

The index to the DDC has the formal name *Relative Index*. Its approach is the reverse of the approach of the schedules. In the schedules, subjects are distributed among disciplines. In the Relative Index all of the indexable terms found in captions and notes, plus terms with literary warrant for concepts represented by the schedules, have been arranged in an alphabetical sequence. The index is called "relative" because it relates subjects to the disciplines in the schedules. Take, for example, the subject amphibians. It has various aspects scattered throughout the schedules. Not all of them are listed in the Relative Index, of course, but we do find the following:

| | |
|---|---|
| Amphibians | 597.8 |
| agriculture | 639.378 |
| art representation | 704.943 278 |
| arts | T3C—362 78 |
| commercial hunting | 639.13 |
| conservation technology | 639.977 8 |
| drawing | 743.676 |
| food | 641.396 |
| cooking | 641.696 |
| paleozoology | 567.8 |
| resource economics | 333.957 8 |
| zoology | 597.8 |

As is obvious, many aspects of amphibians have been brought together from their scattered locations in the schedules.

## SCOPE OF THE INDEX

No index can be totally comprehensive or exhaustive. In using the Relative Index, it is important to know what is included and what is not.[1]

## What the Index Contains

The index is made up of the following kinds of terms in a single alphabetical sequence:

(1)  Indexable terms in the captions and notes of the schedules and tables
(2)  Terms with literary warrant for concepts in the schedules or tables
(3)  Some useful terms for topics represented by built numbers
(4)  Terms for broad concepts covered in Manual notes
(5)  Selected proper names in the following categories:

  (i)  Geographic names (names of countries, names of states and provinces of most countries, names of the counties of the United States, names of capital cities and other important municipalities, and names of important geographic features)

  (ii)  Names of persons (heads-of-state for the purpose of identifying historical periods; founders or revealers of religions; and initiators of schools of thought used to identify the schools)

## What the Index Does Not Contain

The Relative Index is not exhaustive. No index can be expected to contain all names of persons, cities, organizations, minerals, plants, animals, chemical compounds, drugs, manufactured articles, etc. Names are included in the Relative Index selectively. In addition, the following categories of terms are also excluded:

(1)  Phrases beginning with the adjectival form of countries, languages, nationalities, and religions, e.g., English poetry, French architecture, Hindu prayer books, Mexican cooking

(2)  Phrases containing general concepts represented by standard subdivisions such as education, history, maintenance, statistics, laboratories, and management, e.g., Art education, History of science, Automobile maintenance, Educational statistics, Medical laboratories, Restaurant management

A topic falling in either category listed above may be included if there is strong literary warrant for the phrase entry as a term sought by users, e.g., English literature. One of these phrases may also be included if it is a proper name or provides the only form of access to the topic, e.g., English Channel, English horns, English peas.

If a term being sought does not appear in the index, the classifier's first recourse is to look under the index listing for the broader class or term that contains the topic. For example, if the work in hand is a biography of John Milton or Ludwig van Beethoven— names not found in the Relative Index—the classifier should look instead under the

---

[1] The discussion refers to the content of the print version of the Relative Index; the version found in WebDewey contains many additional entries, including some categories of terms systematically excluded from the print version.

broad class to which each belongs: poets for Milton, composers for Beethoven. Similarly, for a work on the Chartered Institute of Library and Information Professionals (CILIP) or Oxford University (names not included in the Relative Index), one might look under "library associations" and "universities." If these terms do not help, one can look at terms in the next level up in the hierarchy, i.e., "organizations" and "higher education." The numbers for these terms will not, of course, provide specific numbers for works, but will point to appropriate general areas in the schedules or tables.

## Interdisciplinary Numbers

When a topic treated from the perspectives of two or more disciplines is represented by multiple numbers, the first class number displayed in the index entry (the number opposite the unindented term) is the number designated for interdisciplinary works. The discipline of the interdisciplinary number may be repeated as a subentry. For example:

| | |
|---|---|
| Elastomers | 678 |
| chemistry | 547.842 |
| manufacturing technology | 678 |
| equipment manufacture | 681.766 8 |
| materials science | 620.194 |
| structural engineering | 624.189 4 |

In the entry above, 678 is the interdisciplinary number for elastomers <u>and</u> the number for the manufacture of elastomers. A work that discusses elastomers from the viewpoint of materials science and manufacturing would be classed in 678, the interdisciplinary number for elastomers; a work on the manufacturing of elastomers would be classed in the same number. A work limited to the materials science aspects of elastomers, on the other hand, would be classed in 620.194.

The Relative Index does not contain interdisciplinary numbers for every entry. The interdisciplinary number is not given in the following cases:

(1) When the first term in the entry is ambiguous
(2) When the index term has no disciplinary focus
(3) When there is little or no literary warrant for the interdisciplinary number

## ORGANIZATION OF THE INDEX

Since Edition 16 (1958), the Relative Index has appeared in a separate volume. In Edition 22, it occupies the whole of volume 4. The text of the Relative Index is prefaced by a list of abbreviations. Detailed guidelines on its use are given in the introduction to Edition 22.[2]

Each page of the index is divided into two columns of entries. An entry is composed of a term, discipline (if any), and a corresponding DDC number. For example:

| | |
|---|---|
| Corn syrup | 641.336 |
| commercial processing | 664.133 |
| food | 641.336 |
| *see also* Sugar | |

---

[2]Dewey, *Dewey Decimal Classification,* Edition 22, v. 1, pp. lix-lxii.

These entries are to be read as follows:

| | |
|---|---|
| Corn syrup, *interdisciplinary works* | 641.336 |
| Corn syrup, *commercial processing* | 664.133 |
| Corn syrup *as food* | 641.336 |

The last line displays an instance of a *see-also* reference to a broader topic. Under the entry referred to, there are additional numbers of possible value.

## READING THE INDEX

Conceptually and typographically the Relative Index is highly structured to yield a maximum amount of information in a minimum amount of space. Some points to keep in mind are:

(1)   American spelling is used, e.g., color, catalog, labor

(2)   All terms are arranged in word-by-word (as distinguished from letter-by-letter) order. A hyphen is treated as a space. For example:

Cross County (Ark.)
Cross-cultural communication
Cross-cultural psychology
Cross dressing
Cross-examination
Cross River languages
Cross River State (Nigeria)
Cross-stitch
Crossbills
Crossbreeding

(3)   Entries with the same word or phrase but with different marks of punctuation are arranged in the following order:

Term
Term. Subheading
Term (Parenthetical qualifier)
Term, inverted term qualifier
Term as part of phrase

For example:

Canada
Canada, Eastern
Canada, Western
Canada goose

Georgia
Georgia (Republic)
Georgia, Strait of (B.C.)

United States
United States. Central Intelligence Agency
United States. Continental Congress
United States. Court of Customs and Patent Appeals
United States. Navy. SEALs
United States. Supreme Court reports
United States Code

(4)     Initialisms and acronyms are entered without punctuation and are filed as if spelled as one word. For example:

ACTH (Hormone)
AIDS (Disease)
CATV systems
PACS (Action committees)
SAT (Assessment test)

(5)     Most numbers are entered in their spelled out form. For example:

Three Rivers (England)
Three wise men (Christian doctrines)
Twentieth century

Proper names containing Arabic or Roman numerals have not been rewritten, and the number files before a letter in the same position, e.g., the entry "100 Mile House (B.C.)" files before A at the beginning of the index.

(6)     Qualifiers, if needed, are added to differentiate homographs:

Biscuits (Breads)
Biscuits (Cookies)
Foundations (Organizations)
Foundations (Structures)
Rays (Fishes)
Rays (Nuclear physics)

(7)     The choice of singular versus plural form follows ISO 999:1996, *Guidelines for the content, organization and presentation of indexes.* Abstract nouns are usually found in the singular, e.g., Divorce, Immortality, Pathology, Truth. Concrete nouns are usually found in the plural form, e.g., Farmers, Libraries, Pianos, Roads. Parts of the body are in the plural only when more than one occurs in a fully formed organism (e.g., Ears, Hands, Nose).

Plants and animals follow scientific convention in the choice of singular versus plural form, with the decision based on whether the taxonomic class has more than one member (e.g., Horses, Lion, Lipizzaner horse). Where usage varies across disciplines, the index entry reflects the form preferred in the discipline where the interdisciplinary works are classed. For example, while there are several kinds of hemp in botany, the index entry is in the singular, because the interdisciplinary number for hemp is 677.12, the number for hemp as a kind of textile fiber.

(8)     Place names and other proper names are generally given in the form specified by the second edition, 2002 revision, of the *Anglo-American Cataloguing Rules*

(*AACR2*), based on the names established in the Library of Congress authority files. If the *AACR2* name is not the common English name, an entry is also included under the familiar form of the name.

(9)  Plants and animals are indexed under their scientific and common names.

## Phrases/Multiword Terms

Subjects commonly represented by phrases are usually entered in adjective-noun form. For example:

> Agricultural banks
> Agricultural credit
> Agricultural law
> Austrian winter peas
> Color television
> Indian Ocean
> Inorganic chemistry
> Islamic calendar
> Reinforced concrete

For many other entries, even though a phrase entry could be imagined, such an entry would separate the particular aspect represented by the phrase entry from the other aspects of the base concept. For example, while "Ancient Egypt" and "Grassland ecology" might be useful phrase headings, entering these concepts as phrases would separate these aspects from other aspects of the topics "Egypt" and " Grasslands." For this reason, these concepts are entered as follows:

| | |
|---|---|
| Egypt | 962 |
| | T2—62 |
|    ancient | 932 |
| | T2—32 |
| | |
| Grasslands | 333.74 |
| | T2—153 |
|    animal husbandry | 636.084 5 |
|    biology | 578.74 |
|    ecology | 577.4 |
|    economics | 333.74 |
|    geography | 910.915 3 |
|    geomorphology | 551.453 |
|    physical geography | 910.021 53 |

If the phrase entry for a topic represents a highly sought term, the topic may be entered as an entry/subentry as well as a phrase entry, e.g., Forest ecology and Forest lands—ecology.

## Looking under Key Terms

As a broad rule: If one term in a phrase refers to an object or a substance and the other refers to a technique or a process or an action, it is better to look under the object/substance, the concrete term, for that is the way most people store information. For example, "Solar flares" is indexed under Solar flares, because "solar" is the adjective pertaining to the sun (an object). Further examples:

> Body mechanics
> Corporate law
> Television transmission

## Use of Capital Letters

Unless there are proper nouns involved, only the main index entry begins with an initial capital letter; its subentries begin with a small letter. The use of capitals for the initial term of main entries is another device to show superordinate and subordinate relations of subjects and/or disciplines in the Index.

## Abbreviations Used in Entries

*AACR2* forms of abbreviations, particularly those used in qualifiers of geographic names, are used in conjunction with entries in the Relative Index. Here are a few examples:

> Bras d'Or Lake (N.S.)
> Colville Lake (N.W.T)
> Hamilton (N.Z.)
> Hamilton (Ont.)
> New York (N.Y.)
> Nicholas County (W. Va.)
> Red Deer (Alta.)

## Initialisms and Acronyms

Topics that can be expressed as initialisms or acronyms are indexed under both the initialism or acronym and the spelled-out form. For example:

| | |
|---|---|
| CDs (Compact discs) | 384 |
| Compact discs | 384 |
| NATO (Alliance) | 355.031 091 821 |
| North Atlantic Treaty Organization | 355.031 091 821 |

## DEPICTING RANK RELATIONS

In the Relative Index some entries stand alone without subentries:

| | |
|---|---|
| Autocracy (Absolute monarchy) | 321.6 |
| Autographs | 929.88 |
| Chin dynasty | 931.04 |
| Lions Bay (B.C.) | T2—711 33 |
| Sheep dogs | 636.737 |
| Siemens process | 669.142 2 |
| Theravada Buddhism | 294.391 |
| Voodooism | 299.675 |

Many entries, on the other hand, have subentries indicating aspects. At first glance such entries, indeed all the entries taken together, seem to make up an involved and tangled alphabetized web. But the web is more approachable than it appears.

## Use of Typographical Indentions

Typographical indentions are used to show the multiplicity of relations and aspects in which a given term figures. Once one learns to read the indentions, there is little difficulty in locating and following the various terms and their relations to one another. Here are two fairly simple entries that tell the classifier a great deal about the nature of the Relative Index:

| | |
|---|---|
| Rates | |
| communications industry | 384.041 |
| insurance | 368.011 |
| transportation services | 388.049 |
| Rates (United Kingdom) | 336.22 |
| law | 343.054 2 |
| public finance | 336.22 |

In the first entry, there is no class number opposite the unindented term "Rates." Rates is a word that appears in many fields of study with a variety of meanings. In the schedules it is a term that is used in the three fields that are indented below its index entry. The actual subjects are communications rates, insurance rates, and transportation rates. Indeed, the term "insurance rates" is so common that it has also been indexed under its natural word order. Rates has no interdisciplinary number opposite its unindented entry because there is no single disciplinary focus for "rates" in its general sense.

"Rates (United Kingdom)," on the other hand, is a genuine subject: the term means local taxes paid by British property owners. Because Rates (United Kingdom) has a distinct meaning, it is a candidate for an interdisciplinary number. "Rates" in the sense of local taxes appears in public finance and law. Interdisciplinary works on taxes are classed in public finance; therefore, the interdisciplinary number for rates in the sense of taxes falls in public finance. In the example, 336.22 is listed as the interdisciplinary number for Rates (United Kingdom) opposite the unindented entry for the term. In the Relative Index, the discipline in which the interdisciplinary number falls may be repeated as a subentry if there are several subentries, or if the meaning of the discipline may not be clear. Under "Rates (United Kingdom)," the name of the discipline in which the interdisciplinary number is located, public finance, is repeated as a subentry.

The first "Rates" entry illustrates an important point about the Relative Index: the classifier cannot depend on the Relative Index for a list of all topics covered by the Classification. The section "What the Index Does Not Contain" found earlier in this chapter describes some of the omissions. Also, as a general rule, the schedules and tables are not recapitulated in the Relative Index. Therefore, "Rates—postal communication" will not be found in the Relative Index. This entry under rates is covered by the broader term Rates—communications industry, of which postal communication is a part.

It is important to keep the foregoing in mind when using the Relative Index. Here is a slightly more complicated entry:

| | |
|---|---|
| Cotton | |
| agricultural economics | 338.173 51 |
| botany | 583.685 |
| fiber crop | 633.51 |
| textiles | 677.21 |
| arts | 746.042 1 |
| *see also* Textiles | |

In this entry, an interdisciplinary number is not given for cotton, because it is unlikely that one disciplinary focus can be determined for general works on cotton as a fabric *and* cotton as a plant species (if such works even exist). Notice, however, the subentry for the discipline "textiles" and sub-subentry for "arts." The number 677.21 is to be used for works on the production of cotton fibers and fabric; the number 746.0421 is to be used for works on the use of cotton fibers and fabrics in the arts. The subindention of "arts" under textiles tells us that works on the production of cotton fibers and the use of cotton fibers in the arts should be classed in the technology number, 677.12. The *see-also* reference is also subindented under the subentry textiles, and leads the classifier to other useful entries under the broader term, Textiles.

Here is another complicated entry:

| | |
|---|---|
| Divorce | 306.89 |
| ethics | 173 |
| religion | 205.63 |
| Buddhism | 294.356 3 |
| Christianity | 241.63 |
| Hinduism | 294.548 63 |
| Islam | 297.563 |
| Judaism | 296.363 |
| Judaism | 296.444 4 |
| law | 346.016 6 |
| psychology | 155.93 |
| religion | 204.41 |
| social theology | 201.7 |
| Christianity | 261.835 89 |
| social welfare | 362.829 4 |
| *see also* Families — social welfare | |
| sociology | 306.89 |

The interdisciplinary number for divorce is 306.89; it is repeated at the end of this long entry opposite its disciplinary entry, sociology. The ethics of divorce is classed in 173; the religious ethics of divorce is classed in 205.63. The number for the ethics of divorce in specific religions is listed opposite the name of the religion at the sub-sub-subentry level. The example also shows how aspects have aspects that may in turn have aspects: Divorce—ethics—religion—Buddhism illustrates this. The entry for Judaism is repeated as a subentry directly under Divorce because Judaism has a special rite for divorce.

Comprehensive works on divorce in Judaism would be classed in 296.4444, not in 296.363. While the Relative Index discloses this information to the astute user, it is always a good idea to verify the interpretation of the number in the schedules and tables. A final point to note in this example is the indented *see also* reference—it refers to social welfare, not to divorce. Had the reference been to divorce, it would have fallen directly under the "s" of sociology.

## ENTRIES FROM THE SIX TABLES

Index entries from the six tables found in volume 1 have the following format:

(1)  The letter T followed by the number of the Table
(2)  An em dash
(3)  The table number for the concept

For example:

Coast Mountains (B.C.)  T2—711 1

This entry tells us that the term is from Table 2 (Geographic Areas, Historical Periods, Persons) and its number is —7111. The em dash before the number indicates that the number is never to be used alone; it must be appended to another number from the schedules or tables.

## REFERENCES TO THE MANUAL

The Relative Index includes index entries for Manual notes. They appear as *see* references under appropriate terms and following entries that carry class numbers and *see-also* references. The "see Manual at" appears in italics, followed by the number of the Manual note. For example:

New Age religions                                  299.93
    *see Manual* at 299.93


Therapeutics                                        615.5
    veterinary medicine                             636.089 55
    *see Manual at* 613 vs. 612, 615.8;
        *also at* 615.8


Voice
    human physiology                                612.78
    music                                           783
        *see Manual at* 782
    preaching                                       251.03
    rhetoric of speech                              808.5

The first example, "*see Manual at* 299.93," refers the classifier to the Manual note for 299.93. The second example refers the classifier to two notes in the Manual pertinent to the topics of therapeutics: 613 vs. 612, 615.8; and 615.8. The reference to the Manual in the third example is subindented under "music," and therefore is limited to a discussion of Voice—music at 782, not voice in general.

## SUMMARY

The Relative Index in volume 4 is a key to the classified (systematic) arrangement of concepts in the schedules and tables. In the Relative Index, the disciplines are subordinated to subject. Therefore, it can be seen at a glance how the various aspects of a subject are scattered by discipline—something that is not possible within the schedules.

The Relative Index contains in a single alphabet and in word-by-word sequence most of the indexable terms found in the schedules and tables, plus some commonly used synonyms and terms with literary warrant for concepts found in the schedules and tables. Subjects in phrase form are usually entered in a direct form, e.g., Civil engineering, not Engineering, Civil. For multiword concepts one should look under all key terms, giving priority to a concrete object over an abstract process, technique, or action. Coordinate and subordinate relations are depicted through indentions and the use of an initial capital letter in the main entry.

Lastly, as a matter of advice, the classifier should not rely too heavily on the Relative Index. Ideally, class numbers should be determined by following the hierarchical structure in the schedules. In reality, most classifiers consult the Relative Index because it provides a shortcut or starting point. However, whenever a number is gleaned from the Relative Index, it must be verified in the schedules.

## EXERCISES

Exercise 1:

Under what terms should you look in the Relative Index for the following subjects?

(1) Ronald Reagan (the actor)

(2) Allstate Insurance Company

(3) John Lennon (the singer-composer of the rock group The Beatles)

(4) AZT (the anti-AIDS drug)

(5) Chlorofluorocarbons

(6) Santa Claus

(7) Sneakers (shoes)

(8) Babe Ruth (the baseball player)

(9) Black widow spider

Exercise 2:

Under which term would you look for the following topics?

(1) Anthology of one-act plays

(2) Libraries for children

(3) Fabian socialism

(4) Dynamics of particles

(5) Air-to-air guided missiles

(6) Modern history

(7) Modeling pottery

(8) History of privateering

## Chapter 7

# SYNTHESIS OF CLASS NUMBERS OR PRACTICAL NUMBER BUILDING

## INTRODUCTION

In its present form, the DDC falls between the two extremes of enumerative and faceted classification. It began as an enumerative classification scheme. Nonetheless, as A. C. Foskett has pointed out, even in the earlier editions of the DDC, "a very clear facet structure" is discernible in some places, notably Class 400 Philology. However, he goes on to say, "Dewey does not appear to have seen the real significance of this, and it was left to Ranganathan some 50 years later to make explicit and generalize the principle which is implicit and restricted in this example; nevertheless, in this as in many other points, Dewey showed the way ahead at a very early stage."[1] From Edition 18 on, with the introduction of more tables and add notes, the DDC has displayed its faceted structure more explicitly.

Edition 22 is even more faceted than earlier editions, with more provisions for the synthesis of class numbers. Needless to say, the DDC has not remained as simple as it was in the beginning, but has become more complex in structure and more sophisticated in its methods. It is now better equipped for the close analysis of knowledge and the subsequent classification of quite narrow (or micro) subjects through synthesis, or number building.

## KINDS OF NUMBER BUILDING IN THE DDC

The DDC schedules include ready-made class numbers for most important subjects. Nevertheless, many subjects are still not explicitly provided for in the schedules; these can be synthesized by the number-building process. Number building is the process of constructing a number by adding notation from the tables or other parts of the schedules to a base number. Broadly speaking, there are two methods of number building in Dewey:

(1)   Building a number as appropriate, without specific instructions
(2)   Building a number according to instructions found under a particular entry

### Building a Number without Specific Instructions

Unless indicated otherwise, any class number in the schedules may be extended by any number taken from Table 1 Standard Subdivisions for a topic that approximates the whole of the number. In other words, a number or its extension from Table 1 may be used where appropriate without a specific instruction to do so. The only restriction is that the classifier must follow the instructions in Table 1 with regard to the correct application of the numbers. The application of Table 1 is discussed in chapter 8.

### Number Building, or Synthesis, upon Instruction

The other kind of number building is done only upon instruction found at an entry in the schedules or tables. When a number is to be extended by any other number, either

---

[1] A. C. Foskett, *The Subject Approach to Information*, 5th ed. (London: Library Association, 1996), p. 258.

from the schedules or from Tables 2–6, there are always specific instructions in the form of add notes that are given at the entry. These add instructions or notes are also called number-building notes. They always include one or more examples in order to ensure that the note is properly understood. The number to be extended is called the *base number*, which can be as brief as one digit or as long as six or seven. It is the unvarying part of the number upon which many class numbers can be built. A base number may be a number from the schedules or from one of the tables. In the latter case, the built number must be added to a base number from the schedules to form a complete class number. Chapters 8–12 discuss number building through the use of Tables 1–6.[2] The remaining part of this chapter explains the process of number building from the schedules only.

## BUILDING CLASS NUMBERS FROM THE SCHEDULES

Upon instruction, a complex number may be built by appending a full number or a segment of a class number taken from anywhere in the schedules to a base number, also taken from the schedules, as shown in the example of mathematics libraries below.

It should be remembered that a complete class number must contain as the first part, or as the base number, a class number from the schedules. The add instructions may be either limited to a given entry or pertain to a span of class numbers.

### Citation Order

In building a number for a complex subject, it is important to determine the proper citation order, i.e., the order in which the parts of the number are strung together into a complete number. In most cases, the base number represents the main focus of the subject. For example, the class number for geology of North America would begin with a base number representing geology; so would the number for a journal of geology. In many other cases, the citation order is less obvious.

Suppose a number is needed for a work on mathematics libraries. Two disciplines are involved, library science and mathematics. The first problem is to determine which discipline is to be considered the primary one, which means that it will be cited (given) first in the DDC number. The classifier has to decide which discipline contains the other, whether to consider the work a treatment of the mathematics of libraries or a treatment of libraries specializing in mathematics. In the example at hand, the primary discipline is library science 020. By scanning the 020 section from 021–029 (either in the third summary or directly in the schedules), the classifier finds the following entry:

> 026      Libraries, archives, information centers devoted to specific subjects and disciplines

This is the proper section, but it is broader than the subject of the work being classified. Numbers or notes that are more specific are needed so that the base number can be particularized down to the subject of the item in hand. At 026.001–.999, the following instruction is found:

> Add to base number 026 notation 001–999, e.g., medical libraries 026.61. . .

---

[2] Chapter 10 contains a brief discussion of cutter numbers, which are often used in combination with a class number to form a complete call number. A call number is a set of letters, numerals, or other symbols (in combination or alone) used by a library to identify a specific copy of a work.

The number for mathematics is easily identified as 510. By appending 510 to 026, as instructed, the classifier creates the proper number: 026.51.

## ADDING A FULL NUMBER

This is the simplest kind of synthesis. Here a full number from anywhere in the schedules is added to another full class number that has been designated the base number. Usually this kind of number-building note is in the form "Add to base number . . . notation 001–999, e.g., . . . ." In other words, add any number in the schedules to the base number. The number 026.51 Mathematics libraries results from adding a full class number 510 to another full class number 026. More examples for 026 are:

(1)  Libraries specializing in the fine arts       $026 + 700 = 026.7$
(2)  Libraries specializing in folklore            $026 + 398 = 026.398$
(3)  Libraries specializing in genealogy           $026 + 929.1 = 026.9291$

Note two things:

(1)  Addition means to append the required number to the end of the base number
(2)  All final zero digits after the decimal point are discarded

In the last example, note also that only one decimal point has been retained in the proper number; it falls, as it always does, after the third digit if there are more than three digits in the number.

Here is a subject that has a slightly longer base number, namely, reporting on diplomatic matters. Again, two fields are involved: journalism and diplomacy. Does the item treat the diplomacy of journalism or journalism about diplomacy? The latter is the case; therefore, the primary field of study is journalism. The Relative Index would be the best place to start in this case because it is not immediately apparent where journalism belongs. The index lists Journalism 070.4. Also, in the schedules at 070, the summary provides the number 070.4 for journalism. Reading through the entries at 070.4, the classifier encounters features and special topics at 070.44. When perusing 070.44, the classifier finds that 070.449 deals with the journalism of specific subjects. The add note follows the standard pattern:

> Add to base number 070.449 notation 001–999, e.g., works about journalistic aspect of health columns 070.449613 . . .

By scanning the third summary or the Relative Index, the classifier can locate the right number for diplomacy. The third summary indicates that International relations is found at 327; the Relative Index lists diplomacy at 327.2. So the proper number for diplomatic journalism is:

> $070.449 + 327.2 = 070.4493272$

More examples for 070.449 are:

(1)  Medical journalism        $070.449 + 610 = 070.44961$
(2)  Legal journalism          $070.449 + 340 = 070.44934$
(3)  Financial journalism      $070.449 + 332 = 070.449332$
(4)  Sports journalism         $070.449 + 796 = 070.449796$

Here is one final set of items, one dealing with the Bible. The first item deals with astronomy in the Bible. Is the subject the effect of the Bible on astronomy or astronomy as found in the Bible? The latter is the case. Therefore, the number for the Bible serves as the base number. The second summary reveals that the Bible has an entire division to itself; unfortunately for the classifier none of its sections seems to fit the topic astronomy in the Bible. That is indeed the case. Here is an instance where the subject deals with the division itself, i.e., the entire Bible, rather than with any of the sections of the division. What must be done here is to look at 220 itself, not 221–229. The summary for 220.1–220.9 lists 220.8 Nonreligious subjects treated in the Bible. At that entry, the following is found among its subdivisions:

> 220.800 1–.899 9    Specific nonreligious subjects
> Add to base number 220.8 notation 001–999, e.g.,
> natural sciences in the Bible 220.85 . . .

Both the second summary and the Relative Index give 520 for Astronomy. The proper number, therefore, is 220.8 + 520 = 220.852. More examples of the treatment of nonreligious topics in the Bible are:

(1)  Women in the Bible          220.8 + 305.4 = 220.83054
     (Use the Relative Index to find the number for women.)

(2)  UFOs in the Bible           220.8 + 001.942 = 220.8001942
     (Use the Relative Index to find the number for UFOs.)

(3)  Mother's love in the Bible   220.8 + 306.8743 = 220.83068743
     (Use the Relative Index. While "Mother's love" is not in the index, "Mothers—family relationships" is.)

## ADDING A PART OF A NUMBER

Sometimes, only a segment of another number can be added to the designated base number. This segment is considered to be the secondary facet in Dewey, or a secondary aspect of the subject.

Suppose a work about wages in textile industries needs to be classified. In this instance, the rule of thumb on separating topic and context is not much help. That is, the question—Is this a work about wages in textile industries or a work about textile industries in the context of wages?—can be answered by saying that both work perfectly well. It is hard to tell which is subsumed under which. The classifier needs to know whether to use the number for textile industries (338.47677) or the number for wages (331.21). Which element of the subject will precede the other?

The DDC provides assistance in this particular situation. At 330 in the schedules, there is a table of preference that directs the classifier to which element should be preferred when two elements of the subject of a work fall within the discipline of economics. The table of preference at 330 shows that 331 Labor economics (a factor of production) precedes 338 Production. This means that wages will precede industry. Next, wages in the Relative Index should be checked. This search leads the classifier to the number for compensation in the schedules, 331.21, since wages are a form of compensation. Reading through the notes in the entry at 331.21 Compensation, the classifier encounters a see reference: ". . . for compensation by industry and occupation, see

331.28." Another way of finding 331.28 Compensation by industry and occupation is to peruse the summary at 331.2 Conditions of employment.

Whichever route (Relative Index vs. summary) is employed to get to 331.28, once there the schedules still need to be read further. At 331.282–.289 Compensation in extractive, manufacturing, construction industries and occupations, an add note is found:

> Add to base number 331.28 the numbers following 6 in 620–690, e.g., compensation in the mining industry 331.2822, average factory compensation 331.287
>> Subdivisions are added for industries, occupations, or both

The note following the add note assures the classifier that building a number for industry only is permitted; this helpful type of note appears in many places in Edition 22 under multiterm headings. Returning to the work in hand, the next step is to find the number for textile manufacturing. The class number for the manufacturing of textiles is 677; this number can be found through either the third summary or the Relative Index. In 677 the number following 6 is 77. Thus, as instructed, 77 is added to 331.28, resulting in 331.2877, the number for wages in textile industries. Wages in agriculture would be 331.28 + 630 = 331.283.

## ADDITION BY WAY OF A FACET INDICATOR

There are times when a whole number or a segment of a number cannot be attached directly to a base number. When this situation arises, a facet indicator is needed to provide access to the base number. The reason is that if a whole or a partial number were attached directly to a base number, there would be a conflict—the same number would mean two different things. For example:

> 778.5   Cinematography, video production, related activities
> 778.52      General topics of cinematography and video production
>> Add to base number 778.52 the numbers following 778.5 in 778.53–778.58, e.g., lighting for cinematography and video production 778.52343

The numbers and captions for some of the numbers in 778.53–778.58 include:

> 778.53      Cinematography (Motion picture photography)
> 778.532      Darkroom and laboratory practice
> 778.534      Specific types and elements of cinematography
> 778.535      Editing films
> 778.538      Cinematography of specific subjects
> 778.55      Motion picture projection
> 778.56      Special kinds of cinematography
> 778.58      Preservation and storage of motion picture films

If the numbers following 778.5 in 778.53–778.58 were added directly to 778.5 (as has been done routinely for number building up to this point), the result would be 778.535 for editing in cinematography and video production. But this number already means editing films in cinematography alone. Because some numbers that arise from the normal process of number building have already been used to represent another topic, a facet indicator is needed to produce a unique number. In the example above, the 2 in

778.52 is the facet indicator.[3] As a result, the number for editing in cinematography and video production is 778.5235. In many cases, the facet indicator is built into the base number: the classifier does not have to add a facet indicator (e.g., zero) to the base number before adding something else. In other cases, the classifier must add a facet indicator before proceeding.

Here are two more examples of base numbers with built-in facet indicators:

(1)  Housing horses                        636.1 $\underline{0}$ + 831 = 636.10831

(2)  Effect of science and technology   701.$\underline{0}$ + 5 = 701.05
     on fine and decorative arts

## COLLECTIVE ADD NOTES

In the print schedules, when all or most of a continuous span of numbers may be expanded by the addition of facets from another continuous span of numbers, the add instruction is given only one time. Since the numbers and the instructions to add to them are found on the same page, all such numbers are asterisked (*), or marked by some other typographical device, and the footnote that corresponds to the asterisk is found at the bottom of the page. For example, on p. 1024 of volume 2 of DDC 22, the terms in the captions in all of the subdivisions of 546.39 Alkaline-earth metals (Group 2) have been marked with an asterisk. The corresponding footnote says to add as instructed under 546. This means that once the appropriate element has been chosen, the classifier should turn to 546 where an add table, or internal table, is found. An excerpt from the table follows:

Add to each subdivision identified by * as follows:
>1–3   The element, compounds, mixtures
           Class theoretical, physical, analytical chemistry of the
           element, compounds, mixtures, in 4–6; class
           comprehensive works in base number for the element in
           546.3–546.7
1        The element
2        Compounds
           Names of compounds usually end in -ide or one of the
           suffixes listed in 22 and 24 below
               *For organo compounds, see 547.01–547.08*
22       Acids and bases
           Names of acids usually end in -ic or -ous
24       Salts
           Names of salts frequently end in -ate or -ite
25       Complex compounds

Suppose the work being classified is on magnesium salts. Through the index, magnesium (546.392) can be found. The footnote at 546.392 leads to the table at 546, where

---

[3] In the DDC, the facet indicator often indicates that what follows represents a different facet, but it does not always indicate the nature of the facet. For a further discussion of facet indicators in the DDC, see chapter 8.

the classifier is told to add the number 24 for salts to the base number (whatever number is to the left of the asterisk). The proper number is:

$$546.392 + 24 = 546.39224$$

This brings up an interesting question: if $546.392 + 1 = 546.3921$ is the number for the element magnesium studied within the context of inorganic chemistry, what is 546.392 to be used for? Isn't it the number for the element magnesium? The answer is that the number 546.3921 is assigned to a work that deals only with magnesium as an element, whereas the number 546.392 is used for a work on magnesium with respect to more than one aspect enumerated in the table, such as compounds, alloys, etc.

Perhaps the following caveat is not necessary, but it remains a useful admonition: A topic that is not asterisked cannot benefit from the extensions provided by a footnote. The salts of americium remain in 546.441 without further identification because there is no provision that allows adding further notation to the base number.

## SUMMARY

Numbers (or parts of numbers) from the schedules or tables may be used to extend (or subdivide) many DDC class numbers in the schedules. This process of extending class numbers is called number building; in general, it can be done only when there are number-building instructions in the schedules or tables. (An exception is the application of notation from Table 1 Standard Subdivisions, a process that will be dealt with in the next chapter.) Number-building instructions may be found at an entry, in a footnote, or under another number or span of numbers to which the footnote has sent the classifier.

Upon instruction, numbers in the schedules may be added to another number to form complex numbers. When two fields of study or two topics are discussed in a work, finding the add instructions efficiently depends upon the classifier's ability to determine the primary field of study. A general rule is that the primary field of study is the one considered to contain or provide a context for the other. Occasionally, a table of preference tells the classifier which one of two fields or subjects takes precedence over the other. When the context/topic relationship is not obvious, and no preference table is available, the classifier will simply have to look at the numbers for both topics and choose the one that allows extension, i.e., the number with an add note.

In all the activity that the classifier engages in with respect to using the DDC, none is so fraught with the possibility of error as the process of number building. When building numbers, we must ascertain that the base number is correct, that a vital digit has not been added or dropped, and that the number being added to the base number is neither more nor less than it should be. After the number is built, it must be checked against the schedules to ensure that the synthesized number does not conflict with any instructions or numbers in the schedules.

The importance of building the right number needs to be considered in the context of providing access to what has been written. There is a long train of effort behind every work that a classifier encounters. If the classifier gives it an inappropriate number, the work will be stored where a user is unlikely to find it. Its reason for being written is thereby much diminished.

## EXERCISES

Exercise 1:

Build class numbers for the following subjects using whole schedule numbers:

(1)  Library classification for economics

(2)  Special libraries devoted to Judaism

(3)  Religion and the theater

(4)  Bibliography of the Dewey Decimal Classification

(5)  Selection and acquisition of art books in libraries

(6)  Bibliography of cool jazz

(7)  Trade in pharmaceutical drugs

(8)  Strikes by professors

(9)  The prices of shoes

Exercise 2:

Build class numbers by adding parts of schedule numbers:

(1)  Trade in diamonds

(2)  Labor market for the leather industry

(3)  Educational guidance in adult education

(4)  Grooming your dog

(5)  The psychology of hyperactive children

(6)  Production efficiency in the manufacturing of passenger automobiles

(7)  Manufacture of volleyball equipment

(8)  Physiology of birds

(9)  Law of bank mergers

(10) A library use study of public libraries

Exercise 3:

Build numbers according to collective add instructions:

(1)  Physical chemistry of gold

(2)  Remodeling warehouses

(3)  Drug therapy for malaria

(4)  Mass of the planet Venus

(5)  Economic utilization of grasslands

(6)  Development of arid land

(7)  Managing railroads

(8)  Public measures to prevent hazardous consequences in the use of agricultural chemicals

(9)  Wasting mineral resources

## Chapter 8

# TABLE 1: STANDARD SUBDIVISIONS

## INTRODUCTION

Libraries deal with knowledge found in documents. Library classification deals with the organization of knowledge found in documents. In addition to the primary element of the subject, library classification also considers the characteristics of documents that indicate how the subject is treated. Documents vary by their form of presentation (such as dictionary, data table, or journal). Their contents also vary according to the particular viewpoint from which they are treated (such as theory, history, or research), and by the medium in which they are published (such as book, electronic resource, or DVD). Library classification may reflect all these elements. It is defined by the equation:

Library classification = Subject (the primary element) + Form of presentation + Author's viewpoint + Physical medium or form.

In practice, however, these aspects or facets are not always expressed in the class number; some facets are emphasized over others.

## DEFINITION OF STANDARD SUBDIVISIONS

Standard subdivisions are numbers found in Table 1 that represent frequently recurring physical forms (dictionaries, periodicals) or approaches (history, research) applicable to any subject or discipline. They may be used with any number in the schedules and tables for topics that approximate the whole of the number unless there are instructions to the contrary. The situations in which topics approximate the whole of a number are discussed later in this chapter on pp. 84–85.

Standard subdivisions were first recognized and listed in the second edition of the DDC (1885). From that edition on they have been a constant feature of the system, though their variety and importance have increased. They were first known as "form divisions," but eventually that phrase became inappropriate. Their present name began in 1965 with Edition 17. The dash before these numbers in Table 1, e.g., —01, —09, means that standard subdivisions (indeed, notation from any table) never stand alone. They convey meaning only when attached to a class number from the schedules.

A standard subdivision consists of at least two digits, of which the initial digit is a zero. In fact, a zero is its constant feature and was the first use of a facet indicator[1] in library classification. In the DDC's standard subdivisions, this featured zero serves as the facet indicator that marks the transition from the primary subject (or primary element of the subject) number to a secondary subject (or a secondary element of the subject) number. For instance, the number 004.09 for a work on the history of computers includes the following elements:

| | |
|---|---|
| 004 | Base number for Computers |
| 0 | Facet indicator |
| 9 | History (the facet specifier) |

---

[1] A facet indicator is a symbol used in a class number to introduce notation representing a characteristic of the subject. In the DDC, the facet indicator is a digit that may or may not signify the nature of the facet.

In this case, the digit 0 after the main number 004 serves as a facet indicator, i.e., a digit that signals a change of facet. The digit 9, the second digit in the standard subdivision, specifies the nature of the facet, i.e., in this case, history.

The following two-level summary gives some sense of the scope and nature of Table 1 Standard Subdivisions as found in Edition 22:

**Standard Subdivisions**

—01 Philosophy and theory
—011 Systems
—012 Classification
—014 Language and communication
—015 Scientific principles
—019 Psychological principles
—02 Miscellany
—020 2–020 8 [Synopses and outlines, humorous treatment, audiovisual treatment]
—021 Tabulated and related materials
—022 Illustrations, models, miniatures
—023 The subject as a profession, occupation, hobby
—024 The subject for persons in specific occupations
—025 Directories of persons and organizations
—027 Patents and identification marks
—028 Auxiliary techniques and procedures; apparatus, equipment, materials
—029 Commercial miscellany
—03 Dictionaries, encyclopedias, concordances
—04 Special topics
—05 Serial publications
—06 Organizations and management
—060 1–060 9 Organizations
—068 Management
—07 Education, research, related topics
—070 1–070 9 Geographic treatment
—071 Education
—072 Research; statistical methods
—074 Museums, collections, exhibits
—075 Museum activities and services   Collecting
—076 Review and exercise
—078 Use of apparatus and equipment in study and teaching
—079 Competitions, festivals, awards, financial support
—08 History and description with respect to kinds of persons
—080 1–080 9 Forecasting, statistics, illustrations, dictionaries, encyclopedias, concordances, serials, museums and collecting, historical and geographic treatment
—081 Men
—082 Women
—083 Young people
—084 Persons in specific stages of adulthood

| | | |
|---|---|---|
| —085 | Relatives   Parents | |
| —086 | Persons by miscellaneous social characteristics | |
| —087 | Persons with disabilities and illnesses, gifted persons | |
| —088 | Occupational and religious groups | |
| —089 | Ethnic and national groups | |
| —09 | Historical, geographic, persons treatment | |
| —090 05 | Serial publications | |
| —090 1–090 5 | Historical periods | |
| —091 | Treatment by areas, regions, places in general | |
| —092 | Persons | |
| —093–099 | Treatment by specific continents, countries, localities; extraterrestrial worlds | |

## Standard Subdivisions in the Schedules

Standard subdivisions are not usually listed in the schedules except where they are needed to fill out three-digit numbers, e.g., 505 Serial publications, and in a few other instances. Standard subdivisions may be listed when subdivisions have special meanings, when extended notation is required for the topic in question, or when notes are required. These special instances will be explained later in the chapter.

Whenever the base digits of a normal standard subdivision are supplied in a schedule, all further subdivisions found in Table 1 are implied. For example, the regular heading of notation 07 from Table 1 Education, research, related topics is supplied at 507. That entry is followed immediately by 507.2 Research; statistical methods, and 507.8 Use of apparatus and equipment in study and teaching, each with the regular heading found in Table 1. These three entries are supplied for technical reasons only: 507 to fill out the three-digit number; 507.2 to supply a reference to 001.4, 001.42, and a Manual note; and 507.8 to supply a note on science fair projects and science projects in schools. The presence of these three entries does not limit the use of other standard subdivisions found under notation 07 in Table 1, e.g., 507.24 Experimental research, 507.6 Review and exercise.

## Kinds of Standard Subdivisions

Standard subdivisions usually represent (a) recurring nonprimary characteristics of a subject and (b) nontopical characteristics that pertain to the document itself rather than to its primary subject. For instance, the primary element of a history of Japan is Japan, with history a nonprimary element—making the full subject the history of Japan. On the other hand, although a dictionary of Japanese history has as its subject Japanese history, the characteristic of being a dictionary does not affect the subject of the item; it pertains to the form the author uses to present the material, not to the information found within the document. Such distinctions may seem esoteric, but they are important in subject analysis and in assigning the proper DDC number when standard subdivisions are appropriate.

There are several kinds of standard subdivisions:

(1)  Subdivisions that bring the methods of other disciplines to bear on the subject, e.g., auxiliary techniques, education, research, management, philosophy and theory

(2)  Subdivisions that relate the subject to its users or to persons in the field, e.g., the subject as a profession, the subject for persons in specific occupations

(3)  Subdivisions that identify a specific kind of information about the subject, e.g., directories, product lists, identification marks, statistics, illustrations

(4)  Subdivisions that treat the whole subject but in a restricted situation, e.g., by kinds of persons, areas, historical periods

(5)  Subdivisions that indicate the bibliographic forms that the information may take, e.g., encyclopedias, periodicals

(6)  Miscellaneous subdivisions, e.g., biography, formulas and specifications, humorous treatment

## APPROXIMATING THE WHOLE

Standard subdivisions are applicable to any class number (however broad or narrow) for any topic that approximates the whole of the number, unless there is a specific instruction to the contrary. Categories of topics that are considered to approximate the whole are as follows:

(1)  Topics in dual headings

(2)  Topics in multiterm headings that are so designated with a standard subdivisions-are-added note (or a subdivisions-are-added note)

(3)  Topics in class-here notes

(4)  Topics that represent more than half the content of a heading

(5)  Topics that cover at least three subdivisions of the number (if the number has only three subdivisions, then topics that cover two)

(6)  Topics coextensive with topics that approximate the whole

The following example illustrates the concept of "approximating the whole":

> 006.32    Neural nets (Neural networks)
>                 Including perceptrons
>
>                 Class here connectionism, neural computers

Standard subdivisions may be added for aspects related to all the topics that approximate the whole of 006.32 plus the topics in the class-here note: neural nets, and its synonym, neural networks; connectionism; and neural computers. Standard subdivisions may not be added for aspects related to perceptrons, since this topic is in an including note.

Here is another example, this time with a standard-subdivisions-are-added note:

> 372.89    History and geography
>                 Standard subdivisions are added for history and geography
>                 together, for history alone
>
>                 Class here civilization

In this example, the note tells the classifier that standard subdivisions may be added for both topics in the heading taken together (history and geography), or for the topic of history alone (but not for the topic of geography alone). Since civilization appears in the class-here note, standard subdivisions may also be added for that topic.

In certain places, there are specific instructions overriding the approximate-the-whole restriction. These instructions are supplied when the nature of the subject or the usefulness of a secondary arrangement (e.g., geographic subarrangement) makes further topical subdivision undesirable. The instructions may take the form of a standard-subdivisions-are-added (or subdivisions-are-added) note, or class-here note. For example:

> 599.367     *Cynomys (Prairie dogs)
> > Subdivisions are added for the genus as a whole and for individual species
>
> *Add as instructed under 592–599

The instructions in the entry for 599.367 Cynomys (Prairie dogs) allow subdivisions to be added for the genus as a whole and for individual species of prairie dogs, even though individual species do not approximate the whole of the genus. Since the number for 599.367 can also be extended by notation from an add table at 592–599, the note is a subdivisions-are-added note, which includes standard subdivisions and other notation from add instructions.

When a number is subdivided, the general rule for determining what topic or combination of topics spelled out in the subdivisions approximates the whole subject of the larger number is that a work covering three subdivisions approximates the whole. If there are only three subdivisions, then generally two subdivisions approximate the whole. However, if a subject consists of a large number of distinct subclasses, e.g., species in biology or kinds of minerals in economic geology, a work on representatives of three or more distinct subdivisions is counted as approximating the whole. For example, a work on coal, gold, and diamond resources in South Africa will be classed in 553.0968, that is, as representative mineral resources (553) of South Africa (standard subdivision —09 in Table 1 plus notation 68 from Table 2).

## HOW TO USE STANDARD SUBDIVISIONS

Unless there are instructions to the contrary, standard subdivisions may be attached to any enumerated (listed) or built number for any topic that approximates the whole of the number without any formal add instructions. In classifying a document, the classifier's first step is to separate the subject proper from the elements represented by standard subdivisions. Identifying these may not be easy at first because some standard subdivisions look like subject elements. Moreover, some topics, such as encyclopedias, dictionaries, bibliography, and classification occur both in the schedules and in Table 1.

The second step is to assign the appropriate class number to the subject proper. If the subject proper approximates the whole of the class number, then one can proceed to consider addition of a standard subdivision unless instructions prohibit it.

The third step is to find the notation for the appropriate standard subdivision from Table 1. Because terms in the tables have been included in the Relative Index, notation for a standard subdivision can be located using that route.

The final step is to append the number for the standard subdivision to the schedule number for the subject proper as in any ordinary add operation. For example, suppose we have an encyclopedia of nuclear engineering. Here the subject proper is obviously nuclear engineering; the corresponding class number for nuclear engineering is 621.48. An encyclopedia is represented by standard subdivision —03 in Table 1:

> 621.48 + 03 = 621.4803

Here are a few more examples:

(1)   Symbols and abbreviations used in arithmetic
$$513 + 0148 = 513.0148$$

(2)   The profession of electrical engineering
$$621.3 + 023 = 621.3023$$

(3)   Research methods in biophysics
$$571.4 + 072 = 571.4072$$

## ADDING A STANDARD SUBDIVISION TO A MAIN CLASS OR A DIVISION

Indicating a standard subdivision for a main class or a division is not as simple as it is for other class numbers in the system because of the terminal zeros that act as space fillers in those numbers. Unless there are contrary instructions, such terminal zeros must be dropped from the class number before appending the standard subdivision. For example, in an encyclopedia of science, science is the core subject; its class number is 500. An encyclopedia is indicated as a standard subdivision by means of the notation 03. Combining the two in the usual fashion would produce the incorrect number: $500 + 03 = 500.03$. The correct procedure is indicated by the equation:

$$500 - 00 + 03 = 503$$

Here are a few more examples:

(1)   An encyclopedia of philosophy
$$100 - 00 + 03 = 103$$

(2)   A journal of philosophy
$$100 - 00 + 05 = 105$$

(3)   Secondary education in science
$$500 - 00 + 0712 = 507.12$$

However, this formula does not work for the following five main classes:

(1)   000 because there is no significant number to work with, and 003–006 are used for systems and computer science

(2)   200 because 201–209 are used for specific aspects of religion

(3)   300 because 301–307 are used for sociology

(4)   700 because 701–709 are limited to the standard subdivisions of fine and decorative arts, and iconography

(5)   900 because 901–909 are limited to the standard subdivisions of history

Standard subdivisions for classes 200, 300, 700, and 900 are found at locations that are one digit longer, i.e., at 200.1–200.9, at 300.1–300.9, at 700.1–700.9, and at 900.1–.9.

In the case of division numbers only one zero needs to be dropped from the three-digit number. For example, for an encyclopedia of mathematics:

$$510 - 0 + 03 = 510.3$$

Further examples:

(1)  Abbreviations and symbols in mathematics
      $510 - 0 + 0148 = 510.148$

(2)  Formulas in astronomy
      $520 - 0 + 0212 = 520.212$

(3)  History of education
      $370 - 0 + 09 = 370.9$

(4)  History of education in the 18th century
      $370 - 0 + 09033 = 370.9033$

(5)  International organizations in chemistry
      $540 - 0 + 0601 = 540.601$

## Number of Zeros

As was mentioned earlier, there are times when the standard subdivision numbers for main classes require more than one zero. The list that follows shows the divisions with irregular standard subdivisions, their headings, and the number of zeros required if more than two.

| | |
|---|---|
| 070 | Documentary media, educational media, news media; journalism; publishing |
| 180 | Ancient, medieval, eastern philosophy |
| 220 | Bible |
| 230 | Christianity    Christian theology (230.002–230.007 Christianity; 230.01–230.09 Christian theology) |
| 270 | Historical, geographic, persons treatment of Christianity    Church history |
| 280 | Denominations and sects of Christian church |
| 320 | Political science (Politics and government) |
| 330 | Economics |
| 340 | Law |
| 380 | Commerce, communications, transportation |
| 390 | Customs, etiquette, folklore |
| 430 | Germanic languages    German |
| 440 | Romance languages    French |
| 460 | Spanish and Portuguese languages |
| 470 | Italic languages    Latin |
| 480 | Hellenic languages    Classical Greek (480.01–480.09 Classical languages) |
| 530 | Physics |
| 620 | Engineering and allied operations (620.001–620.009) |
| 650 | Management and auxiliary services |
| 660 | Chemical engineering and related technologies |
| 690 | Buildings |
| 730 | Plastic arts    Sculpture |
| 760 | Graphic arts    Printmaking and prints |
| 790 | Recreational and performing arts |

| 830 | Literatures of Germanic languages    German literature |
|---|---|
| 840 | Literatures of Romance languages    French literature |
| 860 | Literatures of Spanish and Portuguese languages    Spanish literature |
| 870 | Literatures of Italic languages    Latin literature |
| 880 | Literatures of Hellenic languages    Classical Greek literature |
| | (880.01–880.09 Classical literatures) |
| 920 | Biography, genealogy, insignia (920.001–920.009) |
| 930 | History of ancient world |
| 940 | History of Europe    Western Europe |
| 950 | History of Asia    Orient    Far East |
| 960 | History of Africa |
| 970 | History of North America (970.001–970.009) |
| 980 | History of South America (980.001–980.009) |
| 990 | History of other parts of the world, of extraterrestrial worlds    Pacific Ocean islands |

As the above list is too long to memorize, the classifier must always consult the schedules when using standard subdivisions. In some cases where there are dual or multiterm headings, only the standard subdivisions for the division as a whole require more zeros. For example, the standard subdivisions for the whole of 760 Graphic arts    Printmaking and prints are in 760.01–760.09, but those for Printmaking and prints alone are in 760.1–760.9.

The following kinds of instructions indicate when a different number of zeros must be used:

(1)  Notation in the number column, e.g., 321.001–321.009 for standard subdivisions of Systems of governments and states, 620.009 for history of engineering.

(2)  Footnotes leading to an add table where subdivisions are supplied, e.g., to the add table under 616.1–616.9 where 001–009 are for standard subdivisions. At 616.1 the heading *Diseases of cardiovascular system is governed by a footnote that says to add as instructed under 616.1–616.9. Thus one gets 616.1009 for the history of diagnosis and treatment of cardiovascular diseases.

(3)  Footnotes from the add instruction itself stipulating the use of extra zeros, e.g., the footnote to the add note under 327.3–327.9: "Add 00 for standard subdivisions; see instruction at beginning of Table 1." This instruction directs the classifier to 327.41009 for the history of foreign policy of the United Kingdom. This footnote cites instructions, at the beginning of Table 1, that govern in any case: standard subdivisions must have enough zeros to avoid any possible conflict with a number supplied in the schedules.

## ADDING A STANDARD SUBDIVISION TO A BUILT NUMBER

Standard subdivisions may be added to a built number, but one must remember that the standard subdivision applies to the built number taken as a whole, not to one of its elements. For example, 381.45 means trade in products of secondary industries and services; 687 means manufacturing of clothing, a number that is used for products, i.e., clothing. If 687 is added to 381.45, the resulting built number represents the clothing trade. Periodicals on the clothing trade are represented by adding standard subdivision —05 to the built number 381.45687 to form 381.4568705. This number means periodicals on the clothing trade, not trade in clothing periodicals.

The only exception to the foregoing rule is 016 Bibliographies of works on specific subjects. When a built number is added to 016, bibliography is logically like a standard-subdivision concept in that it applies to the whole of the built number plus any attached standard subdivisions. Thus 016.3814568705 is used only for bibliographies of periodicals on the clothing trade; it is not used for a serial bibliography of the clothing trade.

## Number of Zeros

When building numbers according to add instructions, use the same number of zeros in the segment that is added as are found in the schedule from which the number is taken. For example, under 372.11–372.18 the classifier is instructed to add to 372.1 the numbers following 371 in 371.1–371.8, e.g., administration of elementary schools 372.12 (372.1 for organization and activities in elementary education plus 2 from 371.2 for school administration). The double zeros for standard subdivisions under 371.2 must be carried over to 372.12, e.g., study and teaching of elementary school administration 372.120071. As in most cases where two zeros are used for standard subdivisions, the single zero subdivisions at 371.2 are used for specific topics that might be needed when the 2 is used in elementary education. For example, notation 207 from 371.207 can be used in 372.1207 for works on executive management of elementary schools.

## EXTENDING A STANDARD SUBDIVISION BY AN ADD INSTRUCTION

A few standard subdivisions can be extended according to add instructions. The method for implementing the add instructions in Table 1 is the same as for the schedules. For example, in a work on the scientific principles of civil engineering, the primary or core element of the subject is civil engineering (624). The secondary element is scientific principles. The standard subdivision for scientific principles is —015. Thus:

$$624 + 015 = 624.015$$

For the *mathematical* principles of civil engineering, however, the classifier follows the add note under —015 in Table 1:

> Add to base number —015 the numbers following 5 in 510–590, e.g., mathematical techniques —0151

Therefore, the complete number for mathematical principles of civil engineering is 624.0151:

| | |
|---|---|
| 624 | Base number for Civil engineering |
| 015 | Scientific principles (Table 1) |
| 1 | Number following 5 in 510 Mathematics, with the final zero eliminated |

Further examples:

(1) Directories of businesses in Ohio: 338.7025771

| | |
|---|---|
| 338.7 | Base number for Business enterprises |
| 025 | Directories of persons and organizations (Table 1) |
| 771 | Ohio (Table 2) |

(2) Computer programs for counting carbohydrates in your diet: 613.283028553

| | |
|---|---|
| 613.283 | Base number for Carbohydrates |
| 0285 | Data processing  Computer applications (Table 1) |
| 53 | Number following 00 in 005.3 Computer programs |

(3) Directory of South African breweries: 663.4202968

| | |
|---|---|
| 663.42 | Base number for Beer and ale |
| 029 | Commercial miscellany (Table 1) |
| 68 | South Africa (Table 2) |

## PERSONS TREATMENT USING STANDARD SUBDIVISIONS

There are several ways to describe persons and groups of persons associated with a topic in the DDC by using Table 1. Persons may be treated from a biographical viewpoint as individuals or a collective group, or they may be considered from a "kind of person" viewpoint. In persons treatment, Table 1 notation can be used by itself, or further extended by instructions to add directly from the schedules or from Tables 1, 2, and 5.

### Persons Treatment Using Standard Subdivision —092

The most frequently applied notation for persons is the one designating biographical treatment, standard subdivision —092 from Table 1. Standard subdivision —092 is nearly at the top of the Table 1 preference table, and it can be added to any DDC number (unless there are instructions to the contrary) to indicate biographical treatment of a subject, e.g., a biography of the basketball player Michael Jordan 796.323092. Collective biographical treatment of a subject may be shown through use of standard subdivision —0922, e.g., chemists through the years 540.922. Standard subdivision —0922 can be further extended by the addition of Table 2 notation to —0922 for collected persons treatment in an area, e.g., notable chemists in Italy 540.92245. Standard subdivision —0923 represents collected persons treatment of members of ethnic and national groups; it can be extended by use of Table 5. (The use of Table 5 is discussed in chapter 12.) Standard subdivision —0929 is used to represent animals or plants treated as individuals, e.g., a biography of Secretariat (a famous race horse) 798.400929.

The Relative Index includes many entries for the biographical numbers associated with occupations, e.g., economists 330.092, gamekeepers 639.9092, physicians 610.92. A note of caution: If the work focuses on the role and function of the profession versus biographical treatment of a person or group of persons in the profession, use the number for the profession itself without the addition of notation 092 from Table 1. In certain instances, a special number is provided for the role and function of the profession. For example:

| | |
|---|---|
| Nurses | 610.730 92 |
| role and function | 610.730 69 |

The Manual in Edition 22 includes several important general notes related to use of standard subdivision —092:

| | |
|---|---|
| T1—092 | Persons |
| T1—0922 | Collected persons treatment |
| T1—0922 vs. T1—093–099 | Collected persons treatment vs. Geographic treatment |

In addition, the Manual includes four notes focusing on religious biography at 200.92 and 201–209, 292–299; 220.92; 230–280; and 297.092.

In particular, the classifier should study carefully the Manual note on standard subdivision —092 in order to understand the choice of discipline for persons whose contributions span several fields, for public figures, for systems and laws named after people, for families and close associates of famous people, for partial biographies, and for biographies associated with place. The note also contains a key instruction that is an exception to the general rule for the application of standard subdivisions:

> Add T1—092 even in cases when a person's work may not approximate the whole of the most specific available number. Conversely, do not add T1—092 to extremely minute subjects, e.g., class ball players at the number for the game they played, not in subordinate numbers for specific positions on the field, even if a player filled only one position.

## Kinds of Persons Treatment Using Standard Subdivision —08

Treatment of a topic with respect to kinds of persons is expressed through the application of standard subdivision —08. Standard subdivision —08 provides general notation for kinds of persons (e.g., —082 women, —086942 homeless persons) that can be added to any topic to represent the topic with respect to that kind of person, e.g., women in education 370.82, the sociology of homeless families 306.85086942. Standard subdivision —08 is also used to show discrimination against the kind of person in relation to an area, e.g., discrimination against women in sports 796.082. Again, as in the case of standard subdivision —092, the Manual contains several important notes concerning the use of standard subdivision —08.

The centered heading at —081–088 Miscellaneous specific kinds of persons has an important instruction concerning the application of notation 081–088:

> Unless other instructions are given, class a subject with aspects in two or more subdivisions of —081–088 in the number coming last, e.g., children with disabilities —087 (*not* —083)

Standard subdivision —088 is used to introduce persons in specific occupational and religious groups. Until Edition 22, notation 088 was also extended through use of notation from Table 7. In Edition 22, the notation for specific occupations or religious groups added to standard subdivision —088 is derived directly from the schedules:

> Add to base number —088 notation 001–999, e.g., nondominant religious groups —0882, Catholic teaching on socioeconomic problems 261.8088282 . . .
> Notation 001–999 replaces notation 09–99 from Table 7 with the result that many numbers have been reused with new meanings

Standard subdivision —089 is used to introduce ethnic and national groups. It is also used to express racism in relation to a topic, e.g., racism in sports 796.089. Specific ethnic and national groups associated with a subject can be expressed through use of —089 with Table 5. (Addition to —089 from Table 5 will be discussed in chapter 12.) Notation 081–088 always takes precedence over notation 089, e.g., Vietnamese children —083 (*not* —0899592).

Standard subdivision —08 may be extended by selected standard subdivisions that fall below —08 in the preference table at the beginning of Table 1. These standard subdivisions are listed in the add table in the record for —08 in Table 1. For example, since geographic treatment is permitted, 300.820973 fully expresses the topic "women in social sciences in the U.S."

## The Subject for Persons in Specific Occupations

Instructions for describing the subject for persons in specific occupations are provided under standard subdivision —024. Until Edition 22, numbers for specific occupations were built using Table 7 according to instructions found under standard subdivision —024. In Edition 22, a new instruction under —024 in Table 1 directs the classifier to use notation derived directly from the schedules for occupations:

> Add to base number —024 notation 001–999, e.g., the subject for engineers —02462
> > Notation 001–999 replaces notation 09–99 from Table 7 with the result that many numbers have been reused with new meanings

## STANDARD SUBDIVISIONS WITH EXTENDED OR ALTERED MEANINGS

Sometimes standard subdivisions are not "standard"; their meanings have been altered. An example of a special meaning is found under 540.11, where the number means "Alchemy and systems," not just "Systems." Right below it, 540.28 is printed in brackets to show that the standard subdivision is not used, but that 542 is used instead for auxiliary techniques and procedures, apparatus, equipment, materials. Further examples:

| | | |
|---|---|---|
| 610.69 | Medical personnel and relationships | |
| | (Table 1: —06 Organizations and management; —069 not defined) | |
| 701.9 | Methodology of fine and decorative arts | |
| | (Table 1: —019 Psychological principles) | |

Because these altered "standard subdivisions" are unique to their classes, they do not appear in Table 1, but are enumerated in the schedules. The classifier must be careful, therefore, as there are many such altered standard subdivisions in the DDC.

There is one standard subdivision that does not come close to meeting the definition of a standard subdivision; it just happens to share the same span of numbers as legitimate standard subdivisions. The subdivision —04 Special topics has been used in the past as a device to introduce additional notation in situations where the entire notation available to a class has already been used.

## DISPLACED STANDARD SUBDIVISIONS

As noted earlier in this chapter, standard subdivisions sometimes require more than one zero. Throughout the DDC, there are also special developments for standard subdivision concepts that do not use the regular notation found in Table 1. A displaced standard subdivision is one that has been given special notation in the schedule in place of its regular notation from Table 1. Whenever a standard subdivision is displaced, a do-not-use note is always provided at the regular location of the standard subdivision.

For example:

> 362[.09]    Historical, geographic, persons treatment
> Do not use; class in 362.9

Add instructions at the special notation in the schedule tell the classifier that notation from Table 2 may be added directly to the base number. For example:

> 362.9   Historical, geographic, persons treatment
> Add to base number 362.9 notation 01–9 from Table 2, e.g.,
> social welfare in France 362.944

The addition of a second standard subdivision is permitted with standard subdivision concepts displaced to nonzero numbers (see p. 94).

Many of the displaced standard subdivisions date from early editions of the Dewey Decimal Classification, and they reflect aspects of unusual importance in particular subjects. Thus, there is often a larger and more diverse literature on these displaced concepts than is normal for the regular standard subdivisions. Since Edition 20, there has been a major effort to bring many displaced concepts back to their proper home in the standard subdivision span. This process is called "regularization." Regularization is particularly useful when only a few works have been classified in the irregular location. Regularization makes the Classification easier to apply, and provides consistent representation of standard subdivision concepts throughout the scheme.

## CO-OCCURRENCE OF TWO OR MORE STANDARD SUBDIVISION CONCEPTS IN A DOCUMENT

Occasionally a document includes two or more standard subdivision concepts. For example, a journal of political philosophy involves two standard subdivisions: journal (form of presentation) and philosophy (viewpoint). With few exceptions, only one standard subdivision is used in a class number. It is selected on a preferential basis, and the other is ignored. To choose the appropriate standard subdivision, the classifier should consult the table of preference at the beginning of Table 1. A subdivision that falls earlier in the table of preference is to be preferred over one that falls later. For instance, —072 Research; statistical methods is preferred over —01 Philosophy and theory, which itself is preferred over —03 Dictionaries, encyclopedias, concordances. Looking at the table we observe that preference is generally based on the following order:

(1)   Method
(2)   Viewpoint
(3)   Form of presentation
(4)   Physical medium or form

When selecting one of several standard subdivisions, the classifier should use the table of preference. For a journal on the teaching of political science, the primary subject element is political science and the secondary element is teaching. The fact that the work is a journal has nothing to do with the subject, but everything to do with the document. As standard subdivision —071 Education is preferred over —05 Serial publications, the correct number is 320.071 (320 happens to be a division that requires two zeros to signal a standard subdivision).

The table of preference at the beginning of Table 1 should not be followed when it overrides the basic intention of the author. Suppose the work being classified is about computers in Chinese banking. The primary subject is Chinese banking; therefore, the work should be classed in 332.10951 Chinese banking, not in 332.10285 Computer applications in banking, the number that would be chosen according to the table of preference. If one of the standard subdivisions constitutes an essential or integral part of the primary subject, this subdivision should be chosen, even though the other subdivision may come ahead of it in the table of preference.

Two other rules, the rule of application and the rule of zero (see chapter 4 for a discussion of both rules), override the table of preference at the beginning of Table 1. First, the rule of application instructs one to class a work treating two or more interrelated subjects with the subject that is being acted upon. Therefore, teaching financial management in hospital administration is classed in 362.110681 Financial management in hospital administration, not 362.11071 Education in hospital administration, even though —07 Education, research, related topics is above T1—068 Management in the table of preference at the beginning of Table 1. Second, when standard subdivisions are displaced to nonzero positions, the rule of zero overrides the table of preference, e.g., management of prisons in Great Britain 365.941068, not 365.068 as would be the case if prisons in Great Britain were classed in 365.0941.

## Multiple Standard Subdivisions

Sometimes, the addition of a second standard subdivision is permitted by instructions in the schedules and tables. Do not add one standard subdivision to another standard subdivision unless specifically instructed. In the following cases, addition of a second standard subdivision is allowed:

(1)   With standard subdivision —04 (a special topic subdivision available to permit introduction of a new development when there is no suitable vacant notation in direct 1–9 subdivisions).

(2)   With standard subdivisions that have changed or extended meanings, e.g., encyclopedias on educational psychology 370.1503, on pyrometallurgy 669.028203, on political situations and conditions 320.9003. (In contrast, the encyclopedia subdivision is not added to the true standard subdivisions nearby, e.g., not to psychological principles of political science 320.019, or metallurgical patents 669.0272.)

(3)   Under standard subdivisions —08 and —09, certain other standard subdivisions that are lower in the table of preference are specifically provided. For example, the number for encyclopedias on hospitals in Great Britain is 362.11094103. Although the geographic facet (—09) is higher than the encyclopedia facet (—03) in the table of preference, provision is made under —093–099 in Table 1 for further subdivision by selected standard subdivisions, including —03.

(4)   With standard subdivision concepts displaced to nonzero numbers (usually for geographic treatment), the full range of standard subdivisions is applicable, e.g., management of penal institutions in Great Britain 365.941068. In contrast, management of hospitals in Great Britain is classed in 362.11068.

# WHEN STANDARD SUBDIVISIONS ARE NOT USED

As noted already, standard subdivisions are applicable to almost all of the class numbers in the schedules, and classifiers do not need any special add instructions to use them. However, there are two categories of numbers that should not have standard subdivisions attached to them.

## When a Standard Subdivision Is Already Implied in the Class Number

In some cases a standard subdivision concept is already a part of the class number: —03 is not added to 423 Dictionaries of standard English because 423 already means dictionaries. Nor is —03 added to 031 for *Encyclopedia Americana*; the number already means an encyclopedia in American English. Similarly, —09 is not added in class 900 to the number for the history of a place to show the aspect of history because the nine is already a part of the main number: 973 is a history of the United States, 973.09 is not. Nor is there any point to adding —072 Research; statistical methods to 001.42 Research methods.

In other cases the standard subdivision may be redundant, or nearly so. For example, T1—024694 indicates the subject for carpenters. It is never used with 694 Carpentry, since works on a subject are written primarily for its practitioners. In certain cases a standard subdivision would simply repeat the definition of the base discipline, e.g., T1—01 in its overall meaning of "philosophy and theory" in most of the subdivisions in 100 Philosophy.

Sometimes, only part of a standard subdivision is implied in the class number. In such cases, a broader standard subdivision in the same hierarchy without the redundant meaning is added. For example:

> Plant management for airlines      387.73068

The usual standard subdivision for plant management is —0682; however, 387.73 means "aircraft and facilities," a concept equivalent to "plant." In this case, the standard subdivision —068 Management is added to avoid redundancy.

## When There Is No Specific Class Number for the Subject

Standard subdivisions cannot be used for a subject not provided with a specific class number of its own unless the subject approximates the whole of the contents of the number, or unless there are directions for such addition in the schedules.

*Topics found in including notes cannot have standard subdivisions added; they are considered to be in "standing room" in the number.* For instance, for a work on the philosophy and theory of citation indexing, it is against the rules to add —01 Philosophy and theory to 025.48 (the number for Subject indexing). This is because citation indexing does not have its own number (it is found in an including note), nor does it approximate the whole of 025.48 Subject indexing—it is only a small part of it. Adding —01 to the number would be misleading to the user who would expect 025.4801 to be a work on subject cataloging theory as a whole. On the other hand, standard subdivisions can be added to Marxism, which is in a class-here note at 335.4 Marxian systems. At 301 Sociology and anthropology, the first note instructs: "Standard subdivisions are added for either or both topics in heading." Compare this note to the one at 646.3 Clothing and accessories: "Standard subdivisions are added for clothing and accessories together, for clothing alone." This means that a dictionary of accessories would be classed in 646.3, but a dictionary of clothing (or clothing and accessories together) would be classed in 646.303.

## Use Standard Subdivisions with Caution

The common feature of standard subdivisions is that they identify limited treatment of the subject. This feature leads to the first general rule in applying them: in doubtful cases, do not use standard subdivisions, since they serve to segregate specialized material from works of general interest. For example, avoid using the most recent period subdivision in T1—0905 for "state of the art" works on a subject because most users will expect to find such works in the main number.

Some standard subdivisions used in doubtful situations may be annoying as well as superfluous. For example, many works in social sciences refer mostly to well-developed countries. Use T1—091722 Developed regions sparingly for such works, since it will not be very helpful to users to double the length of the number in order to segregate the material according to aspects that the authors do not emphasize.

## SUMMARY

Standard subdivisions represent frequently recurring physical forms (dictionaries, periodicals) or approaches (history, research) to a topic that are applicable to all fields of study. For the most part, standard subdivisions represent nontopical characteristics of documents. However, at times a standard subdivision may represent a secondary subject.

The list of standard subdivisions is found in Table 1 in volume 1 of the DDC. Standard subdivisions normally consist of at least two digits, of which the first is a zero (the facet indicator) and the next (not a zero) usually specifies the nature of the facet. Like any number in the DDC, notation for standard subdivisions is decimal. Frequently, more than one zero is needed to stipulate a standard subdivision. The proper number of zeros is one, or as many as the instructions indicate.

Generally, only one standard subdivision is used for a document unless there is a specific instruction allowing the use of more than one standard subdivision in the particular case. If two standard subdivisions are applicable to the same work, one is chosen according to the table of preference at the beginning of Table 1. The table of preference should not be followed when it overrides the basic intention of the author.

A standard subdivision is not added to a class number if the viewpoint or form of presentation is an essential part of the main subject and already represented in the class number. Furthermore, standard subdivisions are not added for topics that do not approximate the whole of the number. Such topics may be part of the heading or in an including note. If the topic represents more than half of the contents of the number, it is considered to approximate the whole and may have standard subdivisions added for it.

# EXERCISES

Exercise 1:

Applying standard subdivisions, assign class numbers to the following works:

(1) An encyclopedia of civil and political rights

(2) A dictionary of civil rights

(3) Teaching methods in agriculture

(4) Research methods in milk processing technology

(5) A journal of histology

(6) Marketing management of computer software

Exercise 2:

Build class numbers for the following topics involving main class or division numbers:

(1) Science organizations

(2) Abbreviations and symbols used in science

(3) History of science

(4) History of science in the 16th century

(5) Schools and courses in astronomy

(6) Research methods in philosophy

(7) Dictionary of mathematics

(8) Medical associations

(9) Encyclopedia of architecture

Exercise 3:

Build class numbers for the following topics requiring standard subdivisions with multiple zeros:

(1) Illustrations of human diseases

(2) A history of naval forces

(3) Higher education in Central European history

(4) Tables and formulas in economics

(5) International organizations on human diseases

(6) A dictionary of law

(7) A journal of Christian theology

Exercise 4:

Synthesize numbers for the following subjects:

(1) Mathematics in biophysics

(2) The odds of winning lotteries

(3) Mathematics of human blood flow

(4) A journal of military science

Exercise 5:

Classify the following topics related to persons treatment:

(1) Edward Teller; biography of an atomic physicist

(2) The role of generals in the army

(3) Great physicists of the twentieth century

(4) Seabiscuit: life of a great race horse

(5) Teenagers and the Internet

(6) Discrimination against women in higher education

(7) Racism in sports

(8) Racism in football in the U.K.

(9) Statistical mathematics for librarians

(10) Introduction to law for police officials

Exercise 6:

Assign class numbers to the following subjects, using displaced standard subdivisions:

(1) A history of wages

(2) Apparatus for making plastics

(3) History of painting (art)

(4) Architecture of the modern era

Exercise 7:

Synthesize class numbers for the following topics that involve two standard subdivision concepts:

(1) A journal of higher education in public administration

(2) Encyclopedia of psychological associations

(3) A directory of law schools

(4) A journal of literary history

(5) A biographical dictionary of musicians

Exercise 8:

Provide class numbers for the following subjects that involve standard subdivision concepts but do not use standard subdivision notation:

(1) Management of technology

(2) History of Central Europe

(3) *The New York Public Library Desk Reference*

(4) A general periodical in the English language

# Chapter 9
## TABLE 2: GEOGRAPHIC AREAS, HISTORICAL PERIODS, PERSONS

## INTRODUCTION

Table 2 is the largest of the six tables in the DDC. It is primarily a table of geographic notation that can be added to a Dewey number through instructions in the tables and schedules to represent the geographic focus of a subject. Table 2 also contains notation for historical periods and persons. The main geographic divisions are political; the table also contains certain physical features such as rivers and mountain ranges. In addition, there are other sorts of conceptual divisions of the globe: zones, hemispheres, regions where specific religions or languages dominate, and so on.

The ability to express the geographic aspect of a subject is critical to its representation. Many subjects, especially those in the social sciences and humanities, are best studied in the context of a geographic area. Their intellectual structure often differs markedly from place to place. For example, the education system of France, wages in Canada, the banking system of Switzerland, libraries in South Africa, or the history of science in ancient Egypt are all virtually unique to themselves; they bear the stamp of the place where practiced. Moreover, there are instances in which the area is the subject itself: the history of China is entirely different from the history of Argentina. Equally unlike are the geographies of Saudi Arabia and Alaska.

In the DDC, there are times when the area is so important to a class that the geographic facet is built into the division or section of a class. For example:

| | |
|---|---|
| 181 | Eastern philosophy |
| .2 | Egypt |
| .3 | Palestine    Israel |
| .4 | India |

| | |
|---|---|
| 191 | [Modern western philosophy of] United States and Canada |

In other cases, the geographic aspect is expressed by way of adding notation from Table 2 (also called the area table). Table 2 lists the names and area numbers for all countries, for the provinces and states of many countries, and for the counties and major cities of some countries. Addition of an area number to a class number will help in the complete (close) classification of a document; and it will ultimately help to arrange subjects logically by area and to bring together all studies of a subject within the same area.

## DIVISIONS OF THE AREA TABLE

The major divisions, or the summary, of the area table are given below:

| | |
|---|---|
| —001–009 | Standard subdivisions [not areas, but placed here for number-building purposes] |
| —01–05 | Historical periods [not areas, but placed here for number-building purposes] |
| —1 | Areas, regions, places in general; oceans and seas |
| —2 | Persons [not areas, but placed here for number-building purposes] |
| —3 | The ancient world |

—4    Europe    Western Europe
—5    Asia    Orient    Far East
—6    Africa
—7    North America
—8    South America
—9    Other parts of world and extraterrestrial worlds    Pacific Ocean islands

Notation 1 is used for geophysical and conceptually bound but physically scattered areas, such as oceans, temperate zones, and socioeconomic regions. Notation 2 is used for persons regardless of area, region, or place. Notation 3 is used for the ancient world. The modern world is represented by the span —4–9, divided according to internationally accepted geographic and political divisions. Each set of digits has been hierarchically divided into countries, then provinces or states, then counties or similar jurisdictions, then cities in some cases, and even towns in others. Note the following development:

—4    Europe    Western Europe
—41        British Isles
—42        England and Wales
—43        Central Europe    Germany
—44        France and Monaco
—45        Italian Peninsula and adjacent islands    Italy
—46        Iberian Peninsula and adjacent islands    Spain
—47        Eastern Europe    Russia
—48        Scandinavia
—49        Other parts of Europe

Each of the regions is divided into smaller units:

—43        Central Europe    Germany
—431            Northeastern Germany
—432            Saxony and Thuringia
—433            Bavaria (Bayern)
—434            Southwestern Germany
—435            Northwestern Germany
—436            Austria and Liechtenstein
—437            Czech Republic and Slovakia
—438            Poland
—439            Hungary

And each of these is further divided:

—438        Poland
—438 1            Northwestern Poland
—438 2            North central Poland
—438 3            Northeastern Poland
—438 4            Central Poland
—438 5            Southwestern Poland
—438 6            Southeastern Poland    Polish Galicia

Each area of Poland is further divided into provinces:

| | |
|---|---|
| —438 2 | North central Poland |
| —438 22 | Pomorskie province (Pomorskie Voivodeship) |
| —438 26 | Kujawsko-Pomorskie Province |
| | (Kujawsko-Pomorskie Voivodeship) |

The geographic divisions of the United States, Canada, the United Kingdom, South Africa, Australia, and New Zealand are more detailed than many other areas, because these countries are the major users of the English-language standard edition of the DDC. For example, the geographic divisions for these countries include the names of numerous cities and towns. In many countries, the division is down to province only, although several countries have major cities listed. For example, in Japan there are numbers for Tokyo, Yokohama, Nagoya, Ōsaka, Kyōto, Kōbe, Hiroshima, and Nagasaki. In the United States one can sometimes find an uneven development, e.g., a specific number for a relatively small city (for example, Meridian, Mississippi), but not for larger cities (like Pasadena, California). Certain city numbers were added at a time when there seemed to be literary warrant for the addition, and the reason may not be obvious now. The inclusion of areas in recent editions follows established editorial policies.

Major physical features are included in Table 2 when they span more than one geographic division. Throughout Table 2, see references (often in footnote form) lead from the implied comprehensive number for a jurisdiction, region, or feature to its subordinate parts in other classes in Table 2:

—811  Northern region of Brazil
Class here *Amazon River

*For a specific part of this jurisdiction, region, or feature, see the part and follow instructions under —4–9

## LOCATING AREA NUMBERS IN TABLE 2

Table 2 can be consulted in two ways: hierarchically and systematically, or through the Relative Index. In Table 2, the modern world is divided first into continents, then into regions and countries, then into provinces and states, then into counties, and in some cases, into cities and towns. For example, to find a number for Assam, India, the first thing to know is that it is in northeast India, which is a part of south Asia, which is a part of Asia:

| | | | |
|---|---|---|---|
| —5 | Asia | Orient | Far East |
| —54 | | South Asia | India |
| —541 | | | Northeastern India |
| —5416 | | | Far northeast of India |
| —54162 | | | Assam |

Persons who do not know the general location of Assam can use the Relative Index, where entries for area numbers are simple and direct, and locating a place name delivers a number:

| | |
|---|---|
| Asia | 950 |
| | T2—5 |
| Assam (India) | T2—541 62 |

The index includes a variety of abbreviations:

Calgary (Alta.)          T2—712 338
Calhoun County (Ala.)    T2—761 63

The abbreviation following Calgary is for the province of Alberta and that following Calhoun County is for the state of Alabama. These abbreviations are listed at the beginning of the Relative Index.

Table 2 uses the *AACR2* form of the name without the qualifier if it is in English; if not, the form found in authoritative Anglophone sources is preferred. The *AACR2* form is given after the familiar form in parentheses if it differs in spelling other than diacritics. If the form for the type of jurisdiction differs from the English-language form, both are given. For example:

—435 51    Cologne district (Köln Regierungsbezirk)

—482 1     Oslo county (Oslo fylke)

The *AACR2* form of name as established by the Library of Congress has been used or emulated in the Relative Index. The English form is also listed if the entry term differs significantly in spelling. The index entries for the examples above are as follows:

Cologne (Germany : Regierungsbezirk)
Köln (Germany : Regierungsbezirk)
Oslo fylke (Norway)

## ADDING AREA NUMBERS FROM TABLE 2

As in all number building in the DDC, an area number from Table 2 is appended, not "added" in the mathematical sense, to the class number. An area number can be added in two ways:

(1)  By way of standard subdivision —09

(2)  According to add instructions found under numbers to which area notation is to be added directly. In such cases the add note normally appears in the form: "Add to base number . . . notation . . . from Table 2 . . ."

## ADDING AREA NUMBERS THROUGH STANDARD SUBDIVISION —09

Unless there are instructions to the contrary, area notation may be added to any number for a topic that approximates the whole of a number through the use of standard subdivision —09. Two units of standard subdivision —09 are used for geographic treatment of a subject:

—091      Treatment by areas, regions, places in general
          Add to base number —091 the numbers following —1 in
          notation 11–19 from Table 2, e.g., Torrid Zone —0913 . . .

—093–099  Treatment by specific continents, countries, localities;
          extraterrestrial worlds
          Add to base number —09 notation 3–9 from Table
          2, e.g., the subject in North America —097 . . .

The add notes under these numbers mean that the area numbers covered by —1 or the span —3–9 may be added to the specified base number. The result, for example —0973, then becomes an extended standard subdivision. Since standard subdivision —09, including its extensions, can be added to almost any number in the schedules, virtually any class number may be subdivided geographically without specific add instructions. For example:

> Foreign relations of the former communist bloc countries: 327.091717
> 327    Base number for Foreign relations
> 091    Treatment by areas, regions, places in general (Table 1)
> 717    Number following —1 in —1717 Former communist bloc (Table 2)

To proceed further, take the title *Commercial Banks in Japan*. Here the core subject is commercial banks. The class number for commercial banks is 332.12. Since there is no special provision for geographic treatment under 332.12, the classifier may add area notation through the use of standard subdivision —091 or —093–099. The number for Japan in Table 2 is —52. Therefore:

> Commercial banks in Japan: 332.120952
> 332.12  Base number for Commercial banks
> 09     Historical, geographic, persons treatment (Table 1)
> 52     Japan (Table 2)

Another example:

> Female labor in China: 331.40951
> 331.4   Base number for Women workers
> 09     Historical, geographic, persons treatment (Table 1)
> 51     China (Table 2)

## ADDING AREA NUMBERS ACCORDING TO ADD INSTRUCTIONS

There are times when the geographic treatment of a subject is built directly into the regular subdivisions of a class. That is, the span of numbers .1–.9 has been used to include the standard subdivision concept of place. For example:

> 372[.09]  Historical, geographic, persons treatment [of elementary education]
> Do not use; class in 372.9
>
> 372.9    Historical, geographic, persons treatment of elementary education
> Class here specific schools and school systems
> Add to base number 372.9 notation 01–9 from Table 2, e.g., elementary education in Brazil 372.981

The standard subdivision —09 is displaced from its regular position (372.09) to an alternate provision in the schedule (372.9). Notation from Table 2 may be added directly to the base number 372.9 following the add instruction under that number. The number for elementary education in Brazil (the example in the add instruction) is built from the base number 372.9 plus notation 81 for Brazil in Table 2.

Another example:

    522.109    Historical and persons treatment [of observatories]
                    Do not use for geographic treatment; class in 522.19

    522.19     Geographic treatment [of observatories]
                    Add to base number 522.19 notation 1–9 from Table 2, e.g.,
                    space observatories 522.1919, observatories in China
                    522.1951

Therefore, if one had a work on observatories in Chile, the number would be built as follows:

    Observatories in Chile: 522.1983
        522.19   Geographic treatment [of observatories]
        83       Chile (Table 2)

## A Class, Division, or Section Number Directly Divided by Area

Sometimes a main class, division, or section number, i.e., a one-, two-, or three-digit figure, is directly divided by area. For example:

    History of Wales: 942.9
        9         Base number for History
        429      Wales (Table 2)

    History of Paris: 944.361
        9         Base number for History
        44361   Paris (Table 2)

    Geography of Wales: 914.29
        91        Base number for Geography
        429      Wales (Table 2)

    Geography of Paris: 914.4361
        91        Base number for Geography
        44361   Paris (Table 2)

The full range of Table 2 notation is not always permitted for number-building purposes in such circumstances. For example, under 327.3–.9 (Foreign relations of specific continents and localities, . . . foreign relations of specific countries), one is instructed: "Add to base number 327 notation 3–9 from Table 2 . . . ." The full range of Table 2 notation is —1–9, but, in this case, one is instructed to add the area notation falling only within the span of —3–9. This means, of course, that area —1 cannot be added. If it were added it would produce a number that conflicts with the provisions in the schedules for 327.1 Foreign policy and specific topics in international relations. So, for a work on the foreign relations of the former communist bloc countries, the classifier must start with 327 and add the Table 2 notation (1717) through the use of standard subdivision —09. This example is illustrated on the previous page.

## Adding a Part of a Number from Table 2

There are times when a part of a number from Table 2 is added to the base number. For instance:

063     General organizations in central Europe     In Germany
        Add to base number 063 the numbers following —43 in notation
        431–439 from Table 2, e.g., organizations in Poland 063.8

The number for a work on general organizations in Poland is therefore 063.8:

063     Base number for General organizations in central Europe
8       Number following —43 in —438 Poland (Table 2)

Similarly:

708.3–.8     [Galleries, museums, private collections of fine and decorative
             arts in] Miscellaneous parts of Europe
             Add to base number 708 the numbers following —4 in
             notation 43–48 from Table 2, e.g., galleries, museums,
             private collections in France 708.4

Therefore:

Art galleries in Sweden: 708.85
708     Base number for Galleries
85      Number following —4 in —485 Sweden (Table 2)

## THE DIFFERENCE BETWEEN —009 AND —09

In some cases, geographic treatment may be achieved through two different sets of numbers in the same field of study. The distinctions are explained in the schedules. For example, take the following entries:

330.09          Historical, geographic, persons treatment of economics as a
                discipline
                     Do not use for economic situation and conditions; class
                     in 330.9
330.9           Economic situation and conditions
330.91          Treatment by areas, regions, places in general
330.93–.99      Treatment by specific continents, countries, localities

The entry 330.09 pertains to the discipline of economics as studied in various places. The other entries, 330.91–.99, pertain to the economic conditions that exist in various places. For example, 330.0973 means the discipline of economics as studied in the United States; 330.973 stands for economic situations and conditions of the United States. Note the difference in the schedules between the following pair of numbers:

027.009          Historical and persons treatment [of General libraries,
                 archives, information centers]
027.01–.09       Geographic treatment [of General libraries, archives,
                 information centers]

## AREA NUMBER INTERPOSED BETWEEN TWO SUBJECT FACETS

There are a few places where an area number is interposed between two subject facets; the major one is law. The citation order for law is:

34 + branch of law + jurisdiction + topic within branch + standard subdivision

For example:

History of evidence in criminal law of the Dominican Republic: 345.72930609

| | |
|---|---|
| 34 | Base number for Law |
| 5 | Criminal law |
| 7293 | Dominican Republic (Table 2) |
| 06 | Evidence (added according to the instruction under 345.3–.9) |
| 09 | History (Table 1) |

The first zero that falls between jurisdiction and topic is actually a facet indicator that introduces the specific subject in law subordinate to the branch of law.

## ADDING TWO AREA NUMBERS

There are cases when two areas are considered within a document. This frequently occurs in 300 in such fields as foreign relations, international commerce, and migration. In such cases there is usually a clarifying explanation in the schedules as to which of the two areas should come first. Usually, the two area numbers are joined by a zero. For example, take a work on the foreign relations of the United States with the United Kingdom. It belongs in 327 International relations, specifically at 327.3–.9 Foreign relations of specific continents and localities, foreign relations of specific countries. The instruction there reads:

Add to base number 327 notation 3–9 from Table 2 . . . then, for relations between that nation or region and another nation or region, add 0* and to the result add notation 1–9 from Table 2 . . .

Give priority in notation to the nation or region emphasized. If emphasis is equal, give priority to the nation or region coming first in Table 2

(The asterisk * refers to a footnote in the printed schedules, indicating that in such cases, double zeros are used for standard subdivisions.) Implementing the instruction we arrive at the number 327.73041:

| | |
|---|---|
| 327 | Base number for Foreign relations |
| 73 | United States (nation emphasized) (Table 2) |
| 0 | Facet indicator |
| 41 | United Kingdom (Table 2) |

The entry also contains an option to give priority in notation to the country requiring local emphasis, e.g., if a library in the United Kingdom wished to gather foreign relations with respect to the United Kingdom as the focus of attention, then 327.41073 would be the proper number.

One more example to show a different notation pattern: Suppose one has a work on trade relations between Canada and tropical countries. Under 382.093–.099 International commerce in specific continents, countries, localities, the add instructions are as follows:

> Add to base number 382.09 notation 3–9 from Table 2 . . .; then, for commerce between two continents, countries, localities or between a continent, country, locality and a region, area, place, add 0† and add notation 1–9 from Table 2 . . .

Accordingly, the correct number is 382.0971013:

| | |
|---|---|
| 382 | Base number for International commerce (Foreign trade) |
| 09 | Historical, geographic, persons treatment (Table 1) |
| 71 | Canada (Table 2) |
| 0 | Facet indicator |
| 13 | Torrid zone (Tropics) (Table 2) |

## EXTENDING A TABLE 2 NUMBER BY ANOTHER TABLE 2 NUMBER

Sometimes, a work deals with two or more geographic facets. For example, suppose one has a work that deals with the history of the coastal regions of California. Coastal regions are represented by —146 in Table 2. Should the notation for California be attached to the number for coastal regions, or should the notation for coastal regions be attached to the number for California? Under notation 1 in Table 2, there is an instruction to "class specific continents, countries, localities in —3–9." In the DDC, the particular place is more important than a general area when areas are under consideration. In this case California is more important than coastal regions. For a history of the coastal regions of California, then, the number 979.400946 is built in this way:

| | |
|---|---|
| 9 | Base number for History |
| 794 | California (Table 2) |
| 009 | Areas, regions, places in general (internal table under 930–990) |
| 46 | Number following —1 in —146 Coastal regions and shorelines (Table 2) |

Similarly, place is also transcendent in geography:

Geography of the coastal regions of California: 917.940946

| | |
|---|---|
| 91 | Base number for Geography |
| 794 | California (Table 2) |
| 09 | Areas, regions, places in general (internal table under 913–919) |
| 46 | Number following —1 in —146 Coastal regions and shorelines (Table 2) |

Even when the first area is represented by standard subdivisions —093–099, the number can be further extended by adding the notation for a second area through the instruction given under —093–099 in Table 1:

Add to base number —09 notation 3–9 from Table 2 . . .; then add further as follows:

| | |
|---|---|
| 01 | Forecasts |
| . | |
| . | |
| . | |
| 09 | Historical and geographic treatment |

        Add to 09 the numbers following —09 in notation 090–099 from Table 1 . . .

        Use 093–099 to add notation for a specific continent, country, locality when first area notation is used to specify area of origin, while second identifies area in which subject is found or practiced . . .

For example:

Urban labor market in the United States: 331.120973091732

| | |
|---|---|
| 331.12 | Base number for Labor market |
| 09 | Historical, geographic, persons treatment (Table 1) |
| 73 | United States (Table 2) |
| 09 | Historical and geographic treatment (add table under —093–099 (Table 1) |
| 1 | Number following —09 in —091 Treatment by areas, regions, places in general (Table 1) |
| 732 | Number following —1 in —1732 Urban regions (Table 2) |

Of course, just as elsewhere in the Classification, the area must approximate the whole of the number before a second number can be added. The same guidelines described in chapter 8 for determining topics that approximate the whole of a number apply to areas. For example, specific areas listed in a class-here note approximate the whole of the area number; those listed in an including note do not.

## ADDING AREA NOTATION TO STANDARD SUBDIVISIONS OTHER THAN —09

There are several places in Table 1 where an area number can be attached to a standard subdivision other than the normal —09:

| | |
|---|---|
| —021 8 | Standards |
| —023 | The subject as a profession, occupation, hobby |
| —025 | Directories of persons and organizations |
| —027 2 | Patents |
| —029 1–029 9 | [Geographic treatment of] Commercial miscellany |
| —060 3–060 9 | National, state, provincial, local organizations |
| —070 1–070 9 | Geographic treatment [of Education, research, related topics] |
| —071 01–071 09 | Geographic treatment [of Education] |
| —0711 | [Geographic treatment of] Higher education |
| —0712 | [Geographic treatment of] Secondary education |

—072 01–072 09   Geographic treatment of research and statistical
                 methods together, of research alone
—074             Museums, collections, exhibits
—079             Competitions, festivals, awards, financial support
—092 2           Collected persons treatment

Note that in the table of preference in the beginning of Table 1, the span —093–099 takes precedence over —074. The origin of the item being exhibited takes precedence over the place of the exhibition; however, the place of the exhibition may also be shown by using —074 plus area notation instead of —093–099. For example, Australian aboriginal art exhibited in the United States is classed in 704.039915007473, not 704.03991500973 (for an explanation of the valid number, see chapter 12).

## USING STANDARD SUBDIVISIONS AFTER AN AREA NUMBER

Certain standard subdivisions may be extended by a number from Table 2. At times the converse is true—but only upon instruction. As explained in chapter 8, any built number may have a standard subdivision added to it so long as: 1) there are no instructions to the contrary; 2) the added notation is not redundant; 3) the built number does not already have a standard subdivision attached to it; and 4) the topic approximates the whole of the number. For example:

A journal of elementary education in South Africa: 372.96805
372.9   Historical, geographic, persons treatment of elementary
        education
68      South Africa (Table 2)
05      Serial publications (Table 1)

A journal of higher education in Ghana: 378.66705
378     Base number for Higher education
667     Ghana (Table 2)
05      Serial publications (Table 1)

Research on Japanese economy: 330.9520072
330.9   Base number for Economic situation and conditions
52      Japan (Table 2)
0072    Research (Table 1)

A history of French foreign policy: 327.44009
327     Base number for International relations
44      France (Table 2)
009     History (Table 1)

Note in the last two examples that two zeros are used for standard subdivisions. There are instructions in the schedules to this effect in both cases. In the last example we have to use two zeros because a single zero is used to introduce the second area in those cases where two areas are involved.

## SUMMARY

Table 2 in volume 1 contains the notation for geographic areas. Here the entire world has been covered by the digits —1–9. The world and regions in general are denoted by —1 and its subdivisions. The digit —3 denotes the ancient world. The modern world is denoted by the digits —4–9; it has been divided first into continents, then into regions, countries, provinces, and states. In a few cases, the division continues down to counties and important cities (especially in the United States, the United Kingdom, Canada, South Africa, Australia, and New Zealand). These hierarchical divisions are based on geographic divisions accepted by geographers and historians.

Area numbers are given in the Relative Index. They are preceded by the symbol "T2."

The dash before the area number indicates that it is not to be used alone, but is to be combined with a class number from the schedules. The combining can be done in two ways. The first (and most common) is by adding an area number by way of standard subdivision —09 (which acts as a connecting symbol between the class numbers from the schedules and the area number from Table 2). The second is to add an area number when told to do so in the schedules. Such an instruction is usually found in the form "Add to base number . . . notation 1–9 from Table 2 . . . ."

Two area numbers may be added upon instructions, usually with the interposition of a zero. Sometimes a Table 2 number is added to a standard subdivision other than —09, the normal facet indicator for area.

## EXERCISES

Exercise 1:

In the Relative Index identify the area numbers for the following areas, and then locate and verify them in Table 2:

(1) Genesee County, Michigan

(2) Islāmābād Capital Territory, Pakistan

(3) Suriname

(4) Coast Ranges in Oregon

(5) Cambodia

(6) Unaligned blocs

(7) Eastern Hemisphere

(8) Waterfalls

(9) Antarctic Ocean

(10) Arctic Ocean

(11) Islamic regions

(12) Rural regions

Exercise 2:

Classify the following with direct subdivision by place:

(1) Adult education in Singapore

(2) Education policy in India

(3) General statistics of Finland

(4) General geology of Athens

(5) History of Jammu and Kashmir

(6) History of Jammu and Kashmir during the reign of Aurangzeb

(7) General organizations in Liverpool, England

(8) Journalism and newspapers in Finland

(9) Art galleries in Sweden

(10) Public administration in Canada

Exercise 3:

Assign class numbers to the following, using extensions of area notation 1:

(1) Social welfare programs in developing countries

(2) Democratic political systems in former communist bloc countries

(3) Health insurance systems in the Pacific region

Exercise 4:

Assign class numbers to the following, using standard subdivision —09 and area notation 3–9:

(1) Ambulance services in Washington State

(2) Child labor in Southeast Asia

(3) Taxes in Kuwait

(4) Costume in Belgium

(5) Prices in France: an economic study

(6) Sexual division of labor: a case study in Chicago, Illinois

(7) Broadway musicals: a theatrical history

Exercise 5:

Classify the following subjects requiring area notation between two subject facets:

(1) Physical geography of Mexico

(2) Property law of Nigeria

(3) Public health law of Mozambique

(4) The lower house of the British Parliament

(5) Italian Communist Party

Exercise 6:

Classify the following requiring two area numbers:

(1) Migration from Vietnam to the United States: a sociological study

(2) Trade agreements between Colombia and Venezuela (emphasizes Colombia)

(3) Trade between Venezuela and Colombia (emphasizes Venezuela)

(4) Foreign relations between Australia and countries of the Pacific Rim

(5) Foreign relations between Japan and South Korea

(6) Canadian economic aid to developing countries

(7) Geography of suburban regions of Australia

Exercise 7:

Classify the following topics using an area notation extended by another area notation:

(1) Civil rights in francophone countries of Africa

(2) Male costume in rural Austria

(3) Economic conditions in rural England

Exercise 8:

Classify the following, using a standard subdivision (other than —09) extended by an area notation:

(1) Research in economics in Scotland

(2) Computer science as a profession in the United States

(3) Education in mathematics in Asia

(4) Education of attorneys in Latin America

(5) Higher education in Spain in public administration

(6) Sports curricula in U. S. colleges

Exercise 9:

Classify the following, using a standard subdivision after an area notation:

(1) Journal of Indian geography

(2) Women in the Church of England

(3) Foreign policy of Germany in the 1990s

(4) Sickness and health: Canadian statistics at a glance

(5) Ancient Roman coins [minted in Rome] in the Hobart Classics Museum (Hobart, Tasmania)

(6) A journal of housing programs and services in Argentina

## Chapter 10

# USE OF TABLE 3 WITH LITERATURE AND OTHER CLASSES

## INTRODUCTION

Main class 800 was originally designed for literary works of the imagination by known authors. That is still its basic cast. However, it also contains other types of works. For instance, although anonymous classics, such as the *Mabinogion* and *Tales of the Arabian Nights*, could be classed in folk literature, in the DDC they are classed in 800. Futhermore, section 808 includes topics that are not strictly literature. For example, it includes rhetoric, i.e., material on how to use language to express ideas. This does not mean only material on how to write poetry or prose or fiction or drama, but also material on how to write a legal brief, a medical report, or an engineering analysis. Section 808 also includes editorial techniques.

For literature, the 800 class includes both literary texts and works about literature. For individual authors, Table 3A is used. For works by or about more than one author, Tables 3B and 3C are used. The use of Table 3 is described at length below; first, however, a general discussion of class 800 may be helpful.

## DIVISION OF MAIN CLASS 800 LITERATURE

Main class 800 begins with general works, in 801–809. The remaining notation, 810–890, is divided among the literatures of the world.

Sections 801–807 represent standard subdivisions of literature; 808–809 have been extended to accommodate rhetoric and texts and criticism from more than two literatures. Following is the outline for 801–809:

| | |
|---|---|
| 800 | Literature (Belles-lettres) and rhetoric |
| 801 | Philosophy and theory |
| 802 | Miscellany |
| 803 | Dictionaries, encyclopedias, concordances |
| 804 | [Unassigned] |
| 805 | Serial publications |
| 806 | Organizations and management |
| 807 | Education, research, related topics |
| 808 | Rhetoric and collections of literary texts from more than two literatures |
| 809 | History, description, critical appraisal of more than two literatures |

Classes 801–809 deal with literature in general: 808.8 and 809 are particularly important for several reasons. Class 808.8 contains provisions for collections of texts from more than two literatures, as well as criticism of more than two literatures when a sufficient amount of literary text is present. This makes 808.8 one of the major units in main class 800.

Class 809 deals with history, description, and critical appraisal of more than two literatures. There are many such works, and their classification requires careful handling. Classes 808.8 and 809 will be treated at length later in this chapter.

## Facets of Literature

The 800 class is the most faceted of all the main classes. The main facets represented in the classification of literature are language or nationality, literary genre or form (subdivided by kind of form[1]), and literary period (the time or era when the work was written or when the author flourished). Beyond these main facets are other aspects such as bibliographic form (i.e., collection or history/critical appraisal), literary features (such as naturalism, plot, characters), themes (such as love, friendship, everyday life), and persons (such as for or by women or children).

The general citation order for a class number in literature consists of *language* (except for American literature, which has its own span), *literary form* (such as poetry) or *kind of form* (such as mystery fiction), *period* in which the work is written, and *standard subdivisions*. Literary features, themes, and persons are extensions of subdivisions —08 and —09. This citation order varies slightly for literary works not limited to a particular language.

### LANGUAGE

The literatures of individual languages are classed in 810–899. Each language that at one time was considered to be of importance to western scholars has been allotted a division in 810–880. Consequently, many other important literatures are classed as subdivisions of 890 Literatures of other languages.

Previously, some national literatures, although written in a western language, were not treated as fully as the literature of the mother nation of the tongue. That is, Spanish literature from Spain was treated in detail, but literature from Mexico in Spanish was not. British literature could be gathered by periods, but Australian literature could not. This was a serious shortcoming in Dewey that has been rectified in Edition 22, which allows period subdivisions under affiliated literatures also.

The divisions of the 800s follow:

| | |
|---|---|
| 810 | American literature in English |
| 820 | English and Old English (Anglo Saxon) literatures |
| 830 | Literatures of Germanic languages    German literature |
| 840 | Literatures of Romance languages    French literature |
| 850 | Literatures of Italian, Sardinian, Dalmation, Romanian, Rhaeto-Romanic languages    Italian literature |
| 860 | Literatures of Spanish and Portuguese languages    Spanish literature |
| 870 | Literatures of Italic languages    Latin literature |
| 880 | Literatures of Hellenic languages    Classical Greek literature |
| 890 | Literatures of other specific languages and language families |

### FORM

Most literature is written in a particular form or genre such as poetry or drama. At the head of Tables 3A and 3B, there is a list of the literary forms of literature that the DDC recognizes. They are placed in their order of preference and should be consulted when two or more forms are involved in a work.

---

[1] Kind of form does not apply to works by individual authors.

The following table of preference  appears in Tables 3A and 3B:

| | |
|---|---|
| Drama | —2 |
| Poetry | —1 |
|     Class epigrams in verse in —8 | |
| Fiction | —3 |
| Essays | —4 |
| Speeches | —5 |
| Letters | —6 |
| Miscellaneous writings | —8 |
| Humor and satire | —7 (Table 3B only) |

The form subdivision —7 Humor and satire poses a special problem. Humor and satire are not true literary forms or genres; they are literary styles or devices to make a point. The subdivision —7 does not exist in Table 3A for individual authors. Because a work of humor and/or satire must be written in a particular literary form, it is classed with the form, e.g., satirical poem —1, humorous fiction —3, etc. Humor or satire without identifiable form is classed under —8, as is a collection of satire or humor by an individual author written in more than one form. Subdivision —7 is used only for collections and criticism of works of humor and satire in two or more literary forms (including both verse and prose) by more than one author.

The literary forms represented by —1, —2, —3 and —5 are further subdivided into kinds of forms which are subgenres of literature. These include narrative poetry, lyric and balladic poetry, comedy and melodrama, historical and period fiction, adventure fiction, public speeches (oratory), recitations, etc. They are used only with collections and critical appraisal of works by more than one author, and are not used for individual authors.

## PERIOD

Because literary styles vary in different time periods, the time or period facet is an important consideration in classifying literature. The literature in each major language is divided into recognized time periods. These period subdivisions are found in the schedules under the numbers for individual literatures. For works containing collections from, or critical appraisal of, more than two literatures, the period subdivisions follow those defined in Table 1.

## FEATURE/THEME/PERSONS

Many literary works have identifiable themes or manifest specific features, such as style, mood, and perspective, and literature for and by specific kinds of persons. In the DDC, features, themes, and persons are represented in the class numbers for works by or about more than one author. They are not represented in class numbers for works by or about individual authors.

## INTRODUCTION TO TABLE 3

Few class numbers in literature are found ready-made in the schedules. Most numbers have to be built by way of Tables 3A or 3B and 3C. For this reason class 800 is rightly considered to be one of the most faceted main classes in the DDC. The notation from Tables 3A–3C is to be used only when so instructed in the schedules or tables, and only with base numbers for individual literatures that are listed with add instructions (or a note or asterisk leading to add instructions). The base number may be identified in a note, e.g., in the note at 899: "899.969 Georgian"; otherwise it is the number given for the literature, e.g., 839.31 *Dutch literature.

As mentioned earlier, Table 3A is used with works by or about individual authors, and Table 3B with works by or about more than one author written in the same language. Table 3C contains notation representing aspects of literature other than language and form, and is used where instructed in Table 3B.

## TABLE 3A: WORKS BY AND ABOUT INDIVIDUAL AUTHORS

Class numbers assigned to works by or about individual authors normally contain four component parts in the following citation order:

main class + language + form + period

The procedures for building numbers for individual authors are outlined at the beginning of Table 3A. Detailed explanation of building numbers for individual authors is also found in the Manual notes for Table 3 and Table 3A. In addition, a flow chart is included in the Manual note for Table 3A as an aid to show the step-by-step process.

Table 3A is easy to use primarily because once the form of a literary work and the period during which an author wrote are determined, the classifier's work is essentially completed. There are pitfalls, however: forms are not always apparent, or a work may be juvenilia, or may have been written in the time before the period or periods in which an author is known to have produced his or her major works.

Here is an example of an individual work:

*Cress Delehanty* by Jessamyn West

Jessamyn West is an American writer whose work began to be published in the late 1940s. Because she is an American writer, the base number for her work is 81. Next the literary form or genre of this work has to be determined. *Cress Delehanty* is a series of short stories that are combined to make a novel. Table 3A supplies the notation for the form, which in this case is —3 Fiction. As mentioned earlier, kind of form (e.g., historical fiction) is not used for individual authors. Under —31–39 Specific periods [for fiction] in Table 3A, there is a note to add to —3 notation from the period table for the specific literature in 810–890. Period numbers are found in the schedules under each of the literatures. Jessamyn West's fits nicely in 1945–1999, for which the number 54 is found under 810 American literature in the schedules. Adding the period notation to —3 results in —354, which is then added to base number 81, resulting in the correct number 813.54. That is the end of number building for this work, because there are no instructions to continue further.

Book numbers, also known as item numbers, based on cutter numbers take care of the rest of the needed information. Cutter numbers are devices to subarrange a class— alphabetically by author or subject, or chronologically by date, whatever the occasion demands. In the case of *Cress Delehanty* the number might be W52cr, W52 for West and cr for *Cress Delehanty*. Using such a method to gather works of an author together alphabetically is a help to users. (Cutter numbers are treated in detail in two books, one by John P. Comaromi[2] and the other by Donald J. Lehnus.[3] An automatic Dewey cuttering program is available on the Dewey web site.[4])

To repeat a point made earlier: once the form of the work and the period of an individual author have been selected, the work of the classifier is done.

In the DDC, works by an individual author and critical appraisal of works about the author in general or about a particular work by the author are classed in the same number. In other words, the class number for a work of criticism about *Cress Delehanty* will be the same as the class number for the book itself. Their call numbers will differ slightly through adjustments to book numbers; different libraries follow different practices in this regard.

Here are a few more examples:

### Works by individual authors

*Newspaper days* by Theodore Dreiser [1871–1945]. 813.52
  81  Base number for American literature
  3   Fiction (Table 3A)
  52  Period notation for 1900–1945 from the schedules

*Stories, poems, and other writings* by Willa Cather [1873–1947]. 813.52
  81  Base number for American literature
  3   Fiction (the form with which Cather is chiefly identified)
      (Table 3A)
  52  Period notation for 1900–1945 from the schedules

*The nondramatic works* |poems| *of John Ford* [1586–ca.1640] edited by L.E. Stock et al. 821.3
  82  Base number for English literature
  1   Poetry (Table 3A)
  3   Period notation for Elizabethan period, 1558–1625, from the
      schedules

*Essays: first and second series by Ralph Waldo Emerson* [1803–1882]. 814.3
  81  Base number for American literature
  4   Essays (Table 3A)
  3   Period notation for 1830–1861 from the schedules

Note that collected works of individual authors receive the same class numbers as individual works in the same form. Collections of works in multiple forms are classed with the form with which the author is chiefly identified.

### Works about individual authors

A critical appraisal of an individual author that emphasizes a particular literary form is classed in the same number as the author's works in that form. Notation 092 from

---

[2] John P. Comaromi, *Book Numbers: A Historical Study and Practical Guide to Their Use* (Littleton, CO: Libraries Unlimited, 1981).

[3] Donald J. Lehnus, *Book Numbers: History, Principles, and Application* (Chicago: American Library Association, 1980).

[4] The Dewey Cutter Program (www.oclc.org/dewey/support/program) is a software program that automatically provides cutter numbers from the OCLC Four-Figure Cutter Tables (Cutter Four-Figure Table and Cutter-Sanborn Four-Figure Table) upon input of text.

Table 1 for biography is not used with works about individual authors. For example:

> *Henry James* [1843-1916]: *a study of the short fiction* by Richard A. Hocks. 813.4
>
> | | |
> |---|---|
> | 81 | Base number for American literature |
> | 3 | Fiction (Table 3A) |
> | 4 | Period notation for 1861–1899 from the schedules |

If the critical appraisal does not emphasize a particular form, it is classed with the notation for the form with which the author is chiefly identified.

> *Salem is my dwelling place: a life of Nathaniel Hawthorne* [1804–1864] by Edwin Haviland Miller. 813.3
>
> | | |
> |---|---|
> | 81 | Base number for American literature |
> | 3 | Fiction (the form with which Nathaniel Hawthorne is chiefly identified) (Table 3A) |
> | 3 | Period notation for 1830–1861 from the schedules |

> *In the footsteps of Hans Christian Andersen* [1805–1875] by Kai Chr. Rasmussen. 839.8136
>
> | | |
> |---|---|
> | 839.81 | Base number for Danish literature |
> | 3 | Fiction (Table 3A) |
> | 6 | Period notation for 1800–1899 from the schedules |

> *Charles Baudelaire* [1821–1867] *revisited* by Lois Boe Hyslop. 841.8
>
> | | |
> |---|---|
> | 84 | Base number for French literature |
> | 1 | Poetry (Table 3A) |
> | 8 | Period notation for 1848–1899 from the schedules |

> *The dragon and the dove: the plays of Thomas Dekker* [1572–1632] by Julia Gasper. 822.3
>
> | | |
> |---|---|
> | 82 | Base number for English literature |
> | 2 | Drama (Table 3A) |
> | 3 | Period notation for Elizabethan period, 1558–1625, from the schedules |

## Works about individual works

A work about an individual literary work is assigned the same class number as the work itself:

> *New essays on White noise* [a novel by Don DeLillo, late 20th-century American author] edited by Frank Lentricchia. 813.54
>
> | | |
> |---|---|
> | 81 | Base number for American literature |
> | 3 | Fiction (Table 3A) |
> | 54 | Period notation for 1945–1995 from the schedules |

> *Tristan in the underworld: a study of Gottfried von Strassburg's* [13th cent.] *Tristan together with the Tristan of Thomas* by Neil Thomas. 831.21
>
> | | |
> |---|---|
> | 83 | Base number for German literature |
> | 1 | Poetry (Table 3A) |
> | 21 | Period notation for 1100–1249 from the schedules |

*Love and social contracts: Goethe's* [1749–1832] *Unterhaltungen deutscher Ausgewanderten* by Robin A. Clouser. 833.6

| | |
|---|---|
| 83 | Base number for German literature |
| 3 | Fiction (Table 3A) |
| 6 | Period notation for classical period 1750–1832 from the schedules |

Authors who write in the same language, form, and period share the same class number; for example, poetry by Tennyson and Browning, both being Victorian poets, is assigned the same class number: 821.8.

The language and form of literature are ordinarily obvious to the classifier. The author's period occasionally causes some difficulty. Reference tools, such as the *Oxford Companion to English Literature*, will prove helpful when the classifier is in doubt.

The form subdivision —8 Miscellaneous writings presents a special case. It is used for authors not limited to or chiefly identifiable with one specific form, and also for diaries, journals, notebooks, and reminiscences. Such works are classed with —8 in Table 3A plus period subdivision plus subdivision —02–09 under —81–89. This results in the citation order of 8 + language + 8 + period + special form, as shown in the following examples:

*A moveable feast* by Ernest Hemingway. 818.5203

| | |
|---|---|
| 81 | Base number for American literature |
| 8 | Miscellaneous writings (Table 3A) |
| 52 | Period notation for 1900–1945 from the schedules |
| 03 | Diaries, journals, notebooks, reminiscences (under —81–89 in Table 3A) |

*Indian journals, March 1962–May 1963: Notebooks, diary, blank pages, writings* by Allen Ginsberg. 818.5403

| | |
|---|---|
| 81 | Base number for American literature |
| 8 | Miscellaneous writings (Table 3A) |
| 54 | Period notation for 1945–1999 from the schedules |
| 03 | Journals (under —81–89 in Table 3A) |

Translations of works by individual authors are classed in the same numbers as the original works. For example:

*Souvenirs intimes de David Copperfield: De grandes esperances* by Charles Dickens. 823.8

| | |
|---|---|
| 82 | Base number for English literature |
| 3 | Fiction (Table 3A) |
| 8 | Period notation for English literature, Victorian period, 1837–1899, from the schedules |

## A Word of Caution

If a literature does not have a designated base number, i.e., the name of the literature is not listed with add instructions (or a note or asterisk leading to add instructions), it cannot be extended beyond the base number, i.e., form and literary period cannot be added. For example, the number for the collected works of a Livonian writer (Livonian is a Finnic language found at 894.54) cannot be extended beyond 894.54 because it is not a base number to which Table 3A notation can be added.

Previously, period notation was not added to works by most writers who did not live in the ancestral continent of their mother tongue. That is to say, the periods listed under French literature were not used for authors writing in French who resided in Africa, Canada, or the Caribbean; only French writers living in France or elsewhere in Europe received numbers for such periods. In Edition 22, period notation was extended to works by writers who do not live in the continent of their mother tongue. For example, the period table for English under 820 English and Old English (Anglo-Saxon) literatures is used for literatures from all countries and continents except North America, South America, Hawaii and associated islands. Period extensions for the latter are provided in a table under 810 American literature in English. The period table under 810 for United States in previous editions has been extended in Edition 22 to countries of North, Middle, and South America and to comprehensive works on American literature in English. Edition 22 also retains many of the optional period tables.

## USE OF TABLES 3B AND 3C

Class numbers for general works on literature, such as literary anthologies, literary histories, and critical appraisals of literature, are considerably more difficult to build than those for one author from one literature. However, the introduction to Table 3B, outlining the procedure for number building in eight steps, should ease some of the difficulties in classifying literary anthologies and critical appraisals. Unlike class numbers for works by and about individual authors, which show language, form, and period, class numbers for general collections and criticism also express other facets, such as kind of form, bibliographic form, scope, media, and feature/theme/persons wherever applicable.

### Table 3B: Subdivisions for Works by or about More than One Author

Table 3B contains subdivisions for works by or about more than one author, arranged first by standard subdivisions —01–07 as provided in Table 1 and subdivisions —08 and —09, and then by literary forms —1–8. Subdivisions —08 and —09 warrant special mention.

Subdivision —08 is used to indicate whether the work in hand is a collection. Subdivision —09 in Table 3B is used to indicate whether the document in hand is a work about literature; it covers history, description, or critical appraisal (hereafter also referred to as "criticism"). Subdivisions —08 and —09 may be further extended by notation from Table 1 or Table 3C to accommodate additional facets.

To assist in the complex number building needed for collections or critical appraisals of literature written by more than one author, the Manual note for Table 3B includes a detailed discussion with two flow charts showing the decisions the classifier must make at each step of the number-building process. The flow charts are followed by many examples.

## Table 3C: Notation to Be Added Where Instructed in Table 3B, 700.4, 791.4, and 808–809

Table 3C contains subdivisions used as extensions of the notation in Table 3B and of certain numbers in the schedules. The four main categories in Table 3C are listed below in their order of preference (also listed in the Manual note for Table 3B under "Preference order"):

| | |
|---|---|
| Themes and subjects | —3 |
| Elements | —2 |
| Qualities | —1 |
| Persons | —8–9 |

Each is further divided into greater detail.

## GENERAL COLLECTIONS OF LITERARY TEXTS AND CRITICISM:  MORE THAN TWO LITERATURES

The main class number 800 is usually the beginning point for a general anthology or criticism of world literature or an anthology or criticism of material from literatures in more than two languages.[5] There is one exception to the "more than two" rule described in the note under 808.8:

> . . . class collections of texts from literatures in more than two languages from the same family with the literature of that family, e.g., French, Italian, and Spanish literatures 840

Works of literature not limited to a particular language are classed in 800–809. Note that the second digit after main class number 8 is a zero, which indicates that the language facet is absent. Sections 801–807 carry regular standard subdivisions. Literary texts and criticism are classed in 808.8–809. These numbers can be extended to accommodate literary facets such as literary form, period, and feature/theme/persons.

### General Collections and Criticism with One Facet

The class number for a literary work that manifests only one facet—form, period, or feature/theme/persons—follows the citation order: 808.8 *or* 809 + facet.

### FORM

How would a collection of world poetry be classified? The number for collections of poetry, 808.81, is divided into the spans 808.812–808.818 for specific kinds of poetry. In such situations, there is a note to add to base number 808.81 the numbers following —10 in —102–107 from Table 3B. For example:

| | |
|---|---|
| A collection of epic poetry: 808.8132 | |
| 808.81 | Collections of poetry |
| 32 | Number following —10 in —1032 Epic poetry (Table 3B) |

---

[5] Works in two languages are classed with the language that predominates or that comes first in numerical order.

*The epic circle: allegoresis and the Western tradition : from Homer to Tasso* by Zdenko Zlatar. 809.132

| | |
|---|---|
| 809 | Base number for History, description, critical appraisal of more than two literatures |
| 1 | Number following 808.8 in 808.81 Poetry |
| 32 | Number following —10 in —1032 Epic poetry (Table 3B) |

## PERIOD

How would a work entitled *20th-century literature: a collection* be classified? Instruction for building the number appears under 808.8 Collections of literary texts from more than two literatures:

> 808.8001–808.8005  Collections from specific periods
> Add to base number 808.800 the numbers following —090 in notation 0901–0905 from Table 1, e.g., collections of 18th century literature 808.80033

The number for the 20th century in Table 1 is —0904. Discarding 090 as instructed results in the number 808.8004. Note that, in this case, the period numbers used are taken from Table 1, not from the period subdivisions found under 810–890 for individual literatures. The reason is simple: there is no pattern that works for literature in general, so the pattern of Table 1 is used.

Criticism of world literature by period falls into 809.01–809.05; a single zero is used instead of double zeros. Thus the history of literature in the 20th century falls at 809.04:

> *Twentieth-century literature: critical issues and themes* by Philip Malcolm Waller Thody. 809.04
>
> | | |
> |---|---|
> | 809 | Base number for History, description, critical appraisal of more than two literatures |
> | 0 | Facet indicator for 809.01–.05 Literature from specific periods |
> | 4 | Period notation: number following —090 in —0904 20th century (Table 1) |

## FEATURE/THEME/PERSONS

How would an anthology of literature that features King Arthur be classified? The classifier begins with the base number 808.80, which may be extended with notation 1–3 from Table 3C, which expresses specific features such as style, mood, perspective, themes, and subjects. A person as a character in, or subject of, literature is classed in —351 Literature dealing with specific persons. The number for a collection of literature featuring King Arthur, therefore, is 808.80351:

> | | |
> |---|---|
> | 808.80 | Base number for Collections of literature displaying specific features |
> | 351 | Specific persons (Table 3C) |

Example of an anthology displaying specific features:

> *The love of cats: an illustrated anthology about our love for cats.*
> 808.803629752
>> 808.80 Base number for Collections of literature displaying specific features
>> 362 Animals (Table 3C)
>> 9752 Cats (from 599.752)

For works about literature displaying specific qualities and elements, notation 1–2 from Table 3C is added directly to base number 809.9 without intervening zeros. For works about literature displaying specific themes and subjects, the numbers following —3 in notation 32–38 from Table 3C are added directly to base number 809.933. Therefore, criticism of Arthurian literature is 809.93351; compare this with the number for the Arthurian anthology in our earlier example.

Example of a work about literature displaying specific qualities:

> *Abyss of reason: cultural movements, revelations, and betrayals* by Dan Cottom. 809.911
>> 809 Base number for History, description, critical appraisal of more than two literatures
>> 9 Literature displaying specific features
>> 11 Nontraditional viewpoints (Table 3C)

Notation 8–9 in Table 3C is used for literature for and by specific kinds of persons. For example, a collection of literature by women authors is classed in 808.899287.

## General Collections and Criticism with Two Facets

The class number for a work that is either a general collection or criticism, and contains two facets, has one of the following citation orders:

(1) 808.8 or 809 + form + period
(2) 808.8 or 809 + form + feature/theme/persons
(3) 808.8 or 809 + feature/theme/persons (period is ignored)

## FORM AND PERIOD

When a literary work combines form and period, the period notation follows the form notation. For example:

> *Travels of a genre: the modern novel and ideology* by Mary N. Layoun.
> 809.304
>> 809 Base number for History, description, critical appraisal of more than two literatures
>> 3 Number following 808.8 in 808.83 Fiction
>> 0 Historical periods (added to 808.83 as instructed under 808.81-808.88)
>> 4 Number following —090 in —0904 20th century (Table 1)

## FORM AND FEATURE/THEME/PERSONS

A collection of poetry that features King Arthur is classed in base number 808.819, where the classifier is instructed to add notation from Table 3C. As seen above, King Arthur is classed in —351; therefore, a collection of poems from more than two literatures about King Arthur or the Arthurian ideal is classed in 808.819351. (Of course, the number is shared with a number of other heroes from many times and climes.) Another example:

> *The landscapes of alienation: ideological subversion in Kafka, Céline, and Onetti* by Jack Murray. 809.39353

| | |
|---|---|
| 809 | Base number for History, description, critical appraisal of more than two literatures |
| 39 | Number following 808.8 in 808.839 Fiction displaying specific features |
| 353 | Alienation (Table 3C) |

## PERIOD AND FEATURE/THEME/PERSONS

How would a collection or criticism of literature from a particular period on a specific theme or quality be classified? What can be done? Here is as good a place as any to introduce the rule of fewest zeros. When a work contains several facets but there is no instruction in the DDC to combine them, the classifier is faced with the problem of choosing among several single-facet numbers. Given a series of numbers that share the first few digits, the classifier should choose the class number that has the least number of zeros following the common digits. For example, anthologies from more than two literatures have the base number 808.8 to which other facets are added. Anthologies by period are introduced by two zeros, e.g., 808.8004. Anthologies by theme or feature are introduced by one zero, e.g., 808.8036 and therefore are to be preferred to an anthology by period. For example:

> A collection of 18th-century world literature about friendship: 808.80353

| | |
|---|---|
| 808.80 | Base number for Collections displaying specific features |
| 353 | Friendship (Table 3C) |

The number 808.80353, meaning a collection of world literature about friendship, is preferred to the number 808.80033 meaning a collection of 18th-century literature because the former has fewer zeros. Furthermore, the standard subdivision —09033 18th century cannot be added after 808.80353 to bring out the period because the theme "friendship" is in an including note and therefore does not approximate the whole meaning of —353 in Table 3C.

## ANTHOLOGIES OF AND CRITICISM OF LITERATURE IN A SPECIFIC LANGUAGE

Literature written in a specific language is classed in 810–899. Moreover, both anthologies and criticism partake of subdivision —08 (collections) and subdivision —09 (history, description, critical appraisal from Table 3B), when appropriate. For example, an anthology of English literature not limited by form is classed in base number 82 plus —08 for collections, resulting in 820.8. Similarly, a history or criticism of English literature is classed in 820.9, and a history of Polish literature in 891.8509 (891.85 + 09). Further examples:

*From sea to shining sea* [a collection of American songs, tales, poems, and stories]. 810.8

| | |
|---|---|
| 81 | Base number for American literature |
| 08 | Collections of literary texts in more than one form (Table 3B) |

*The Oxford illustrated history of English literature* by Pat Rogers. 820.9

| | |
|---|---|
| 82 | Base number for English literature |
| 09 | History, description, critical appraisal of works in more than one form (Table 3B) |

## Anthologies of and Criticism of Literature in a Specific Language and Another Facet

The number for a collection or study of literature in a specific language that contains one other facet is built according to one of the following citation orders:

8 + language + (form) + (—08 *or* —09)

8 + language + (—08 *or* —09) + period

8 + language + (—08 *or* —09) + feature/theme/person

## FORM

For an anthology of literature in a specific form written in a specific language, the notation for the form (—1 for poetry, —2 for drama, etc.) with the subdivision —008 or —009 as displayed in Table 3B is added to the base number for the individual literature. For example:

An anthology of German poetry: 831.008

| | |
|---|---|
| 83 | Base number for German literature |
| 100 | Poetry (Table 3B) (includes facet indicator 00) |
| 8 | Collections of literary texts (internal table under —1–8 in Table 3B) |

A study of Japanese drama: 895.62009

| | |
|---|---|
| 895.6 | Base number for Japanese literature |
| 200 | Drama (Table 3B) (includes facet indicator 00) |
| 9 | History, description, critical appraisal (internal table under —1–8 in Table 3B) |

A history of Spanish fiction: 863.009

| | |
|---|---|
| 86 | Base number for Spanish literature |
| 300 | Fiction (Table 3B) (includes facet indicator 00) |
| 9 | History, description, critical appraisal (internal table under —1–8 in Table 3B) |

## Kind of Form

Some works contain specimens of or deal with the literature of a specific language and a kind of literary form, i.e., a subgenre such as lyric poetry or historical fiction. Table 3B provides specific numbers for these kinds of literary forms. For example:

An anthology of English epic poetry: 821.03208

| | |
|---|---|
| 82 | Base number for English literature |
| 1032 | Epic poetry (Table 3B) |
| 08 | Collections of literary texts (internal table under —102–107 in Table 3B) |

A critical study of American historical fiction: 813.08109

| | |
|---|---|
| 81 | Base number for American literature |
| 3081 | Historical and period fiction (Table 3B) |
| 09 | History, description, critical appraisal (internal table under —102–107 in Table 3B) |

Standard subdivisions —01–07 may be added to a kind of literary form if the work consists equally of literary texts and history, description, critical appraisal. For example:

A journal of English dramatic poetry: 821.0205

| | |
|---|---|
| 82 | Base number for English literature |
| 102 | Dramatic poetry (Table 3B) |
| 05 | Serial publications (Standard subdivision —05 as instructed in internal table under —102–107 in Table 3B) |

## PERIOD

For a history of 20th-century English literature, the class number begins with the base number 82, expanded by notation from Table 3B. The instructions in Table 3B say to add to —0900 notation for the appropriate period for each specific literature given in the schedules. The number for the 20th century under 820 English literature is 91, thus yielding —090091. The result is therefore 82 + —0900 + 91 = 820.90091. Another example:

German literature from the classical period: a collection: 830.8006

| | |
|---|---|
| 83 | Base number for German literature |
| 080 | Collections of literary texts in more than one form (Table 3B) (includes facet indicator 0) |
| 0 | Additional facet indicator for —01–09 Specific periods (Table 3C) |
| 6 | Classical period (Period table under 830 German literature) |

## FEATURE/THEME/PERSONS

Table 3C enables classifiers to extend notation 08 anthology and 09 criticism from Table 3B to represent specific themes, features, and persons. For example:

An anthology of English literature illustrating Romanticism: 820.80145

| | |
|---|---|
| 82 | Base number for English literature |
| 080 | Collections of literary texts in more than one form (Table 3B) (includes facet indicator 0) |
| 145 | Romanticism (Table 3C) |

For literature written for and by specific kinds of persons, notation 8–9 from Table 3C is used. For example:

An anthology of Polish literature for children: 891.850809282

| | |
|---|---|
| 891.85 | Base number for Polish literature |
| 080 | Collections of literary texts in more than one form (Table 3B) (includes facet indicator 0) |
| 9282 | [Literature for and by] Children (Table 3C) |

Similarly, for a criticism or history of the literature in a specific language displaying specific features, themes, or persons, notation 09 from Table 3B may be extended by adding notation from Table 3C to express such themes and features, but in this case without the second 0 facet indicator. For example:

> *Language in her eye : views on writing and gender by Canadian women writing in English.* 810.99287
>
> | | |
> |---|---|
> | 81 | Base number for Canadian literature |
> | 09 | History, description, critical appraisal of works in more than one form (Table 3B) |
> | 9287 | Women (Table 3C) |

Likewise:

> A critical appraisal of Romanticism in English literature: 820.9145
>
> A critical appraisal of English literature for children: 820.99282

In Table 3C, under —93–99 Literature for and by persons resident in specific continents, countries, localities, there is an instruction to add to —9 notation 3–9 from Table 2. For example:

> An anthology of American literature by residents of New England: 810.80974
>
> | | |
> |---|---|
> | 81 | Base number for American literature |
> | 080 | Collections of literary text in more than one form (Table 3B) (includes facet indicator 0) |
> | 9 | Literature for and by persons resident in specific continents, countries, localities (from —93–99 in Table 3C) |
> | 74 | New England (Table 2) |

## Anthologies of and General Criticism of Literature in a Specific Language with Two Other Facets

The class number for a literary work in a specific language that contains two other facets has one of the following citation orders:

> 8 + language + form + period + —08 or —09
> 8 + language + form + —08 or —09 + feature/theme/persons
> 8 + language + —08 or —09 + feature/theme/persons + —09 + period
> (from Table 1)

### FORM AND PERIOD

The following examples illustrate the number-building process:

> An anthology of 20th-century French poetry: 841.9108
>
> | | |
> |---|---|
> | 84 | Base number for French literature |
> | 1 | Poetry (Table 3B) |
> | 91 | 1900–1999 (Period table under 840.1–848) |
> | 0 | Facet indicator as instructed under —11–19 in Table 3B |
> | 8 | Collections of literary texts (internal table under —1–8 in Table 3B) |

Similarly:

A critical study of 20th-century French poetry: 841.9109

## FORM AND FEATURE/THEME/PERSONS

If the anthology or criticism focuses on a particular literary form, the form is expressed before adding the subdivision —008 or —009. In Table 3B, under —1–8 Specific forms, both —008 and —009 can be further extended by adding notation from Table 3C to express specific features, themes, or persons.

An anthology of German poetry illustrating classicism: 831.0080142
83      Base number for German literature
100     Poetry (Table 3B) (includes facet indicator 00)
80      Collections of literary texts displaying specific features (internal
        table under —1–8 in Table 3B)
142     Classicism (Table 3C)

Similarly, for poems written for or by specific kinds of persons, notation 1008, 1009, 2008, etc. from Table 3B may be extended by notation 8–9 from Table 3C:

A critical study of American drama written for teenagers: 812.0099283
81      Base number for American literature
200     Drama (Table 3B) (includes facet indicator 00)
9       History, description, critical appraisal (internal table under
        —1–8 in Table 3B)
9283    Literature for and by young people twelve to twenty (Table 3C)

An anthology of American poetry by residents of New England:
811.0080974
81      Base number for American literature
100     Poetry (Table 3B) (includes facet indicator 00)
80      Collections displaying specific features or emphasizing specific
        subjects, for and by specific kinds of persons (internal table
        under —1–8 in Table 3B) (includes facet indicator 0)
9       Literature for and by persons resident in specific continents,
        countries, localities (from —93–99 in Table 3C)
74      New England (Table 2)

A critical study of American poetry by residents of New England:
811.009974
81      Base number for American literature
100     Poetry (Table 3B) (includes facet indicator 00)
9       History, description, critical appraisal of texts displaying
        specific features or emphasizing specific subjects, for and by
        specific kinds of persons (internal table under
        —1–8 in Table 3B)
9       Literature for and by persons resident in specific continents,
        countries, localities (from —93–99 in Table 3C)
74      New England (Table 2)

If the work is in a particular kind of literary form, the notation for collections —08 requires only one zero as instructed under —102–107 in Table 3B. For example:

>   *Tales of the diamond: selected gems of baseball fiction* [short stories] by
>   William Price Fox [et al.].  813.0108357
>
>   | | |
>   |---|---|
>   | 81 | Base number for American literature |
>   | 301 | Short stories (Table 3B) |
>   | 08 | Collections of literary texts (internal table under —102–107 in Table 3B) |
>   | 357 | Sports (Table 3C) |

## PERIOD AND FEATURE/THEME/PERSONS

If the collection or criticism of literature in one language relates to a period and a feature, or a theme, or is for and/or by specific kinds of persons, but is not in a particular form, the citation order in the class number varies slightly from those for other combinations. For example:

>   An anthology of 16th-century British literature on Ireland:
>   820.93241509031
>
>   | | |
>   |---|---|
>   | 82 | Base number for English literature |
>   | 09 | History, description, critical appraisal (Table 3B) |
>   | 32 | Literature dealing with places (Table 3C) |
>   | 415 | Ireland (Table 2) |
>   | 09031 | 16th century, 1500–1599 (Table 1) |

In this case, because Tables 3B and 3C do not have provision to combine period and feature/theme/persons under —09, the feature/theme/persons facet takes precedence because the number 820.932415 contains fewer zeros than the number 820.9003 study of 16th-century English literature.  The period is then added through standard subdivision —0901–0905.

## LITERATURE IN A PARTICULAR LANGUAGE WITH ALL FACETS

For works involving all facets (language, form, period, and feature/theme/persons), the citation order for the class number is:

>   8 + language + form (Table 3B) + period (from period tables under the
>   base number in the schedules) + —08 or —09 + feature/theme/persons
>   (Table 3C)

For example:

>   An anthology of 20th-century French poetry depicting seasons:
>   841.9108033
>
>   | | |
>   |---|---|
>   | 84 | Base number for French literature |
>   | 1 | Poetry (Table 3B) |
>   | 91 | 1900–1999 (Period table under 840.1–848) |
>   | 0 | Facet indicator as instructed under —11–19 (Table 3B) |
>   | 80 | Collections of literary texts displaying specific features (internal table under —1–8 in Table 3B) (includes facet indicator 0) |
>   | 33 | Times (Table 3C) |

A critical study of 20th-century French poetry depicting seasons: 841.910933

| | |
|---|---|
| 84 | Base number for French literature |
| 1 | Poetry (Table 3B) |
| 91 | 1900–1999 (Period table under 840.1–848) |
| 0 | Facet indicator as instructed under —11–19 (Table 3B) |
| 9 | History, description, critical appraisal of texts displaying specific features (internal table under —1–8 in Table 3B) |
| 33 | Times (Table 3C) |

*Narrative time/descriptive time: lying, forgetting, and beyond in the* [19th century] *French realist novel* by James H. Reid. 843.70912

| | |
|---|---|
| 84 | Base number for French literature |
| 3 | Fiction (Table 3B) |
| 7 | 19th century (Period table under 840.1–848) |
| 0 | Facet indicator as instructed under —31–39 (Table 3B) |
| 9 | History, description, critical appraisal of texts displaying specific features (internal table under —1–8 in Table 3B) |
| 12 | Realism (Table 3C) |

## USE OF TABLE 3C WITH OTHER CLASSES

Table 3C was originally designed for use with main class 800 only. Beginning with Edition 20, it has also been used with base numbers from main class 700. For example:

The grotesque in the arts: 700.415

| | |
|---|---|
| 700.41 | Base number for Arts displaying specific qualities of style, mood, viewpoint |
| 5 | Number following —1 in notation 15 Symbolism, allegory, fantasy, myth (Table 3C—the grotesque is in an including note at —15) |

Urban themes in the arts: 700.421732

| | |
|---|---|
| 700.4 | Base number for Arts displaying specific themes and subjects |
| 2 | Number following —3 in notation 32 Places (Table 3C) |
| 1732 | Urban regions (Table 2) |

Comedy films: 791.43617

| | |
|---|---|
| 791.4361 | Base number for Films displaying specific qualities |
| 7 | Number following —1 in notation 17 Comedy (Table 3C) |

Films portraying the Bible: 791.436822

| | |
|---|---|
| 791.436 | Base number for Films dealing with specific themes and subjects |
| 82 | Number following —3 in —382 Religious themes (Table 3C) |
| 2 | Number following 2 in 220 Bible |

## SUMMARY

Literary works of the imagination are classed in main class 800. Collections of literary texts from more than two literatures are classed in 808.8, and the history, description, and critical appraisal (criticism) of such literature are classed in 809. Literatures written in specific languages are classed in 810–890. Most of these numbers may be extended by adding notation from Tables 3A–3C on instruction. Tables 3A–3C provide notation for bibliographic forms (e.g., collections); approaches (e.g., history); literary forms (e.g., poetry, drama) and kinds of literary forms (e.g., narrative poetry, comedy); and specific features (symbolism, plot) and themes (e.g., chivalry, travel), or persons (e.g., for and by children, women). Each literature that may be extended by using tables 3A–3C is listed with add instructions (or a note or asterisk leading to add instructions). These tables are not used with numbers for literatures lacking such instructions.

Class numbers for works of individual authors reflect the facets of language, form, and period. The base number for a literature is taken from the schedules, and is followed by the form notation from Table 3A, and the period notation that is given in the schedules under the base number for the specific literature in 810–890. Literary works by and literary criticism of individual authors (including criticism about their individual works) that are written in the same language, the same form, and the same period share the same number. Subdivisions —08 and —09 are not used for works by or about individual authors.

Class numbers for collections and critical appraisal of literature in a particular language written by more than one author reflect the facets of language, form, period, and feature, theme, or persons. Notation for form and kind of form comes from Table 3B, and the period notation is given in the schedules under the base number for the individual language in 810–890. Subdivisions —08 and —09 given in Table 3B many be extended by notation representing feature, theme, and persons from Table 3C, which in turn may be further extended by notation from other tables.

Notation from Table 3C may also be added directly to certain numbers in 808.8–809 and in main class 700 The arts.

## EXERCISES

Exercise 1:

Classify the following works by or about individual authors:

(1)  Poems of Charles Baudelaire (French poet, 1821–1867)

(2)  The collected plays of Thomas Dekker (British, 1572–1632)

(3)  Selected poetry of William Butler Yeats (Irish author, 1865–1939, writing in the English language)

(4)  Dramatic works of Eugene O'Neill (American, 1888–1953)

(5)  *Murder on the Orient Express* by Agatha Christie (1890–1976)

(6)  *The Adventures of Huckleberry Finn* by the American novelist Mark Twain (1835–1910)

(7)  A biography of Claus Silvester Dörner (German writer not limited to or chiefly identifiable with one specific form, 1913–   )

(8)  A collection of jokes by the American author, Nancy Gray (1959–   )

Exercise 2:

Classify the following topics from more than one literature:

(1) A collection of sonnets
(2) A collection of poetry by women
(3) An anthology of nineteenth-century literature
(4) A critical appraisal of lyric poetry
(5) A collection of poetry displaying realism
(6) A collection of poetry with marriage as the theme
(7) A critical appraisal of romantic literature

Exercise 3:

Classify the following topics from one literature:

(1) A study of symbolism in French literature
(2) A history of twentieth-century English literature
(3) A study of French women authors
(4) A study of social themes in 15th-century English literature
(5) A study of Portuguese literature by African authors
(6) Discourses of Christian salvation in English literature; an historical study

Exercise 4:

Classify the following works from one literature and in a particular form:

(1) Collection of English lyric poetry on love
(2) An anthology of English allegorical narrative poetry
(3) A critical study of plots in American historical fiction
(4) A study of English horror tales
(5) A study of heroism in the English novel

Exercise 5:

Classify the following works from one literature with multiple facets:

(1) Collection of Elizabethan English poetry
(2) Love in twentieth-century American drama: a critical study
(3) Collection of late twentieth-century American drama by teenagers
(4) A study of the Berlin wall in East German fiction
(5) A bibliography of English romantic poetry by women authors, 1770–1835

Exercise 6:

Classify the following works, using Table 3C with 700 numbers:

(1) Fantasy films
(2) Horror programs on television
(3) Werewolves in the arts
(4) Atlantis in art and literature

## Chapter 11

# TABLE 4: SUBDIVISIONS OF INDIVIDUAL LANGUAGES AND TABLE 6: LANGUAGES

## INTRODUCTION

Tables 4 and 6 are treated together in this chapter because they both deal with languages. Table 4 is used with a limited span of numbers, 420–490 Specific languages (plus 419 Sign languages). It provides notation for specific aspects, such as etymology and grammar, of individual languages. Table 6, on the other hand, is used throughout the Classification. It provides notation for groups of languages (such as Hellenic languages and Bantu languages) and for individual languages (such as Spanish and Zulu) as an aspect of a subject. The relationship between Table 6 and Table 5 Ethnic and National Groups is discussed in chapter 12.

## INTRODUCTION TO TABLE 4

Table 4 Subdivisions of Individual Languages and Language Families is the simplest table in the DDC. Simple in structure and application, it is used exclusively with the main numbers for individual languages and language families (419 and 420–490) in class 400 Language. In Table 4, linguistic elements, problems, and other aspects of linguistics are provided for separately. A summary of Table 4 is reproduced below:

**Summary of Table 4**

| | |
|---|---|
| —01–09 | Standard subdivisions |
| —1 | Writing systems, phonology, phonetics of the standard form of the language |
| —2 | Etymology of the standard form of the language |
| —3 | Dictionaries of the standard form of the language |
| —5 | Grammar of the standard form of the language    Syntax of the standard form of the language |
| —7 | Historical and geographic variations, modern nongeographic variations |
| —8 | Standard usage of the language (Prescriptive linguistics) Applied linguistics |

Notation from this table for recurring aspects such as etymology and grammar is to be combined, on instruction, with designated base numbers for individual languages in the schedules. The base number in this context is a compound number comprised of the main class digit 4 followed by the number for that particular language. For example, in base number 42 English, 4 is the main class digit and 2 is the notation for English. For such reasons, 400 Language is one of the most highly faceted classes in the DDC. The base numbers for all the major languages of the world are enumerated and listed with add instructions (or a note or asterisk leading to add instructions). With a few minor exceptions, there is a close parallel between the base numbers for languages in main classes 400 Language and 800 Literature:

| Language | Base number Language 400 | Base number Literature 800 |
|---|---|---|
| English | 4<u>2</u> | 8<u>2</u> |
| German | 4<u>3</u> | 8<u>3</u> |
| French | 4<u>4</u> | 8<u>4</u> |
| Hindi | 49<u>1.43</u> | 89<u>1.43</u> |
| Bengali | 49<u>1.44</u> | 89<u>1.44</u> |

A base number from main class 400 combined with notation from Table 4 results in the complete class number. However, only those numbers that are listed with add instructions (or a note or asterisk leading to add instructions) may be extended by a notation from Table 4.

## DIVISION OF MAIN CLASS 400

The division of main class 400 Language is also similar to that of class 800 Literature. 401–409 are used for general works of languages resulting from adding standard subdivisions (Table 1) to base number 400. For example:

> 401 Philosophy and theory [of language]
> 402 Miscellany
> 405 Serial publications

The span 410–418 is designated for Linguistics in general, regardless of language. For example:

| Etymology | 412 |
|---|---|
| Dictionaries | 413 |
| Grammar | 415 |

419, previously designated for structured verbal language other than spoken and written, has been renamed "Sign languages" in Edition 22. Numbers for specific sign languages may be built by adding to base number 419 notation 4–9 from Table 2 for the supranational region or country where the language is used. For example:

> 419.41 British Sign Language
> 419.44 French Sign Language
> 419.7 American Sign Language
> 419.87 Venezuelan Sign Language

According to instructions in the schedule, certain sign languages may be further extended by adding the facet indicator 0 (zero) followed by notation from Table 4 to the number for the specific sign language, e.g., grammar of British Sign Language 419.4105.

Specific Indo-European languages (except for East Indo-European and Celtic languages) are accommodated in the span 420–480. Within this span, each major Indo-European language family with its predominant language is assigned its own division

*Table 4 and Table 6: Languages* / 135

represented by a three-digit number with two meaningful digits:

| | |
|---|---|
| 420 | English and old English (Anglo-Saxon) |
| 430 | Germanic languages    German |
| 440 | Romance languages    French |
| 450 | Italian, Sardinian, Dalmatian, Romanian, Rhaeto-Romanic languages |
| 460 | Spanish and Portuguese languages |
| 470 | Italic languages    Latin |
| 480 | Hellenic languages    Classical Greek |

East Indo-European, Celtic, and other languages have been grouped together at 490 Other languages. Examples include 491.7 Russian, 492.4 Hebrew, 492.7 Arabic, and 495.1 Chinese.

## USING TABLE 4

As with all of the tables, notation in Table 4 Subdivisions of Individual Languages and Language Families is never used alone, but may be used as required with the base numbers for individual languages that are listed with add instructions (or a note or asterisk leading to add instructions) under 420–490.

Numbers from Table 4 and their subdivisions can be combined with base numbers in the schedules according to instruction under 420–490. The citation order of 420–490 is straightforward and regular:

Language + language subdivision from Table 4 + standard subdivision from Table 1

### Using Table 4 with Designated Base Numbers

In the print schedules, the asterisk by a number in the 400 class leads, through the footnote at the bottom of each page, to the instructions under 420–490 Specific languages. The relevant instruction at 420–490 reads:

Except for modifications shown under specific entries, add to base number for each language identified by * notation 01–8 from Table 4, e.g., grammar of Japanese 495.65. The base number is the number given for the language unless the schedule specifies a different number

Some examples of base numbers include:

| | |
|---|---|
| 429 | *Old English (Anglo-Saxon) |
| 469 | *Portuguese |
| 495.7 | *Korean |

In these cases, the base number for the language is the one shown in the number column.

In other cases, the use of Table 4 with the base number is given through an add instruction:

491.701–.75    Standard subdivisions, writing systems, phonology, phonetics, etymology, dictionaries, grammar of Russian
Add to base number 491.7 notation 01–5 from Table 4, e.g., grammar of Russian 491.75

In each case, it is the specified base number to which notation from Table 4 is added. For example, to build a number for a work on Portuguese grammar, we begin with the asterisked base number 469, since the language is the main subject. "Grammar" is a linguistic aspect whose number in Table 4 is —5. Hence the complete class number for the work is 469.5, analyzed as follows:

469      Base number for Portuguese
5      Grammar (Table 4)

The following table, showing the use of different notation from Table 4 with different base numbers, illustrates its simple but efficacious use:

**Language Elements**

| Language | Base Number | Etymology —2 | Dictionary —3 | Grammar —5 |
|---|---|---|---|---|
| English | 42 | 42<u>2</u> | 42<u>3</u> | 42<u>5</u> |
| German | 43 | 43<u>2</u> | 43<u>3</u> | 43<u>5</u> |
| French | 44 | 44<u>2</u> | 44<u>3</u> | 44<u>5</u> |
| Hindi | 491.43 | 491.43<u>2</u> | 491.43<u>3</u> | 491.43<u>5</u> |
| Bengali | 491.44 | 491.44<u>2</u> | 491.44<u>3</u> | 491.44<u>5</u> |

Further examples:

Foreign words in English: 422.4
42      Base number for English
24      Foreign elements (Table 4)

A study of Russian spelling: 491.7152
491.7    Base number for Russian
152      Spelling (Table 4)

Hausa dialects: 493.727
493.72   Base number for Hausa
7      Dialects (Table 4)

German dictionary of synonyms: 433.12
43      Base number for German
312      Dictionaries of synonyms and antonyms (Table 4)

Some of the numbers listed in the 420–490 schedules result from using extensions of notation from Table 4:

| | |
|---|---|
| 421.52 | Spelling (Orthography) and pronunciation [of standard English] |
| 421.54 | Standard American (U.S.) spelling and pronunciation |
| 425 | Grammar of standard English    Syntax of standard English |
| 427 | Historical and geographic variations, modern nongeographic variations |
| 451 | Writing systems, phonology, phonetics, of standard Italian |
| 465 | Grammar of standard Spanish    Syntax of standard Spanish |

*Table 4 and Table 6: Languages* / 137

Some composite numbers can be further extended by notation from Table 2. For example:

> 427.1–.8   Geographic variations [dialects of English] in England
>              Add to 427 the numbers following —42 in notation
>              421–428 from Table 2, e.g., dialects of London 427.1

> North Yorkshire dialect of English: 427.84
>   427     Historical and geographic variations [of English]
>   84      Number following —42 in —4284 for North Yorkshire (Table 2)

Variations in English in other parts of the world are classed in 427.9, which may be further subdivided by area:

> Indian English: 427.954
>   427     Historical and geographic variations [of English]
>   9       Geographic variations in other places
>   54      India (Table 2)

> African English: 427.96
>   427     Historical and geographic variations [of English]
>   9       Geographic variations in other places
>   6       Africa (Table 2)

As usual, these built numbers may be further extended by standard subdivisions from Table 1:

> An outline of German grammar for foreigners written in the 17th century:
> 438.2409032
>   43      Base number for German
>   824     Structural approach to expression for persons whose native
>            language is different (Table 4)
>   09032  Standard subdivision for 17th century (Table 1)

Some of the subdivisions in Table 4 can be further extended by notation from Table 6. Such cases will be taken up later in the chapter.

## Numbers That Cannot Be Extended by Table 4

It follows that a number in 420–490 without add instructions in the entry or an asterisk leading to add instructions cannot be extended by Table 4. For example:

> A grammar of Middle English: 427.02

427.02 is in fact the number for Middle English proper. The notation for grammar from Table 4 cannot be added, because there is no add instruction for 427.02 Middle English. In other words, any language aspect of Middle English will get the number 427.02. For example, a work on the etymology of Middle English is also classed in 427.02.

## INTRODUCTION TO TABLE 6

Table 6 Languages contains notation for language families and major languages. Notation from this table may be added, when instructed, to numbers from the schedules or from other tables. The most important use of Table 6 is to provide the basis for building numbers in 490 and 890 for specific languages and literatures. In addition, numbers from Table 6 are used to extend Table 2 notation —175 Regions where specific languages predominate; to extend Table 5 notation to represent peoples who speak, or whose ancestors spoke, specific languages; and in combination with various numbers scattered throughout the tables and schedules to designate specific languages as an aspect of a subject.

Table 6 consists of a systematic list of various languages of the world grouped according to language family. Its summary is reproduced below:

—1 Indo-European languages
—2 English and Old English (Anglo-Saxon)
—3 Germanic languages
—4 Romance languages
—5 Italian, Sardinian, Dalmatian, Romanian, Rhaeto-Romanic
—6 Spanish and Portuguese
—7 Italic languages
—8 Hellenic languages
—9 Other languages

Each of these families is further subdivided hierarchically. The existence of this language table has made possible the representation of language as an aspect of a subject; examples include general serial publications in a particular language, or translations of the Bible in a particular language.

The main outline of the notation in Table 6 parallels that of the main numbers for languages in class 400 and for literatures in class 800. However, the Table 6 numbers for some languages may not correspond exactly to those in classes 400 and 800. For example, although in the schedules, the base number for the German language is 43 and for German literature is 83, the number for German in Table 6 is —31, not —3.

## USING TABLE 6

Unlike Tables 3 and 4, which are used only with specific spans of numbers from the schedules, Table 6 is applicable in many places throughout the schedules and tables. However, like other tables (except Table 1), notation from Table 6 is used only where there is an explicit instruction in the schedules or other tables. For example, for a Bible in languages other than English, the classifier follows the instruction given under 220.53–.59:

220.53–.59 Versions in other languages [other than English]
        Add to base number 220.5 notation 3–9 from Table 6

Following this instruction, the classifier can build the following numbers:

Bible in the French language: 220.541
    220.5   Base number for Bible versions in other languages [other
            than English]
    41      French language (Table 6)

*Table 4 and Table 6: Languages* / 139

Bible in the Ibo language: 220.596332
220.5     Base number for Bible versions in other languages [other than English]
96332   Ibo language (Table 6)

Similarly:

The New Testament in the Chinese language: 225.5951
225    Base number for the New Testament
5      The number following 220 in 220.5 Modern versions and translations (with .53–.59 for versions in other languages [other than English])
951    Chinese language (Table 6)

Talmudic literature in English: 296.120521
296.12  Base number for Talmudic literature
05     Translations (from internal table under 296.12–296.14)
21     English language (Table 6)

## Table 6 Notation in the Relative Index

Table 6 is a relatively long table, and the name of a particular language may often be unfamiliar. In such cases, the Relative Index can be of great assistance. In the index the numbers for all entries from Table 6 are preceded by the designation T6. For example:

Mon-Khmer languages          495.93
T6—959 3

This means that in addition to the number 495.93 in main class 400, Mon-Khmer languages appear in Table 6 with the notation —9593. The Relative Index also lists many built language numbers not enumerated in main class 400. For example:

Mambwe language            496.391
T6—963 91

The major source of information about language families in Table 6 is *Ethnologue*.[1] The classifier should check Table 6 and the Relative Index first to find a specific language or group of languages. If nothing is found, consult *Ethnologue* to find the appropriate language group.

## Examples Illustrating the Use of Table 6

The numbers 031–039 General encyclopedic works in specific languages and language families are divided on the basis of language. Class numbers for some general encyclopedias in major languages have been given ready-made numbers:

031       General encyclopedic works in American English
032       General encyclopedic works in English
037.1     General encyclopedic works in Russian

---

[1] *Ethnologue*, 14th ed. (Dallas, TX: Summer Institute of Linguistics, 2000). Also available at www.sil.org/ethnologue.

Other numbers in this span can be further specified with notation from Table 6. For example, the schedules list the number 036 for General encyclopedias in Spanish and Portuguese, with the instruction to add to base number 036 the numbers following —6 in notation 61–69 from Table 6. Hence:

General encyclopedia in Spanish: 036.1
036　　　Base number for General encyclopedic works in Spanish and Portuguese
1　　　　Spanish (from —61 in Table 6)

General encyclopedia in Portuguese: 036.9
036　　　Base number for General encyclopedic works in Spanish and Portuguese
9　　　　Portuguese (from —69 in Table 6)

General encyclopedias[2] in languages other than those provided for in 031–038 are classed in 039, which may be further extended by Table 6. For example:

General encyclopedia in Japanese: 039.956
039　　　Base number for General encyclopedic works in Italic, Hellenic, other languages
956　　　Japanese (Table 6)

Similarly, 051–059 General serial publications in specific languages and language families are divided by language patterned after 031–039 General encyclopedias:

General serial publications in Spanish: 056.1
General periodicals in Chinese: 059.951

Table 6 is also used with 305.7, 372.65, and 398:

A social study of Spanish-speaking people: 305.761
305.7　　Base number for [Social] Language groups
61　　　Spanish (Table 6)

French as a second language in elementary schools: 372.6541
372.65　Base number for Foreign languages in elementary education
41　　　French language (Table 6)

Judeo-Spanish folktales: 398.20467
398.204　Base number for Folk literature by language
67　　　Judeo-Spanish (Table 6)

English proverbs: 398.921
398.9　　Base number for Proverbs
21　　　English (Table 6)

---

[2] It should be noted that while general encyclopedias are classed in 031–039, subject encyclopedias are classed with their respective subjects further extended by standard subdivision —03 from Table 1. For example, an encyclopedia of mathematics is classed at 510.3.

*Table 4 and Table 6: Languages* / 141

One of the most important uses of Table 6 is to provide the basis for building certain specific language numbers in 490 Other languages and to provide the basis for building certain specific literature numbers in 890 Literature of other specific languages and language families.

Main class 400 provides many broad numbers for language families. In order to specify comparatively minor languages from a language family, the main numbers given in the schedules are extended with the use of notation from Table 6. For example:

> 496.33    Igboid, Defoid, Edoid, Idomoid, Nupoid, Akpes, Oko,
> Ukaan languages; Kwa languages; Kru languages
> > Add to 496.33 the numbers following —9633 in notation
> > 96332–96338 from Table 6 . . .

Therefore:

> The Ewe language: 496.3374
> > 496.33    Base number for Igboid, Defoid . . . languages
> > 74    Number following —9633 in —963374 Ewe (Table 6)

Similarly, under 495.92–.97 Viet-Muong, Mon-Khmer, Munda, Hmong-Mien (Miao-Yao) languages we are instructed to add to the base number 495.9 the number following —959 in notation 9592–9597 from Table 6. The number for Munda languages in Table 6 is —9595. Hence a work about Munda languages is classed in 495.95.

Following the same pattern, class numbers in 800 for literatures in minor languages can be built:

> Swazi literature: 896.3987

## USE OF TABLE 6 WITH TABLE 4: CLASSIFYING BILINGUAL DICTIONARIES

Upon instruction, Table 6 may also be used in combination with other tables. Its notation is often combined with notation from Table 4 to represent subjects that manifest two languages, as do bilingual dictionaries in which the entry words are given in one language and their meanings in another. The number-building formula for representing such dictionaries is:

> Base number for first language + 3 (dictionaries from Table 4) + number for second language from Table 6

The first language is the one with entry words arranged alphabetically; its base number is found in main class 400 in the schedules. The number for the second language (the one in which meanings are given) is taken from Table 6. For example, for an English-French dictionary, English is the primary language, and the base number is taken from main class 400 Language. French, the language in which meanings are given, is taken from Table 6. Hence:

> English-French dictionary: 423.41
> > 42    Base number for English from the schedules
> > 3    Dictionaries (Table 4)
> > 41    French (Table 6)

Similarly:

> French-English dictionary: 443.21
> English-Dutch dictionary: 423.3931
> French-Korean dictionary: 443.957
> Ibo-English dictionary: 496.332321

In fact, to build the number shown in the last example, Table 6 was used twice. The following analysis of the number illustrates the number-building process:

| | |
|---|---|
| 496 | Base number for African languages |
| 332 | Number following 96 in —96332 Ibo (Table 6) |
| | (496.332 is also enumerated in the schedule) |
| 3 | Dictionaries (Table 4) |
| 21 | English language (Table 6) |

As instructed under —32–39 in Table 4, a bilingual dictionary with entry words in both languages is classed with the language in which it will be more useful, with the addition of the notation for the second language after —3. For example, in most libraries in English-speaking regions, an English-Spanish, Spanish-English dictionary is classed with Spanish in 463.21. If classification with either language is equally useful, preference is given to the language coming later in the 420–490 sequence, for example, a French-Korean, Korean-French dictionary: 495.7341.

In addition to its use with notation 32–39 in Table 4, Table 6 is also used with the following Table 4 numbers:

| | |
|---|---|
| —042 | Bilingualism |
| —24 | Foreign elements |
| —802 | Translation to and from other languages |
| —824 | Structural approach to expression for persons whose native language is different |
| —834 | Audio-lingual approach to expression for persons whose native language is different |
| —864 | Readers for persons whose native language is different from the language of the reader |

The following examples illustrate the use of Table 6 with these numbers:

> French words and phrases used in the Italian language: 452.441

| | |
|---|---|
| 45 | Base number for Italian language |
| 24 | Foreign elements (Table 4) |
| 41 | French (Table 6) |

Similarly:

> Latin elements in the French language: 442.471
> German grammar for English-speaking people: 438.2421
> Audio-lingual approach to German for English-speaking people: 438.3421
> German reader for English-speaking people: 438.6421

*Table 4 and Table 6: Languages* / 143

## Caution

The class number for a language or literature built by using notation from Table 6 cannot be further extended by Table 4 (or Table 3 as the case may be) unless the built number is listed with add instructions (or a note or asterisk leading to add instructions) in the schedule. For example, the following numbers cannot be further extended:

| | |
|---|---|
| Elamite languages: | 499.93 |
| Elamite grammar: | 499.93 |
| Elamite etymology: | 499.93 |

On the other hand, in cases where the synthesized number for a particular language resulting from the combination of a base number and a notation from Table 6 is enumerated (precombined) in the schedules and listed with add instructions (or a note or asterisk leading to add instructions), the number may be further extended through the use of Table 4. For example:

> 494　　Altaic, Uralic, Hyperborean, Dravidian languages
> 　　　　　　Add to 494 the numbers following —94 in notation 941–948
> 　　　　　　from Table 6, e.g., Mongolian 494.23, Altai 494.33; then to the
> 　　　　　　number given for each language listed below add notation 01–8
> 　　　　　　from Table 4, e.g., grammar of Mongolian
>
> .
> .
> .
>
> 　　　　494.83 Brahui

Therefore:

> Brahui grammar
> 　　494.83 + 5 (Table 4) = 494.835
>
> Brahui dictionary
> 　　494.83 + 3 (Table 4) = 494.833

## USING TABLE 6 WITH OTHER TABLES

In addition to its use with Table 4, Table 6 may also be used in conjunction with other tables. For example, Table 6 notation is used to extend Table 2 notation 175 Regions where specific languages predominate to define an area where a particular language predominates. Thus, regions of the world where English is spoken is represented by —17521, i.e., —175 (Table 2) + —21 (Table 6). As shown in the following cases, this subdivision can be used whenever there is any instruction to add area notation —1:

> Wages in English-speaking countries of the world: 331.2917521
> 　331.29　Historical, geographic, persons treatment of compensation
> 　175　　Regions where specific languages predominate (Table 2)
> 　21　　　English (Table 6)
>
> General libraries in the French-speaking world: 027.017541
> 　027.0　Base number for Geographic treatment [of General libraries]
> 　　　　　(final 0 is facet indicator)
> 　175　　Regions where specific languages predominate (Table 2)
> 　41　　　French (Table 6)

In literature, a number resulting from the use of Table 6 may be further subdivided by notation from Table 3 as long as there are add instructions or a note or asterisk leading to add instructions. For example:

896     African literatures
          Add to 896 the numbers following —96 in notation 961–965 from Table 6 . . . then to the number given for each literature listed below add further as instructed at beginning of Table 3

.

.

.

          896.3985         Xhosa

Xhosa poetry: 896.39851
    896     Base number for African literatures
    3985    Number following —96 in —963985 Xhosa (Table 6)
           (896.3985 is also enumerated in the schedule)
    1       Poetry (Table 3A or 3B)

The use of Table 6 with Table 5 is discussed in chapter 12.

## SUMMARY

Tables 4 and 6 have been treated together in this chapter because of the complementary relationship between the two. Table 4 contains numbers representing various problems, aspects and tools of linguistics as they relate to individual languages; it is patterned after sections 411–419 of the schedules. It is used exclusively with 420–490 Specific languages (plus 419 Sign languages). Only those entries in 420–490 that contain add instructions, or a note or asterisk leading to add instructions, may be extended by notation from Table 4. The divisions 420–490 represent the major languages of the world. Class numbers for some languages that are not enumerated in 420–490 can be built with the use of Table 6. In application, Table 4 is the simplest of all the six tables in the DDC. In some cases Table 4 can be further extended by Table 6, e.g., for classifying bilingual dictionaries.

Table 6 contains a systematic listing of all the major and many minor languages of the world grouped according to language families. The outline of Table 6 parallels that of 420–490, but it provides greater detail for individual languages. Notation from Table 6 is used with many numbers in the schedules as well as with other tables, but only where specifically instructed. In many cases, it is added to a base number to specify the language in which a subject is treated in a document. In other cases, it may be used to extend a number from another table.

*Table 4 and Table 6: Languages* / 145

# EXERCISES

Exercise 1:

Classify the following topics using Table 4:

(1)  Phonology of Slovak

(2)  An introduction to Middle Dutch

(3)  Noun phrases in Norwegian

(4)  English verb tables for ESL [English as a second language] speakers

(5)  Portuguese word formation with suffixes

Exercise 2:

Classify the following topics using Table 6:

(1)  German-language encyclopedia

(2)  A study of Sauk (a North American native language)

(3)  Arabic folktales from Israel

(4)  French-speaking people in Africa: a social study

(5)  General encyclopedia in Thai

(6)  General periodicals in Norwegian

(7)  Spanish quotations

(8)  Introduction to Samoan

Exercise 3:

Classify the following topics using both Table 4 and Table 6:

(1)  Chinese-English dictionary

(2)  Finnish-English dictionary

(3)  Spanish reader for English-speaking people

(4)  Latin words in the German language

(5)  Conversational English for Russian-speaking people

Exercise 4:

Classify the following topics using Table 6 through Table 2:

(1)  School enrollment in the French-speaking world

(2)  Conservation of economic resources in the Portuguese-speaking world

## Chapter 12

# TABLE 5: ETHNIC AND NATIONAL GROUPS

## INTRODUCTION

Table 5 lists groups of persons systematically according to their ethnic and national origins. Its notation can be added to any class number through standard subdivision —089 Ethnic and national groups, or according to an add instruction given in the schedules. When Table 5 notation is applied using standard subdivision —089, the 089 serves as a facet indicator.

In Edition 22, Table 5 was renamed from "Racial, Ethnic, National Groups" to "Ethnic and National Groups." The name change and the discontinuation of the provisions for basic races were introduced to reflect the de-emphasis on race in modern scholarship. A summary of Table 5 follows:

| | |
|---|---|
| —05–09 | [Persons of mixed ancestry with ethnic origins from more than one continent; Europeans and people of European descent] |
| —1 | North Americans |
| —2 | British, English, Anglo-Saxons |
| —3 | Germanic people |
| —4 | Modern Latin peoples |
| —5 | Italians, Romanians, related groups |
| —6 | Spanish and Portuguese |
| —7 | Other Italic peoples |
| —8 | Greeks and related groups |
| —9 | Other ethnic and national groups |

Each division listed above is further divided hierarchically. The name of each ethnic and national group listed in the table is indexed in the Relative Index, where each notation from Table 5 is preceded by the symbol T5. For example:

| | |
|---|---|
| African Americans | T5—960 73 |
| Asians | T5—95 |
| Indo-Europeans | T5—09 |
| Russians | T5—917 1 |
| Swedes | T5—397 |

In Table 5, "ethnic group" normally refers to a group with linguistic ties; it can also mean a group with cultural or racial ties. Notation is provided at the beginning of the table for persons of mixed ancestry with ethnic origins from more than one continent (—05); this notation is only used for works that stress mixed ancestry. Table 5 also includes notation for Europeans and persons of European descent (—09); this number provides a comprehensive number for such persons, and persons who refer to themselves as "white."

### Citation and Preference Order in Table 5

Because some people can be categorized by more than one characteristic, e.g., national groups of foreign origins and noncitizen residents, a citation order (in cases where numbers can be combined to show multiple facets) or a preference order (in cases where numbers cannot be combined and a choice must be made between two or more numbers) is needed to maintain consistency in treatment. In Table 5, ethnic group is generally preferred over nationality. For example, T5—13 means people of the United States, but T5—68073 means Spanish Americans in the United States (where —68 means Spanish Americans and —73 means United States). In a few cases, however, the citation order is reversed to nationality over ethnic group, for example, T5—114 Canadians of French origin, where —11 denotes Canadians and —4 denotes French origin.

When choosing between two ethnic groups, preference is given to the group for which the notation is different from that of the nationality of the people. For example, a work treating equally the Hispanic and native American heritage of bilingual Spanish-Guaraní mestizos of Paraguay is classed in —983820892 Guaraní-speaking people in Paraguay (not —68892 Paraguayans as a Spanish-American national group). When choosing between two national groups, preference is given to the former or ancestral national group instead of the current national group. For example, a work dealing with people from Ukraine who have become United States citizens is classed in —91791073 Ukrainians in the United States (not —13 People of the United States).

## USING TABLE 5 ON SPECIFIC INSTRUCTIONS

Upon instruction, Table 5 notation may be added directly to a base number. Here is an example: Ethnopsychology of the Jewish people. The class number for ethno-psychology given in the Relative Index is 155.82. Upon consulting the schedules, the classifier finds that the ethnopsychology of specific ethnic groups is classed in 155.84.

> 155.84 [Ethnopsychology of] Specific ethnic groups
> Add to base number 155.84 notation 05–9 from Table 5,
> e.g., ethnopsychology of African Americans 155.8496073

The notation for Jews in Table 5 is —924. Hence the complete class number is: 155.84924. Further examples:

> A sociological study of the German people: 305.831
> 305.8    Base number for [Sociology of] Ethnic and national groups
> 31       Germans (Table 5)

> Australian native art: 704.039915
> 704.03   Base number for History and description [of Fine and
>          decorative arts] with respect to ethnic and national groups
> 9915     Australian native peoples (Table 5)

> Polish folk music: 781.629185
> 781.62   Base number for Folk music of specific ethnic and national
>          groups
> 9185     Polish people (Table 5)

> A history of literature by African authors: 809.8896
> 809.889  Base number for Literature for and by persons of other ethnic
>          and national groups
> 6        Number following —9 in —96 Africans and people of African
>          descent (Table 5)

When Table 5 notation is added directly to a schedule number without the use of standard subdivision —089, other standard subdivisions may be used to extend the number. For example:

Australian aboriginal art exhibited in the United States: 704.039915007473

| | |
|---|---|
| 704.03 | Base number for History and description [of Fine and decorative arts] with respect to ethnic and national groups |
| 9915 | Australian native peoples (Table 5) |
| 00 | Facet indicator to introduce standard subdivisions (double zeros used according to instructions at beginning of Table 5) |
| 74 | Museums, collections, exhibits (Table 1) |
| 73 | United States (Table 2) |

## EXTENDING TABLE 5 NUMBERS BY NOTATION FROM TABLES 2 AND 6

Numbers from Table 5 may be extended by area notation from Table 2 and partial notation from Table 6. Extensions using area notation can be achieved in two ways:

(1) through 0 (zero) as instructed in a general note at the beginning of Table 5;

(2) by adding an area notation directly to a Table 5 notation when specifically instructed. In such cases there is no need of a zero as a facet indicator.

### Extending Table 5 Notation Using Zero as a Facet Indicator

Instructions given at the beginning of Table 5 indicate that each number from this table may be further extended by adding a notation from Table 2, unless there is specific instruction to do otherwise or unless it is redundant. The general instruction at the beginning of Table 5 reads:

Except where instructed otherwise, and unless it is redundant, add 0 to the number from this table and to the result add notation 1 or 3–9 from Table 2 for area in which a group is or was located . . . If notation from Table 2 is not added, use 00 for standard subdivisions . . .

As a result, almost any number in Table 5 may be extended by area notation through 0, and there is no need for a specific instruction under the particular number. For example, the number for the Chinese in Brazil is —951081: —951 (Table 5) + 0 + 81 (Table 2). On the other hand, the number for the Chinese in China is —951, since adding —051 here would be redundant.

Here are more examples:

A study of the social status of Jews in Germany: 305.8924043

| | |
|---|---|
| 305.8 | Base number for [Sociology of] Ethnic and national groups |
| 924 | Jews (Table 5) |
| 0 | Facet indicator (as instructed at the beginning of Table 5) |
| 43 | Germany (Table 2) |

Civil rights of Jews in Germany: a political study: 323.11924043

   323.11    Base number for [Civil rights and political rights of] Specific
             ethnic and national groups

   924       Jews (Table 5)

   0         Facet indicator (as instructed at the beginning of Table 5)

   43        Germany (Table 2)

Similarly:

A social study of German nationals in the United States: 305.831073

Civil rights of African Americans in the United States: a political study:
323.1196073

## Extending Table 5 Notation by Direct Addition of Table 2 Notation

Upon instruction, some of the numbers in Table 5 may be further subdivided directly by notation from Table 2, without using the facet indicator 0. For example, under —687–688 [Spanish-American] Regional and national groups, the classifier is instructed to add to base number —68 notation 7–8 from Table 2 to get the number for a specific national group. Therefore, the number for Chilean nationals is: —68 (Table 5) + 83 (Table 2) = —6883.

Under 909.04 [World] History with respect to ethnic and national groups, the classifier finds the following instruction:

Add to base number 909.04 notation 05–9 from Table 5, e.g.,
world history of Jews 909.04924; then add 0* and to the result add
the numbers following 909 in 909.1–909.8, e.g., world history of
Jews in 18th century 909.0492407

Therefore:

World history of Romany people in the 20th century: 909.0491497082

   909.04     Base number for World history with respect to ethnic and
             national groups

   91497     Romany people (Table 5)

   0         Facet indicator as instructed under 909.04

   82        The number following 909 in 909.82, 20th century

## Extending Table 5 Notation by Table 6

Table 5 notation 94, 96, 97, 98, and 99 may be extended on instruction with notation from Table 6 to represent peoples who speak, or whose ancestors spoke, specific languages. In this way, the detailed development for languages in Table 6 does not have to be repeated in Table 5. For example:

   —98       South American native peoples
                  Add to base number —98 the numbers following —98 in
                  notation 982–984 from Table 6, e.g., Quechua —98323;
                  then add further as instructed at beginning of Table 5, e.g.,
                  Quechua in Bolivia —98323084

Therefore:

>Arawakans in Colombia: —98390861
>—98    Base number for South American native peoples (Table 5)
>39      Number following —98 in —9839 Arawakan languages
>          (Table 6)
>0        Facet indicator for area notation
>861    Colombia (Table 2)

Note that notation for a people built by using Table 5 + Table 6 may be further extended by Table 2 as explained above.

## ADDING A PART OF A NUMBER FROM TABLE 5

In some cases, a part of a Table 5 number is added to a base number. For instance, some religions are not listed explicitly under 292–299 in the schedules but are built by using a portion of Table 5 notation. For example, in the schedules one finds:

>299.683-.685    Religions of peoples who speak, or whose ancestors spoke,
>                        Niger-Congo, Nilo-Saharan languages
>                        Add to base number 299.68 the numbers following
>                        —96 in notation 963–965 from Table 5, e.g., religion
>                        of the Yoruba 299.68333 . . .

Hence:

>Traditional Zulu religion: 299.683986
>299.68    Base number for Religions of peoples who speak, or whose
>              ancestors spoke, Niger-Congo, Nilo-Saharan languages
>3986      Number following —96 in —963986 Zulu (Table 5)

## USE OF TABLE 5 THROUGH STANDARD SUBDIVISION —089

In Edition 18, Table 5 could be used only according to specific instructions in the schedules. Since Edition 19, however, the use of Table 5 has been universalized through standard subdivision —089.[1] The combination of Table 1 and Table 5 notation can be freely added to any class number in the schedules when appropriate:

>—08905–0899    [History and description with respect to] Specific ethnic
>                          and national groups
>                          Add to base number —089 notation 05–9 from Table 5,
>                          e.g., the subject with respect to Chinese —089951, with
>                          respect to Chinese in United States —089951073

For example:

>Dolls made by Pueblo Indians: 745.59221089974
>745.59221    Base number for Dolls
>089            Standard subdivision for Specific ethnic and national
>                  groups (Table 1)
>974            Pueblo Indians (Table 5)

---

[1] See chapter 8 for a general discussion and examples of persons treatment in the DDC

Reading interests and habits of Spanish Americans in the United States: 028.908968073

| | |
|---|---|
| 028.9 | Base number for Reading interests and habits |
| 089 | Specific ethnic and national groups (Table 1) |
| 68 | Spanish Americans (Table 5) |
| 0 | Facet indicator as instructed at the beginning of Table 5 |
| 73 | United States (Table 2) |

## USE OF TABLE 5 THROUGH TABLE 3C

In Table 3C the subdivision —8 Literature for and by persons of ethnic and national groups is further subdivided by using notation from Table 5 to specify individual groups. For example:

A collection of African American literature: 810.80896073

| | |
|---|---|
| 81 | Base number for American literature |
| 080 | Collections of literary texts in more than one form (Table 3B) (includes facet indicator 0) |
| 8 | Literature for and by persons of ethnic and national groups (Table 3C) |
| 96073 | African Americans (United States) (Table 5) |

## SUMMARY

Table 5 contains a list of persons categorized by their ethnic or national characteristics. It is used throughout the schedules and other tables, and is not exclusive to any one class. Table 5 notation may be used upon instruction in two ways: directly with numbers in the schedules or tables, and through standard subdivision —089. In earlier additions, some notation for persons was derived from Table 7. In Edition 22, Table 7 has been replaced by use of notation already available in the schedules and in notation 08 from Table 1.

## EXERCISES

Classify the following topics using Table 5:

(1) Folksongs of the Romany people

(2) Italians around the world (a social study)

(3) Jewish art

(4) Religion of the Hittites

(5) Navajo religion

(6) Contemporary Australian aboriginal paintings

(7) Chinese American scientists

## Chapter 13

# NUMBER BUILDING FOR COMPLEX SUBJECTS

## INTRODUCTION

In the Dewey Decimal Classification (DDC), multitopical or multi-aspect subjects are referred to as *complex subjects*. Because of its provisions for building numbers, the DDC is able to accommodate many complex subjects. Although the system does not allow for unlimited synthesis, many aspects of a subject can be expressed through number building. Previous chapters discussed and illustrated the number-building processes that use notation from the schedules and from one or more tables simultaneously. This chapter discusses and provides examples for cases where multiple elements taken from both the schedules and the tables are put together to form complex numbers.

With each edition of the DDC, especially since Edition 17, the Classification has featured the progressive use of *multiple synthesis*, in other words, the combining of multiple elements to form complex numbers. Multiple synthesis has been made possible both by the increasing number of "add" notes and tables within the schedules, and by the provision of separate tables. Theoretically speaking, multiple synthesis is a simple extension of add instructions or number building (discussed in chapter 7 and elaborated in chapters 8–12). The basic problem again is how to identify the correct base number, locate the notation to be added, and decide on the citation order. In a complex subject, many aspects may seem equal contenders for the base number. Choice of the appropriate one will depend upon the classifier's knowledge of the structure of the Classification and his or her perception of the facet of primary importance. One simple test is that the correct base number is often followed by an add note, except, of course, for those cases in which standard subdivisions are appropriate. In building numbers, one must proceed slowly and follow instructions carefully. At times it may be necessary to move forward and backward among different parts of the DDC schedules and tables. Once a number is built, the schedules must be checked again to ensure that the resulting number does not conflict with any number or instructions in the schedules.

The following discussion illustrates complex number building with multiple notation from the schedules and tables. The discussions and examples are grouped by main classes. The examples are not exhaustive, and the classifier should study each area of the DDC to understand specific number-building instructions.

## MULTIPLE SYNTHESIS IN 000, 100, 200, AND 300

In the topic Administration of science libraries, there are two main facets:

(1)   Library administration
(2)   Science library

The second facet in turn comprises two subfacets:

(1)   Special libraries
(2)   Science

Two relevant entries are found in the schedules:

025.19    Administration of specific types of institutions [i.e. libraries, archives, information centers]

026    Libraries, archives, information centers devoted to specific subjects and disciplines

Class 025.19 can be extended by type of library, and 026 can be extended by the subject or discipline of the library. Under 026.001–.999 the instruction reads:

Add to base number 026 notation 001–999, e.g., medical libraries 026.61; however, do not add notation 068 from Table 1 for organizations and management; class in 025.19

Since the work is on administration (management), the second part of the add instruction leads the classifier back to 025.19. The following instruction is found at 025.19:

Add to base number 025.19 the numbers following 02 in 026–027 . . .

This leads the classifier back to 026. Adding the number for science (500) without the zero fillers (00) to —6 (the number following 02 in 026) results in:

6 + 500 = 65 (the number for libraries devoted to science subjects)

Adding notation 65 to 025.19 results in the correct class number: 025.1965. The number may also be analyzed as:

025.19    Base number for Administration of specific types of libraries
6    Number following 02 in 026 Libraries devoted to specific subjects and disciplines
5    Number 500 Science with the zeros removed

This number can be extended further by standard subdivisions from Table 1:

Journal of administration of science libraries
025.1965 + 05 (Table 1) = 025.196505

Another example:

Law of international commerce in agricultural products: 343.0871
343.087 Base number for International commerce [law] in specific commodities
1    Number following 381.4 in 381.41 Products of agriculture

To proceed further, say to classify a work on law pertaining to international trade in wheat, under 381.413–.418 Specific products the classifier is instructed to add the number following 63 in 633–638. Following the instruction, we arrive at the number for the specific commodity wheat:

Law of international trade in wheat: 343.0871311
343.087 Number built previously
311    Number following 63 in 633.11 Wheat

One more example of multiple synthesis in class 300:

International trade of industrial chemicals by Hamburg, Germany, 1990–2000: 382.456610094351509049

| | |
|---|---|
| 382.4 | Base number for International commerce by specific products and services |
| 5 | Number following 381.4 in 381.45 for Specific products and services |
| 661 | Industrial chemicals (comprehensive works number) |
| 009 | Historical, geographic, persons treatment (Table 1) (extra zero from 661.001–.009) |
| 43515 | Hamburg, Germany (Table 2) |
| 09 | Historical and geographic treatment (add instruction found in internal table under —093–099 in Table 1) |
| 049 | Number following —09 in —09049 [1990–1999] (Table 1) |

## Data Processing    Computer Science

A completely new computer science schedule was published as an update to Edition 19 in 1985.[1] The current computer science schedule in Edition 22 still features the same basic structure as the original schedule, but has been updated and revised to reflect current topics and relationships in the field. There are no internal tables in 004–006, but the schedule uses add notes to support multiple synthesis. For example:

Operating systems for IBM mainframe servers: 005.4425

| | |
|---|---|
| 005.44 | Base number for Operating systems for Specific computers |
| 2 | Number following 005.3 in 005.31–005.39 for Mainframe computers |
| 5 | Number following 005.36 in 005.362–005.368 for Specific computers |

## Religion

In Edition 22, the editors completed the two-edition plan that was initiated in Edition 21 to reduce Christian bias in the 200 Religion schedule. In Edition 21, comprehensive works on Christianity were moved from 200 to 230, and the standard subdivisions for Christianity were relocated from 201–209 to specific numbers in 230–270. The standard subdivisions of comparative religion were integrated with those for religion in general in 200.1–.9. Also, the schedules for two major religions, 296 Judaism and 297 Islam, were revised and expanded.

Edition 22 contains the rest of the relocations and expansions outlined in the two-edition plan. The specific aspects of religion have been moved from 291 to the 201–209 span vacated in Edition 21. These numbers are now used for general topics in religion, and as the source for notation to address specific aspects of religions in 292–299. In 299.6–.8, the preference order has been reversed between topic and ethnic group, and a fuller array of topical aspects can now be added to the ethnic group numbers. The following example illustrates multiple synthesis in the revised 200 Religion schedule:

---

[1] Melvil Dewey, *004–006 Data Processing and Computer Science and Changes in Related Disciplines*, prepared by Julianne Beall et al. (Albany, NY: Forest Press, 1985).

Marriage rites of the Yoruba traditional religion: 299.683330385:

| | |
|---|---|
| 299.68 | Base number for Religions of specific groups and peoples |
| 333 | Number following —96 in —96333 Yoruba (Table 6) |
| 0 | Facet indicator for Specific aspects (internal table under 299.683–.685) |
| 385 | Number following 20 in 203.85 Marriage rites |

## Public Administration

The schedule for public administration was completely revised in Edition 21. The citation order is topic/jurisdiction, and the schedule features significant use of facet indicators and notational synthesis. The basic structure of the schedule is as follows:

| | |
|---|---|
| 351 | Public administration |
| 352 | General considerations of public administration |
| 353 | Specific fields of public administration |
| 354 | Public administration of economy and environment |

The subdivisions of 351 Public administration are at coordinate notation in 352–354. At 352–354, the classifier is instructed to class a subject with aspects in two or more subdivisions of 352–354 in the number coming last unless there are instructions to the contrary. The schedule also features a "retroactive" citation order in number building. Retroactive citation order means that one starts with a number coming later in the schedule as the base number, and then adds as instructed from numbers earlier in the sequence. For example:

Personnel management in provincial governments in Canada: 352.62130971

| | |
|---|---|
| 352.6 | Base number for Personnel management |
| 21 | Jurisdictional level (internal table under 352–354) |
| 3 | Number following 352.1 in 352.13 State and provincial administration |
| 09 | Historical, geographic, persons treatment (Table 1 notation as instructed in internal table under 352.13–352.19) |
| 71 | Canada (Table 2) |

In the example above, the topic precedes the jurisdiction. Though not listed as such in the number-building steps, the initial digit (2) of the notation for jurisdictional level is a facet indicator for general considerations in public administration. Another example:

Government corporations dealing with railroad passenger transportation: 354.76732266

| | |
|---|---|
| 354.767 | Base number for Administration of railroad transportation |
| 3 | Passenger service (internal table under 354.765–354.79) |
| 2 | General considerations of public administration (internal table under 352–354) |
| 266 | Number following 352 in 352.266 Government corporations |

In both examples one is instructed to add notation from a number earlier in the sequence to a base number later in the sequence.

## MULTIPLE SYNTHESIS IN 500 AND 600

Because scientific and technical studies in a particular field or discipline often borrow concepts and techniques from other fields and disciplines, the basic concepts and techniques enumerated under the basic sciences in the DDC are often used to build numbers in related fields. For example:

Thermochemistry of uranium: 546.43156

| | |
|---|---|
| 546.431 | Base number for Uranium |
| 5 | Physical chemistry (internal table under 546) |
| 6 | Number following 541.3 in 541.36 Thermochemistry |

Molecular structure of aliphatic hydrocarbons: 547.410442

| | |
|---|---|
| 547.41 | Base number for Aliphatic hydrocarbons |
| 044 | Theoretical chemistry (internal table under 547) |
| 2 | Number following 541.2 in 541.22 Molecular structure |

Animal pests of apple orchards: 634.1196

| | |
|---|---|
| 634.11 | Base number for Apple orchards |
| 9 | Injuries, diseases, pests (internal table under 633–635) |
| 6 | Number following 632 in 632.6 Animal pests |

As instructed further under 632.6 the particular kind of pests can be specified by adding to 632.6 the number following 59 in 592–599, hence:

Worms as pests of apple orchards: 634.119623

| | |
|---|---|
| 634.11 | Base number for Apple orchards |
| 9 | Injuries, diseases, pests (internal table under 633–635) |
| 6 | Number following 632 in 632.6 Animal pests |
| 23 | Number following 59 in 592.3 Worms |

Further examples:

Anatomy of horses: 636.10891

| | |
|---|---|
| 636.10 | Base number for Horses (includes facet indicator 0) |
| 89 | Number following 636.0 in 636.089 Veterinary sciences |
| 1 | Number following 61 in 611 Anatomy |

Anatomy of the lungs of horses: 636.1089124

| | |
|---|---|
| 636.10 | Base number for Horses (includes facet indicator 0) |
| 89 | Number following 636.0 in 636.089 Veterinary sciences |
| 124 | Number following 61 in 611.24 Anatomy of the lungs |

Diseases of the digestive system of horses: 636.108963

| | |
|---|---|
| 636.10 | Base number for Horses (includes facet indicator 0) |
| 89 | Number following 636.0 in 636.089 Veterinary sciences |
| 63 | Number following 61 in 616.3 Diseases of the digestive system |

# Life Sciences

The life sciences were significantly revised in Edition 21. The 570 schedule was completely revised, along with 583 Dicotyledons. The rest of 560–590 was extensively revised. The citation order for internal biological processes is process/organism, and facet indicators are used to introduce the organism. As in 351 Public administration and 780 Music, 570 features retroactive citation order in number building.

The mammalian brain: 573.8619

| | |
|---|---|
| 573.86 | Base number for Brain |
| 1 | Facet indicator for Animals (number following 571 in 571.1 animals as instructed in internal table under 573) |
| 9 | Number following 59 in 599 Mammals |

Circulation in monkey brains: 573.8621198

| | |
|---|---|
| 573.86 | Base number for Brain |
| 21 | Circulation in the system (internal table under 573) |
| 1 | Facet indicator for animals (number following 571 in 571.1 Animals) |
| 98 | Number following 59 in 599.8 Monkeys |

In the examples above, the process precedes the organism, and the organism (an animal) is introduced by the facet indicator for Animals (1). The facet indicator is derived from a schedule earlier in the sequence (571.1). In the second example, intermediate number building takes place using retroactive citation order to specify the process.

When the focus of the work is on the biology of the whole organism (as opposed to an internal process in the organism), the number building begins with the organism as the base number. The distinction between the biology of the whole organism vs. the biology of internal processes is explained in depth in the Manual note at 579–590 vs. 571–575. The following examples illustrate use of the organism as the base number, with addition from the schedules for aspects related to general topics in the natural history of the organism:

Behavior of monkeys: 599.815

| | |
|---|---|
| 599.8 | Base number for Monkeys |
| 1 | Facet indicator for General topics in natural history of animals (from instruction in internal table under 592–599) |
| 5 | Number following 591 in 591.5 Behavior |

Mammals of the prairie and savannah: 599.174

| | |
|---|---|
| 599 | Base number for Mammals |
| 1 | Facet indicator for General topics in natural history of animals (from instruction in internal table under 592–599) |
| 7 | Number following 591 in 591.7 Animals characteristic of specific environments |
| 4 | Number following 577 in 577.4 Grassland ecology |

## Medicine and Health

The 610 Medicine and health schedule features three key add tables that have been revised and expanded in Edition 22:

| | | |
|---|---|---|
| 616.1–.9 | Specific diseases | |
| 617 | Miscellaneous branches of medicine | Surgery |
| 618.1–.8 | Gynecology and obstetrics | |

The three add tables are generally parallel with each other, but each contains special notation required by the specific branch of medicine that it covers. These tables, along with notation found elsewhere in the schedule, support number building to represent complex medical subjects. For example:

Journal of diabetes nursing: 616.462023105

616.462 Base number for Diabetes

0231     Nursing with respect to specific diseases (internal table under 616.1–616.9)

05       Standard subdivision for Serial publications (Table 1)

Diet therapy for osteoporosis: 616.7160654

616.716 Base number for Osteoporosis

06       Therapy (internal table under 616.1–616.9)

54       Number following 615.8 in 615.854 Diet therapy

Cytodiagnosis for cancer of the salivary glands: 616.99431607582

616.994 Base number for Cancer

316      Number following 611 in 611.316 Salivary glands

07       Pathology (internal table under 618.1–618.8)

582      Number following 616.07 in 616.07582 Cytological examination (as instructed at 075–079 in internal table under 618.1–618.8)

Restorative plastic surgery for hand injuries: 617.575044592

617.575 Base number for Hands

044      Injuries (internal table under 617)

592      Number following 0 in 0592 for Restorative plastic surgery (as instructed at 044 and 0425–0428 in internal table under 617)

Ultrasound for diagnosis of diseases of the fetal nervous system: 618.326807543

618.3268 Base number for Diseases of fetal nervous system

07       Pathology (internal table under 618.1–618.8)

543      Number following 616.07 in 616.07543 Diagnostic ultrasound (as instructed at 075–079 in internal table under 618.1–618.8)

## MULTIPLE SYNTHESIS IN 400, 700, 800, AND 900

In certain fields in the humanities (such as fine arts, music, and language and literature), class numbers must accommodate various facets such as forms and genres, themes, and performing agents. Number building can therefore be rather complicated. The following examples illustrate complex number building in these fields.

# Arts

Crucifixion of Jesus Christ in Renaissance art: 704.9485309409024

| | |
|---|---|
| 704.94853 | Base number for Jesus Christ [in art] (Manual note at 704.9 and 753–758 instructs to prefer iconography over historical and geographic treatment; the note also instructs that standard subdivisions may be added for topics that do not approximate the whole) |
| 09 | Historical, geographic, persons treatment (Table 1) |
| 4 | Europe (Table 2) |
| 09 | Historical and geographic treatment (internal table under —093–099 in Table 1) |
| 024 | Number following —09 in —09024 15th century (Table 1) |

Exhibition of book illustrations at Yale Center for British Art: 741.6409410747468

| | |
|---|---|
| 741.64 | Base number for [Graphic design, illustration, commercial art for] Books and book jackets |
| 09 | Historical, geographic, persons treatment (Table 1) |
| 41 | Great Britain (Table 2) |
| 074 | Museums, collections, exhibits (internal table under —093–099 in Table 1) |
| 7468 | New Haven, Connecticut [the location of the exhibit] (Table 2) |

The portrayal of publishers in motion pictures: 791.4365280705

| | |
|---|---|
| 791.436 | Base number for Films dealing with specific themes and subjects |
| 52 | Number following —3 in —352 Specific kinds of persons (Table 3C) |
| 8 | Number following —08 in —088 Occupational and religious groups (Table 1) |
| 0705 | Publishing[2] |

125 years of musical theatre in New York City: an exhibition at the IBM Gallery of Science and Art in New York City: 792.60974710747471

| | |
|---|---|
| 792.6 | Base number for Musical plays |
| 09 | Historical, geographic, persons treatment (Table 1) |
| 7471 | New York City (Table 2) |
| 074 | Museums, collections, exhibits (internal table under —093–099 in Table 1) |
| 7471 | New York City (Table 2) |

---

[2] Notation 092 from 070.5092 Publishers is redundant, since persons treatment has already been expressed by T3C—352 Specific kinds of persons.

## Music

In Edition 20, the schedule for 780 Music was completely revised. The schedule for 780 Music represents one of the most faceted classes in the DDC. Number building in 780 Music is often complicated. To assist classifiers, the Manual note for 780 in volume 1 offers a detailed discussion with examples.

In building numbers for musical works, the classifier should bear in mind the following citation order:

| | |
|---|---|
| Voices and instruments | 782–788 |
| Musical forms | 781.8 |
| Sacred music | 781.7 |
| Traditions of music | 781.6 |
| Kinds of music | 781.5 |
| Techniques of music | 781.4 |
| Composition | 781.3 |
| Elements of music | 781.2 |
| Basic principles of music | 781.1 |
| Standard subdivisions | 780.1–.9 |

Notice that this citation order is the reverse of the order in which these elements are listed in the schedules. In building numbers in music, unless other instructions are given, always begin with the later number and work backwards. The following examples illustrate this retroactive citation order:

American (U.S.) popular songs: 782.421640973

| | |
|---|---|
| 782.42 | Songs |
| 1 | Facet indicator for General principles (internal table under 782.1–782.4) |
| 64 | Number following 781 in 781.64 Western popular music |
| 09 | Geographic treatment (Table 1) |
| 73 | United States (Table 2) |

Rhythm of the barrio: Mexican-American music in Los Angeles: 781.626872079494

| | |
|---|---|
| 781.62 | Base number for Folk music of specific ethnic and national groups |
| 68 | Spanish Americans (Table 5) |
| 72 | Mexico (Table 2) |
| 0 | Facet indicator for Geographic subdivision (instructions in note at beginning of Table 5) |
| 79494 | City of Los Angeles (Table 2) |

Treatises on sound recordings of rock ballet music: 781.6615560266

| | |
|---|---|
| 781.66 | Rock (Rock 'n' roll) |
| 1 | Facet indicator for General principles (internal table under 781.63–781.69) |
| 556 | Number following 781 in 781.556 Ballet music |
| 0266 | Modified standard subdivision for Sound recordings of music (as modified at 780.266) |

# Language and Literature

Numbers for literary works and works about literature are built with the use of Tables 3A–3C. In many cases, these numbers are extended with notation from other Tables. Chapter 10 contains examples illustrating number building for works of and about literature. The following examples illustrate more complicated numbers:

A collection of African American poetry: 811.0080896073

| | |
|---|---|
| 81 | Base number for American literature |
| 100 | Poetry (Table 3B) (includes facet indicator 00) |
| 80 | Collections for and by specific kinds of persons (internal table under —1–8 in Table 3B) (includes facet indicator 0) |
| 8 | Literature for and by persons of ethnic and national groups (Table 3C) |
| 96073 | African Americans (United States Blacks) (Table 5) |

A critical study of African American fiction: 813.009896073

| | |
|---|---|
| 81 | Base number for American literature |
| 300 | Fiction (Table 3B) (includes facet indicator 00) |
| 9 | History, description, critical appraisal (internal table under —1–8 in Table 3B) |
| 8 | Literature for and by persons of ethnic and national groups (Table 3C) |
| 96073 | African Americans (United States Blacks) (Table 5) |

American gay and lesbian literary history: 810.9920664

| | |
|---|---|
| 81 | Base number for American literature |
| 09 | History, description, critical appraisal of works in more than one form (Table 3B) |
| 920 | Literature for and by persons of specific classes (includes facet indicator 0) (Table 3C) |
| 664 | Number following —08 in —08664 Gays (Table 1) |

Portrayal of Berlin in late 19th-century German fiction: 833.8093243155

| | |
|---|---|
| 83 | Base number for German literature |
| 3 | Fiction (Table 3B) |
| 8 | 1856–1899 (period table under 830.1–838) |
| 0 | Facet indicator as instructed under —31–39 (Table 3B) |
| 9 | History, description, critical appraisal (internal table under —1–8 in Table 3B) |
| 32 | [Literature dealing with specific] Places (Table 3C) |
| 43155 | Berlin (Table 2) |

Similarly, in 400 Language, numbers may be built with the use of multiple tables, as illustrated in the following example showing the use of three tables:

Conversational Spanish for English-speaking library employees: 468.342102402

| | |
|---|---|
| 46 | Base number for Spanish |
| 834 | Audio-lingual approach to expression for those whose native language is different (Table 4) |
| 21 | English (Table 6) |
| 024 | The subject for persons in specific occupations (Table 1) |
| 02 | Library and information sciences [The final 0 in 020 is dropped] |

## History and Geography

In support of multiple synthesis for topics related to history and geography, main class 900 features three important add tables at 913–919, 930–990, and 940–990, plus additional add instructions throughout the schedule. Some examples:

Bed and breakfasts in South Africa, 2003: 916.806466

| | |
|---|---|
| 91 | Base number for Geography and travel |
| 68 | South Africa (Table 2) |
| 064 | Bed and breakfast accommodations (internal table under 913–919) |
| 66 | Number following 968.0 in 968.066 1999– |

A pictorial work portraying Turks in Vorarlberg, Austria: 943.645004943500222

| | |
|---|---|
| 9 | Base number for History of specific localities (internal table at 930–990) |
| 43645 | Vorarlberg province, Austria (Table 2) |
| 004 | Ethnic and national groups (internal table under 930–990) |
| 943 | Turkic peoples (Table 5) |
| 5 | Number following —943 in notation 9435 Turkish (Table 6) |
| 00222 | Pictorial works (Table 1) |

## SUMMARY

The term multiple synthesis has not been used in a formal sense in the DDC. We may define it as a process requiring the addition of two or more facets, one after the other, to the same base number. There are many situations and provisions in the DDC where the classifier follows the add operation more than once to arrive at the synthesized number. It is this feature of Dewey that provides for the close classification of many minute and specific subjects.

To repeat: The first task for classifying a complex subject is to identify the base number; the second is to follow the instructions for adding segments from auxiliary tables and/or other parts of the schedules to the number chosen. This operation can be long and involved, requiring considerable manipulation of the schedules and tables. It is extremely important to keep track of each step in the number-building process to ensure that notation is assembled in the correct citation order.

Examples in this chapter are restricted to multiple synthesis through the addition of two or more subdivisions to the same base number, with one add instruction leading to another. In such cases, the first and foremost step is the choice of the appropriate base number. The citation formula is generally entity/operation/agent; choosing the correct base number enables the classifier to combine maximum facets through add instructions. It is important to follow such instructions step-by-step. The operation, though sometimes long and involved, uses the same technique as simple synthesis. Proficiency comes with practice.

## EXERCISES

Classify the following topics involving multiple synthesis:

(1)   Social reform movement for heroin addicts in the United States

(2)   African-American college students

(3)   Behavior of chipmunks

(4)   Administration of architecture libraries in New York State

(5)   Paratroop training in France

(6)   Annual administrative reports on proposed budgets of New York State

(7)   Viral diseases in maize

(8)   The rulers of Yemen; a collected biography

(9)   A 2003 guide to youth hostels in Queensland, Australia

(10) Jewish art in the Victoria and Albert Museum (South Kensington, London)

(11) A critical study of teenagers in British comedy (dramatic literature)

(12) A study of late nineteenth-century German novels about Berlin

(13) A list of journals on German literature for children

(14) Discography of bluegrass songs

(15) German opera written in the eighteenth century

# APPENDIX
## ANSWERS TO EXERCISES

## ANSWERS TO EXERCISES

### CHAPTER 4

Exercise 1:                                    Answers to Exercise 1:
Identify the class numbers for the
following subjects:

(1) Aves: a zoological study                   (1) 598

(2) Human heart diseases                       (2) 616.12

(3) Nursing interventions for patients         (3) 616.82 (*not* 610.73)
    with meningitis

(4) 20th-century sculpture                     (4) 735.23

(5) Reign of Elizabeth I of England            (5) 942.055


Exercise 2:                                    Answers to Exercise 2:
Classify the following subjects by using
the appropriate table of preference:

(1) Preparing lunches for schools              (1) 641.571 (*not* 641.53)

(2) Deportation for political offenses         (2) 364.68 (*not* 364.131)

(3) Decorative lighting for weddings           (3) 747.92 (*not* 747.93)

(4) Miniature portrait paintings of            (4) 757.7 (*not* 757.4)
    women

(5) Compensation of working mothers            (5) 331.44 (*not* 331.21)


Exercise 3:                                    Answers to Exercise 3:
Identify the class numbers for the
following subjects:

(1) Educational services in adult women        (1) 365.66 (*not* 365.43)
    prisons

(2) Retired immigrant labor                    (2) 331.5 (*not* 331.62)

(3) Economics of production efficiency         (3) 338.16
    in agriculture

(4) Public safety programs about the           (4) 363.1799 (*not* 363.12)
    transportation of radioactive materials

## CHAPTER 4 *(continued)*

Exercise 4:

Identify the class numbers for the following subjects:

(1) Curricula in elementary schools

(2) Color printing by photomechanical techniques

(3) Manufacture of metallic chairs

(4) Atomic weight of curium (chemical element)

(5) Breeding of Oriental horses

(6) Diseases of arrowroot (starch crop)

Answers to Exercise 4:

(1) 372.19 (*not* 375.001)

(2) 686.232 (*not* 686.23042)

(3) 684.13 (*not* 684.105)

(4) 546.442 (*not* 541.242)

(5) 636.11 (*not* 636.082)

(6) 633.68 (*not* 632.3)

## CHAPTER 6

Exercise 1:

Under what terms should you look in the Relative Index for the following subjects?

(1) Ronald Reagan (the actor)

(2) Allstate Insurance Company

(3) John Lennon (the singer-composer of the rock group The Beatles)

(4) AZT (the anti-AIDS drug)

(5) Chlorofluorocarbons

(6) Santa Claus

(7) Sneakers (shoes)

(8) Babe Ruth (the baseball player)

(9) Black widow spider

Answers to Exercise 1:

(1) Actors—motion picture

(2) Insurance companies

(3) Rock musicians—singers or Rock singers

(4) AIDS (Disease)—medicine

(5) Chlorine—organic chemistry or Fluorine—organic chemistry

(6) Christmas—customs

(7) Shoes

(8) Baseball players

(9) Spiders

## CHAPTER 6 *(continued)*

Exercise 2:

Under which term would you look for the following topics?

Answers to Exercise 2:

(1) Anthology of one-act plays

(2) Libraries for children

(3) Fabian socialism

(4) Dynamics of particles

(5) Air-to-air guided missiles

(6) Modern history

(7) Modeling pottery

(8) History of privateering

(1) One-act plays

(2) Children's libraries

(3) Fabian socialism

(4) Dynamics—particles or Particles (Matter)—classical mechanics

(5) Air-to-air guided missiles

(6) Modern history

(7) Modeling—pottery or Pottery

(8) Privateering

## CHAPTER 7

Exercise 1:

Build class numbers for the following subjects using whole schedule numbers:

Answers to Exercise 1:

(1) Library classification for economics

(2) Special libraries devoted to Judaism

(3) Religion and the theater

(4) Bibliography of the Dewey Decimal Classification

(5) Selection and acquisition of art books in libraries

(6) Bibliography of cool jazz

(7) Trade in pharmaceutical drugs

(8) Strikes by professors

(9) The prices of shoes

(1) $025.46 + 330 = 025.4633$

(2) $026 + 296 = 026.296$

(3) $201.6 + 792 = 201.6792$

(4) $016 + 025.431 = 016.025431$

(5) $025.27 + 700 = 025.277$

(6) $016 + 781.655 = 016.781655$

(7) $381.45 + 615.1 = 381.456151$

(8) $331.89281 + 378.12 =$ $331.8928137812$

(9) $338.43 + 685.31 = 338.4368531$

**CHAPTER 7** *(continued)*

Exercise 2:

Build class numbers by adding parts of schedule numbers:

(1) Trade in diamonds

(2) Labor market for the leather industry

(3) Educational guidance in adult education

(4) Grooming your dog

(5) The psychology of hyperactive children

(6) Production efficiency in the manufacturing of passenger automobiles

(7) Manufacture of volleyball equipment

(8) Physiology of birds

(9) Law of bank mergers

(10) A library use study of public libraries

Answers to Exercise 2:

(1) 381.42 + 82 (from 553.[82]) = 381.4282 (381 is the comprehensive number for domestic and international trade)

(2) 331.129 + 75 (from 6[75]) = 331.12975

(3) 374.1 + 422 (from 371.[422]) = 374.1422

(4) 636.70 + 833 (from 636.0[833]) = 636.70833

(5) 155.45 + 4 (from 371.9[4]) = 155.454

(6) 338.456 + 29222 (from 6[29.222]) = 338.45629222

(7) 668.76 + 325 (from 796.[325]) = 668.76325

(8) 571.1 + 8 (from 59[8]) = 571.18

(9) 346.082 + 16 (from 332.[16]) = 346.08216

(10) 025.58 + 74 (from 02[7.4]) = 025.5874

## CHAPTER 7 *(continued)*

Exercise 3:

Build numbers according to collective add instructions:

(1) Physical chemistry of gold

(2) Remodeling warehouses

(3) Drug therapy for malaria

(4) Mass of the planet Venus

(5) Economic utilization of grasslands

(6) Development of arid land

(7) Managing railroads

(8) Public measures to prevent hazardous consequences in the use of agricultural chemicals

(9) Wasting mineral resources

Answers to Exercise 3:

(1) 546.656 + 5 (from table under 546) = 546.6565

(2) 725.35 + 0286 (from table under 721–729) = 725.350286

(3) 616.9362 + 061 (from table under 616.1–616.9) = 616.9362061

(4) 523.42 + 1 (from 523.3[1]) = 523.421

(5) 333.74 + 13 (from table under 333.7–333.9) = 333.7413

(6) 333.736 + 15 (from table under 333.7–333.9) = 333.73615

(7) 385 + 068 (from table under 380) = 385.068

(8) 363.1792 + 7 (from table under 362–363) = 363.17927

(9) 333.85 + 137 (from table under 333.7–333.9) = 333.85137

## CHAPTER 8

Exercise 1:

Applying standard subdivisions, assign class numbers to the following works:

(1) An encyclopedia of civil and political rights

(2) A dictionary of civil rights

(3) Teaching methods in agriculture

(4) Research methods in milk processing technology

(5) A journal of histology

(6) Marketing management of computer software

Answers to Exercise 1:

(1) 323.03

(2) 323.03

(3) 630.71

(4) 637.1072

(5) 571.505

(6) 005.30688

**CHAPTER 8** *(continued)*

Exercise 2:

Build class numbers for the following topics involving main class or division numbers:

Answers to Exercise 2:

(1)  Science organizations

(2)  Abbreviations and symbols used in science

(3)  History of science

(4)  History of science in the 16th century

(5)  Schools and courses in astronomy

(6)  Research methods in philosophy

(7)  Dictionary of mathematics

(8)  Medical associations

(9)  Encyclopedia of architecture

(1)  506

(2)  501.48

(3)  509

(4)  509.031

(5)  520.71

(6)  107.2

(7)  510.3

(8)  610.6

(9)  720.3

Exercise 3:

Build class numbers for the following topics requiring standard subdivisions with multiple zeros:

Answers to Exercise 3:

(1)  Illustrations of human diseases

(2)  A history of naval forces

(3)  Higher education in Central European history

(4)  Tables and formulas in economics

(5)  International organizations on human diseases

(6)  A dictionary of law

(7)  A journal of Christian theology

(1)  616.00222

(2)  359.009

(3)  943.000711

(4)  330.021

(5)  616.00601

(6)  340.03

(7)  230.05

## CHAPTER 8 *(continued)*

Exercise 4:

Synthesize numbers for the following subjects:

(1) Mathematics in biophysics
(2) The odds of winning lotteries
(3) Mathematics of human blood flow




(4) A journal of military science


Answers to Exercise 4:


(1) 571.40151
(2) 795.38015192
(3) 612.1181 (Since blood flow does not have its own number, standard subdivisions cannot be added for it. See "approximating the whole" in chapter 8.)
(4) 355.005


Exercise 5:

Classify the following topics related to persons treatment:

(1) Edward Teller; biography of an atomic physicist
(2) The role of generals in the army
(3) Great physicists of the twentieth century
(4) Seabiscuit: life of a great race horse
(5) Teenagers and the Internet
(6) Discrimination against women in higher education
(7) Racism in sports
(8) Racism in football in the U.K.
(9) Statistical mathematics for librarians
(10) Introduction to law for police officials


Answers to Exercise 5:


(1) 539.7092

(2) 355.331
(3) 530.0922

(4) 798.400929
(5) 004.6780835
(6) 378.0082

(7) 796.089
(8) 796.33408900941
(9) 519.502402
(10) 340.0243632

## CHAPTER 8 *(continued)*

Exercise 6:

Assign class numbers to the following subjects, using displaced standard subdivisions:

(1) A history of wages

(2) Apparatus for making plastics

(3) History of painting (art)

(4) Architecture of the modern era

Answers to Exercise 6:

(1) 331.29

(2) 668.41

(3) 759

(4) 724

Exercise 7:

Synthesize class numbers for the following topics that involve two standard subdivision concepts.

(1) A journal of higher education in public administration

(2) Encyclopedia of psychological associations

(3) A directory of law schools

(4) A journal of literary history

(5) A biographical dictionary of musicians

Answers to Exercise 7:

(1) 351.0711 (*not* 351. 05)

(2) 150.6 (*not* 150.3)

(3) 340.0711

(4) 809.005

(5) 780.922

Exercise 8:

Provide class numbers for the following subjects that involve standard subdivision concepts but do not use standard subdivision notation:

(1) Management of technology

(2) History of Central Europe

(3) *The New York Public Library Desk Reference*

(4) A general periodical in the English language

Answers to Exercise 8:

(1) 658

(2) 943

(3) 031

(4) 052

## CHAPTER 9

Exercise 1:

In the Relative Index identify the area numbers for the following areas, and then locate and verify them in Table 2.

(1) Genesee County, Michigan

(2) Islāmābād Capital Territory, Pakistan

(3) Suriname

(4) Coast Ranges in Oregon

(5) Cambodia

(6) Unaligned blocs

(7) Eastern Hemisphere

(8) Waterfalls

(9) Antarctic Ocean

(10) Arctic Ocean

(11) Islamic regions

(12) Rural regions

Answers to Exercise 1:

(1) —77437

(2) —549149

(3) —883

(4) —7951

(5) —596

(6) —1716

(7) —1811

(8) —1694

(9) —167

(10)—1632

(11) 1767

(12) —1734

Exercise 2:

Classify the following with direct subdivision by place:

(1) Adult education in Singapore

(2) Education policy in India

(3) General statistics of Finland

(4) General geology of Athens

(5) History of Jammu and Kashmir

(6) History of Jammu and Kashmir during the reign of Aurangzeb

(7) General organizations in Liverpool, England

(8) Journalism and newspapers in Finland

(9) Art galleries in Sweden

(10) Public administration in Canada

Answers to Exercise 2:

(1) 374.95957

(2) 379.54

(3) 314.897

(4) 554.9512

(5) 954.6

(6) 954.60258

(7) 062.753

(8) 078.97

(9) 708.85

(10)351.71

**CHAPTER 9** *(continued)*

Exercise 3:

Assign class numbers to the following, using extensions of area notation 1:

(1) Social welfare programs in developing countries

(2) Democratic political systems in former communist bloc countries

(3) Health insurance systems in the Pacific region

Answers to Exercise 3:

(1) 362.91724

(2) 321.8091717

(3) 368.3820091823

Exercise 4:

Assign class numbers to the following, using standard subdivision —09 and area notation 3–9:

(1) Ambulance services in Washington State

(2) Child labor in Southeast Asia

(3) Taxes in Kuwait

(4) Costume in Belgium

(5) Prices in France: an economic study

(6) Sexual division of labor: a case study in Chicago, Illinois

(7) Broadway musicals: a theatrical history

Answers to Exercise 4:

(1) 362.18809797

(2) 331.310959

(3) 336.20095367

(4) 391.009493

(5) 338.520944

(6) 306.36150977311

(7) 792.6097471

Exercise 5:

Classify the following subjects requiring area notation between two subject facets:

(1) Physical geography of Mexico

(2) Property law of Nigeria

(3) Public health law of Mozambique

(4) The lower house of the British Parliament

(5) Italian Communist Party

Answers to Exercise 5:

(1) 917.202

(2) 346.66904

(3) 344.67904

(4) 328.41072

(5) 324.245075

**CHAPTER 9** *(continued)*

Exercise 6:                                    Answers to Exercise 6:

Classify the following requiring two area
numbers:

(1) Migration from Vietnam to the          (1) 304.8730597
    United States: a sociological study

(2) Trade agreements between Colombia      (2) 382.9861087
    and Venezuela (emphasizes Colombia)

(3) Trade between Venezuela and            (3) 382.09870861
    Colombia (emphasizes Venezuela)

(4) Foreign relations between Australia    (4) 327.9401823
    and countries of the Pacific Rim

(5) Foreign relations between Japan and    (5) 327.5195052
    South Korea

(6) Canadian economic aid to developing    (6) 338.917101724
    countries

(7) Geography of suburban regions of       (7) 919.409733
    Australia


Exercise 7:                                    Answers to Exercise 7:

Classify the following topics using an
area notation extended by another area
notation:

(1) Civil rights in francophone countries  (1) 323.0960917541
    of Africa

(2) Male costume in rural Austria          (2) 391.109436091734

(3) Economic conditions in rural England   (3) 330.9420091734

## CHAPTER 9 *(continued)*

| Exercise 8: | Answers to Exercise 8: |
|---|---|

Classify the following, using a standard subdivision (other than —09) extended by an area notation:

| | | | |
|---|---|---|---|
| (1) | Research in economics in Scotland | (1) | 330.0720411 |
| (2) | Computer science as a profession in the United States | (2) | 004.02373 |
| (3) | Education in mathematics in Asia | (3) | 510.7105 |
| (4) | Education of attorneys in Latin America | (4) | 340.07118 |
| (5) | Higher education in Spain in public administration | (5) | 351.071146 |
| (6) | Sports curricula in U. S. colleges | (6) | 796.071173 |

| Exercise 9: | Answers to Exercise 9: |
|---|---|

Classify the following, using a standard subdivision after an area notation:

| | | | |
|---|---|---|---|
| (1) | Journal of Indian geography | (1) | 915.4005 |
| (2) | Women in the Church of England | (2) | 283.42082 |
| (3) | Foreign policy of Germany in the 1990s | (3) | 327.43009049 |
| (4) | Sickness and health: Canadian statistics at a glance | (4) | 614.4271021 |
| (5) | Ancient Roman coins [minted in Rome] in the Hobart Classics Museum (Hobart, Tasmania) | (5) | 737.493760749461 |
| (6) | A journal of housing programs and services in Argentina | (6) | 363.58098205 |

## CHAPTER 10

Exercise 1:

Classify the following works by or about individual authors:

(1) Poems of Charles Baudelaire (French poet, 1821–1867)

(2) The collected plays of Thomas Dekker (British, 1572–1632)

(3) Selected poetry of William Butler Yeats (Irish author, 1865–1939, writing in the English language)

(4) Dramatic works of Eugene O'Neill (American, 1888–1953)

(5) *Murder on the Orient Express* by Agatha Christie (1890–1976)

(6) *The Adventures of Huckleberry Finn* by the American novelist Mark Twain (1835–1910)

(7) A biography of Claus Silvester Dörner (German writer not limited to or chiefly identifiable with one specific form, 1913–   )

(8) A collection of jokes by the American author, Nancy Gray (1959–   )

Answers to Exercise 1:

(1)  841.8

(2)  822.3

(3)  821.8

(4)  812.52

(5)  823.912

(6)  813.4

(7)  838.91409

(8)  818.5402

## CHAPTER 10 *(continued)*

Exercise 2:
Classify the following topics from more
than one literature:

Answers to Exercise 2:

(1) A collection of sonnets

(1) 808.8142

(2) A collection of poetry by women

(2) 808.810082

(3) An anthology of nineteenth-century
literature

(3) 808.80034

(4) A critical appraisal of lyric poetry

(4) 809.14

(5) A collection of poetry displaying
realism

(5) 808.81912

(6) A collection of poetry with marriage
as the theme

(6) 808.8193543

(7) A critical appraisal of romantic
literature

(7) 809.9145

Exercise 3:
Classify the following topics from one
literature:

Answers to Exercise 3:

(1) A study of symbolism in French
literature

(1) 840.915

(2) A history of twentieth-century
English literature

(2) 820.90091

(3) A study of French women authors

(3) 840.99287

(4) A study of social themes in 15th-
century English literature

(4) 820.935509024

(5) A study of Portuguese literature by
African authors

(5) 869.0996

(6) Discourses of Christian salvation in
English literature; an historical study

(6) 820.938234

## CHAPTER 10 *(continued)*

Exercise 4:

Classify the following works from one literature and in a particular form:

(1) Collection of English lyric poetry on love

(2) An anthology of English allegorical narrative poetry

(3) A critical study of plots in American historical fiction

(4) A study of English horror tales

(5) A study of heroism in the English novel

Answers to Exercise 4:

(1) 821.04083543

(2) 821.030815

(3) 813.0810924

(4) 823.0873809

(5) 823.009353

Exercise 5:

Classify the following works from one literature with multiple facets:

(1) Collection of Elizabethan English poetry

(2) Love in twentieth-century American drama: a critical study

(3) Collection of late twentieth-century American drama by teenagers

(4) A study of the Berlin wall in East German fiction

(5) A bibliography of English romantic poetry by women authors, 1770–1835

Answers to Exercise 5:

(1) 821.308

(2) 812.5093543

(3) 812.540809283

(4) 833.91409358

(5) 016.8216080145082

Exercise 6:

Classify the following works, using Table 3C with 700 numbers:

(1) Fantasy films

(2) Horror programs on television

(3) Werewolves in the arts

(4) Atlantis in art and literature

Answers to Exercise 6:

(1) 791.43615

(2) 791.456164

(3) 700.474

(4) 700.472

## CHAPTER 11

Exercise 1:

Classify the following topics using Table 4:

(1) Phonology of Slovak

(2) An introduction to Middle Dutch

(3) Noun phrases in Norwegian

(4) English verb tables for ESL [English as a second language] speakers

(5) Portuguese word formation with suffixes

Answers to Exercise 1:

(1) 491.8715

(2) 439.317

(3) 439.8255

(4) 428.24

(5) 469.592

Exercise 2:

Classify the following topics using Table 6:

(1) German-language encyclopedia

(2) A study of Sauk (a North American native language)

(3) Arabic folktales from Israel

(4) French-speaking people in Africa: a social study

(5) General encyclopedia in Thai

(6) General periodicals in Norwegian

(7) Spanish quotations

(8) Introduction to Samoan

Answers to Exercise 2:

(1) 033.1

(2) 497.3149

(3) 398.204927095694

(4) 305.74106

(5) 039.95911

(6) 058.82

(7) 086.1

(8) 499.462

Exercise 3:

Classify the following topics using both Table 4 and Table 6:

(1) Chinese-English dictionary

(2) Finnish-English dictionary

(3) Spanish reader for English-speaking people

(4) Latin words in the German language

(5) Conversational English for Russian-speaking people

Answers to Exercise 3:

(1) 495.1321

(2) 494.541321

(3) 468.6421

(4) 432.471

(5) 428.349171

## CHAPTER 11 *(continued)*

Exercise 4:

Classify the following topics using Table 6 through Table 2:

(1) School enrollment in the French-speaking world

(2) Conservation of economic resources in the Portuguese-speaking world

Answers to Exercise 4:

(1) 371.21917541

(2) 339.4917569

## CHAPTER 12

Exercises:

Classify the following topics using Table 5:

(1) Folksongs of the Romany people

(2) Italians around the world (a social study)

(3) Jewish art

(4) Religion of the Hittites

(5) Navajo religion

(6) Contemporary Australian aboriginal paintings

(7) Chinese American scientists

Answers to Exercises:

(1) 782.4216291497

(2) 305.851

(3) 704.03924

(4) 299.199

(5) 299.7826

(6) 759.9940899915

(7) 509.23951073

## CHAPTER 13

| Exercises: | Answers to Exercises: |
|---|---|
| Classify the following topics involving multiple synthesis: | |
| (1) Social reform movement for heroin addicts in the United States | (1) 362.2935240973 |
| (2) African-American college students | (2) 378.1982996073 |
| (3) Behavior of chipmunks | (3) 599.36415 |
| (4) Administration of architecture libraries in New York State | (4) 025.1967209747 |
| (5) Paratroop training in France | (5) 356.16650944 |
| (6) Annual administrative reports on proposed budgets of New York State | (6) 352.497470105 |
| (7) Viral diseases in maize | (7) 633.1598 |
| (8) The rulers of Yemen; a collected biography | (8) 953.30099 |
| (9) A 2003 guide to youth hostels in Queensland, Australia | (9) 919.430667 |
| (10) Jewish art in the Victoria and Albert Museum (South Kensington, London) | (10) 704.03924007442134 |
| (11) A critical study of teenagers in British comedy (dramatic literature) | (11) 822.05230935235 |
| (12) A study of late nineteenth-century German novels about Berlin | (12) 833.8093243155 |
| (13) A list of journals on German literature for children | (13) 016.83080928205 |
| (14) Discography of bluegrass songs | (14) 016.7824216420266 |
| (15) German opera written in the eighteenth century | (15) 782.1094309033 |

**GLOSSARY**

# GLOSSARY

The glossary includes the terms and definitions found in the glossary in volume 1 of *Dewey Decimal Classification and Relative Index*, Edition 22. The glossary also contains additional terms used in this book.

**Abridged edition:** A shortened version of the Dewey Decimal Classification (DDC) system that is a logical truncation of the notational and structural hierarchy of the corresponding full edition on which it is based. The abridged edition is intended for general collections of 20,000 titles or less. *See also* **Broad classification; Full edition.**

**Add note:** A note instructing the classifier to append digits found elsewhere in the DDC to a given base number. *See also* **Base number.**

**Add table:** *See* **Tables (2).**

**Application:** *See* **Rule of application.**

**Approximate the whole:** When a topic is nearly coextensive with the full meaning of a DDC class, the topic is said to "approximate the whole" of the class. The term is also used to characterize topics that cover more than half the content of a class. When a topic approximates the whole of a class, standard subdivisions may be added. Topics that do not approximate the whole are said to be in "standing room" in the number. *See also* **Class-here note; Standard-subdivisions-are-added note; Standing room.**

**Area table:** An auxiliary table (Table 2) that gives geographic areas primarily, but also lists historical periods and several numbers for persons associated with a subject. Areas of the world are listed systematically, not alphabetically. Area table notation may be used with other numbers in the schedules and tables when explicit instructions permitting such use are given. *See also* **Tables.**

**Arrange-alphabetically note:** A note suggesting the option of alphabetical subarrangement when identification by specific name or other identifying characteristic is desired. *See also* **Option.**

**Arrange-chronologically note:** A note suggesting the option of chronological subarrangement when identification by date is desired. *See also* **Option.**

**Artificial digit:** A letter or other symbol used optionally as a substitute for digits 0–9 to provide a more prominent location or shorter notation for a jurisdiction, language, literature, religion, ethnic or national group, or other characteristic. *See also* **Option.**

**Aspect:** An approach to a subject, or characteristic (facet) of a subject. *See also* **Discipline; Facet; Subject.**

**Attraction:** *See* **Classification by attraction.**

**Author number:** *See* **Book number.**

**Base number:** A number of any length to which other numbers are appended. *See also* **Add note.**

**Book number:** The part of a call number that distinguishes a specific item from other items within the same class number. A library using the Cutter-Sanborn system can have D548d indicate David Copperfield by Dickens (where D stands for the D of Dickens, 548 stands for "ickens," and d stands for David Copperfield). *See also* **Call number; Cutter number; Work mark.**

**Broad classification:** The classification of works in broad categories by logical abridgment, even when more specific numbers are available, e.g., the use of 641.5 Cooking instead of 641.5972 Mexican cooking for a cookbook of Mexican recipes. Broad classification is the opposite of close classification. *See also* **Abridged edition; Close classification.**

**Built number:** A number constructed according to add instructions stated or implied in the schedules or tables. *See also* **Number building.**

**Call number:** A set of letters, numerals, or other symbols (in combination or alone) used by a library to identify a specific copy of a work. A call number may consist of the class number; book number; and other data such as date, volume number, copy number, and location symbol. *See also* **Book number; Class number.**

**Caption:** *See* **Heading.**

**Category:** *See* **Class** *(Noun).*

**Centered entry:** An entry representing a subject covered by a span of numbers, e.g., 372–374 Specific levels of education. The entry is called "centered" because the span of numbers appears in the center of the page in the print version of the DDC rather than in the number column on the left side of the page. Centered entries are identified by the symbol > in the number column.

**Characteristic of division:** *See* **Facet.**

**Citation order:** The order in which two or more characteristics (facets) of a class are to be combined in number building. When number building is not permitted or possible, instructions on preference order with respect to the choice of facets are provided. *See also* **Facet; Number building; Preference order.**

**Class:** (Noun) (1) A group of objects exhibiting one or more common characteristics, identified by specific notation. *See also* **Entry (1).** (2) One of the ten major groups of the DDC numbered 0–9. *See also* **Main class.** (3) A subdivision of the DDC of any degree of specificity. *See also* **Subdivision.** (Verb) To assign a class number to an individual work. *See also* **Classify.**

**Class-elsewhere note:** A note instructing the classifier about the location of interrelated topics. The note may show preference order, lead to the interdisciplinary or comprehensive number, override the first-of-two rule, or lead to broader or narrower numbers in the same hierarchical array that might otherwise be overlooked. *See also* **Comprehensive number; Interdisciplinary number; Preference order.**

**Class-here note:** A note that identifies topics that are equivalent to the whole of the class under which the note appears. The topic as a whole is classed in the number under which the note appears; parts of the topic are classed in the most appropriate subdivision of the number. Topics identified in class-here notes, even if broader or narrower than the heading, are said to "approximate the whole" of the number; therefore, standard subdivisions may be added for topics in class-here notes. Class-here notes also may identify the comprehensive or interdisciplinary number for a subject. *See also* **Approximate the whole; Comprehensive number; Interdisciplinary number.**

**Class number:** Notation that designates the class to which a given item belongs. *See also* **Call number.**

**Classification:** A logical system for the arrangement of knowledge.

**Classification by attraction:** The classification of a specific aspect of a subject in an inappropriate discipline, usually because the subject is named in the inappropriate discipline but not mentioned explicitly in the appropriate discipline.

**Classified catalog:** A catalog arranged according to the notational order of a classification system.

**Classifier:** A person who applies a classification system to a body of knowledge or a collection of documents.

**Classify:** (1) To arrange a collection of items according to a classification system. (2) To assign a class number to an individual work.

**Close classification:** The classification of works to the fullest extent permitted by the notation. Close classification is the opposite of broad classification. *See also* **Broad classification; Full edition.**

**Coextensive:** Describes a topic equal in scope to the concept represented by the number.

**Comparative table:** A table provided for a complete or extensive revision that lists in alphabetical order selected topics accompanied by their previous number and their number in the current edition. *See also* **Equivalence table; Revision.**

**Complete revision:** *See* **Revision** *(Complete revision).*

**Complex subject:** A complex subject is a subject that has more than one characteristic. For example, "unemployed carpenters" is a complex subject because it has more than one characteristic (employment status and occupation). *See also* **Preference order.**

**Comprehensive number:** A number (often identified by a "Class here comprehensive works" note) that covers all the components of the subject treated within that discipline. The components may be in a span of consecutive numbers or distributed throughout the schedule or table. *See also* **Interdisciplinary number.**

**Coordinate:** Describes a number or topic at a level equal to another number or topic in the same hierarchy.

**Cross classification:** The accidental placement of works on the same subject in two different class numbers. This tends to happen when works being classified deal with two or more characteristics of a subject in the same class. Notes on preference order should prevent cross classification. *See also* **Preference order.**

**Cross reference:** *See* **Class-elsewhere note; See-also reference; See reference.**

**Cutter number:** The notation in a book number derived from the Cutter Three-Figure Author Table, the Cutter-Sanborn Three-Figure Author Table, or the OCLC Four-Figure Cutter Tables. The OCLC Four-Figure Cutter Tables are revised and expanded versions of the Cutter Three-Figure Author Table and the Cutter-Sanborn Three-Figure Author Table. *See also* **Book number.**

**DDC:** Dewey Decimal Classification.

**DDC Summaries:** A listing of the first three levels (main classes, divisions, and sections) of the Dewey Decimal Classification system. The headings associated with the numbers in the summaries have been edited for browsing purposes, and may not match the complete headings found in the schedules. *See also* **Division; Main class; Section; Summary.**

**Decimal point:** The dot that follows the third digit in a DDC number. In strict usage the word "decimal" is not accurate; however, common usage is followed in this edition's explanatory material.

**Definition note:** A note indicating the meaning of a term in the heading.

**Digit:** The smallest individual unit in a notational system. For example, the notation 954 has three digits: 9, 5, and 4.

**Discipline:** An organized field of study or branch of knowledge, e.g., 200 Religion, 530 Physics, 364 Criminology. In the DDC, subjects are arranged by disciplines. *See also* **Subject.**

**Discontinuation:** The shifting of a topic or the entire contents of a number to a more general number in the same hierarchy, or the complete removal of the topic or number. A topic or number is discontinued because the topic or concept represented by the number has a negligible current literature or represents a distinction that is no longer valid in the literature or common perception of the field. A note explaining its shift or removal accompanies a discontinued topic or number. Discontinued numbers appear in square brackets. *See also* **Relocation; Schedule reduction.**

**Displaced standard subdivision:** A standard subdivision concept given special notation in the schedule in place of its regular notation from Table 1. A do-not-use note is always provided at the regular location of the standard subdivision concept. *See also* **Do-not-use note; Standard subdivisions.**

**Division:** The second level of subdivision in the DDC, represented by the first two digits in the notation, e.g., 64 in 640 Home and family management. *See also* **DDC Summaries; Main class; Section.**

**Do-not-use note:** A note instructing the classifier not to use all or part of a regular standard subdivision notation or an add table provision, but instead to use a special provision or standard subdivision notation at a broader number. *See also* **Displaced standard subdivision.**

**Document:** A generic term for all media capable of conveying, coding, and preserving knowledge. Documents may be books, journals, electronic resources, reports, sound recordings, motion pictures, etc.

**Dual heading:** A heading with two separate terms, the first of which is the main topic and the second of which is a major subordinate topic, e.g., 570 Life sciences   Biology. A dual heading is used when the subject as a whole and the subordinate topic as a whole share the same number and most of its subdivisions. Standard subdivisions may be added for either or both topics in a dual heading.

**Dual provision:** The inadvertent provision of more than one place in the DDC for the same aspect of a subject.

**Entry:** (1) In the schedules and tables, a self-contained unit consisting of a number or span of numbers, a heading, and often one or more notes. (2) In the Relative Index, a term or phrase usually followed by a DDC number. (3) In the Manual, a self-contained unit consisting of a number or group of numbers, the associated headings or topics, and an extended instruction or discussion.

**Enumerative scheme:** A classification system in which numbers for complex subjects are precombined and listed.

**Equivalence table:** A table provided for a complete or extensive revision that lists in numerical order the classes of the current edition with their equivalent numbers in the previous edition (and vice versa). *See also* **Revision.**

**Expansion:** The development of a class in the schedules or tables to provide further subdivisions. *See also* **Revision.**

**Extensive revision:** *See* **Revision** *(Extensive revision).*

**Facet:** Any of the various categories into which a given class may be divided, e.g., division of the class "people" into the categories of ethnicity, age, education, and language spoken. Each category contains terms based on a single characteristic of division, e.g., children, adolescents, and adults are characteristics of division of the "ages" category. *See also* **Citation order.**

**Facet analysis:** The division of a subject into its component parts (facets).

**Facet indicator:** A digit used to introduce notation representing a characteristic of the subject. For example, "0" is often used as a facet indicator to introduce standard subdivision concepts.

**Faceted scheme:** A classification scheme that identifies subjects by their component parts (facets). The appropriate facets need to be fitted together in order to provide a class number for a work. *See also* **Enumerative scheme.**

**First-of-two rule:** The rule instructing that works dealing equally with two subjects that are not used to introduce or explain one another are classed in the number coming first in the schedules or tables.

**Fixed location:** System of marking and arranging library materials by shelf and book numbers so that their absolute position in room or tier and on the shelf is always the same. *See also* **Relative location.**

**Footnote:** An instruction that applies to many subdivisions of a class, or to a topic within a class. The affected subdivision or topic is marked with a symbol such as an asterisk. In the print version of the DDC, the footnote is located at the bottom of the page. In the electronic version, the footnote is included in the notes section of each class to which the instruction applies.

**Former-heading note:** A note listing the heading associated with the class number in the previous edition. The note is used when the heading has changed so much that it bears little or no resemblance to the previous heading, even though the meaning of the number has remained substantially the same.

**Full edition:** The complete version of the Dewey Decimal Classification (DDC) system. *See also* **Abridged edition; Close classification.**

**Heading:** The word or phrase used as the description of a given class. Also called "caption."

**Hierarchical force:** The principle that the attributes of a class as defined in the heading and in certain basic notes apply to all the subdivisions of the class, and to all other classes to which reference is made.

**Hierarchy:** The arrangement of a classification system from general to specific. In the DDC, the length of the notation and the corresponding depth of indention of the heading usually indicate the degree of specificity of a class. Hierarchy may also be indicated by special headings, notes, and centered entries.

**Hook number:** A number in the DDC without meaning in itself, but used to introduce examples of the topic. Hook numbers have headings that begin with "Miscellaneous," "Specific," or "Other"; and do not contain add notes, including notes, or class-here notes. Standard subdivisions are always bracketed under hook numbers.

**Including note:** A note enumerating topics that are logically part of the class but are less extensive in scope than the concept represented by the class number. These topics do not have enough literature to warrant their own number. Standard subdivisions may not be added to the numbers for these topics. *See also* **Literary warrant; Standing room.**

**Indention:** Typographical setting of notes and subheadings below and to the right of the main entry term.

**Influence:** *See* **Rule of application.**

**Interdisciplinary number:** A number (often identified by a "Class here interdisciplinary works" note) to be used for works covering a subject from the perspective of more than one discipline, including the discipline where the interdisciplinary number is located, e.g., the interdisciplinary number for marriage is 306.81 in Sociology. *See also* **Comprehensive number.**

**Literary form:** A mode of literary expression such as poetry, drama, fiction, etc. Each form can be subdivided into kinds of forms, e.g., lyric poetry, comedy, science fiction, etc.

**Literary warrant:** Justification for the development of a class or the explicit inclusion of a topic in the schedules, tables, or Relative Index, based on the existence of a body of literature on the topic.

**Main class:** One of the ten major subdivisions of the DDC, represented by the first digit in the notation, e.g., 3 in 300 Social sciences. *See also* **DDC Summaries; Division; Section.**

**Manual:** A guide to the use of the DDC that is made up primarily of extended discussions of problem areas in the application of the DDC. In the schedules and tables, see-Manual references indicate where relevant discussions are located in the Manual. *See also* **Manual note.**

**Manual note:** An individual entry in the Manual. *See also* **Entry (3); Manual; See-Manual reference.**

**Notation:** Numerals, letters, and/or symbols used to represent the main and subordinate divisions of a classification scheme. In the DDC, Arabic numerals are used to represent the classes, e.g., notation 07 from Table 1 and 511.3 from the schedules.

**Notational synthesis:** *See* **Number building.**

**Note:** An instruction, definition, or reference that explains the contents and use of a class, or the relationship of the class to other classes. *See also* **Add note; Arrange-alphabetically note; Arrange-chronologically note; Class-elsewhere note; Class-here note; Definition note; Discontinuation; Do-not-use note; Footnote; Former-heading note; Including note; Manual note; Number-built note; Preference order; Relocation; Revision note; Scope note; See-also reference; See-Manual reference; See reference; Standard-subdivisions-are-added note; Subdivisions-are-added note.**

**Number building:** The process of constructing a number by adding notation from the tables or other parts of the schedules to a base number. *See also* **Base number; Citation order.**

**Number-building note:** *See* **Add note.**

**Number-built note:** A note that states where the number building instructions may be found for a built number that is explicitly listed in the schedules or tables. Typically, such built numbers are listed for two reasons: to provide an entry for a built number under which other notes are required; or to provide an entry for a three-digit built number.

**Number column:** In the print version of the DDC, the column of numbers that appears in the left margin of the schedules and tables, and to the right of the alphabetical entries in the Relative Index.

**Option:** An alternative to standard notation provided in the schedules and tables to give emphasis to an aspect in a library's collection not given preferred treatment in the standard notation. In some cases, an option may provide shorter notation for the aspect. *See also* **Optional number.**

**Optional number:** (1) A number listed in parentheses in the schedules or tables that is an alternative to the standard notation. (2) A number constructed by following an option. *See also* **Option.**

**Order of preference:** *See* **Preference order.**

**Period table:** A table giving chronological time periods with their notation. For many literatures, period tables are given in the schedules. For works not limited to a particular language, the period notation is taken from Table 1 —0901–0905. *See also* **Tables.**

**Phoenix schedule:** *See* **Revision** *(Complete revision).*

**Preference order:** The order indicating which one of two or more numbers is to be chosen when different characteristics of a subject cannot be shown in full by number building. A note (sometimes containing a table of preference) indicates which characteristic is to be selected for works covering more than one characteristic. When a notation can be synthesized to show two or more characteristics, it is a matter of citation order. *See also* **Citation order.**

**Preference table:** *See* **Preference order.**

**Prime marks:** *See* **Segmentation.**

**Reduction of schedules:** *See* **Schedule reduction.**

**Regularization:** The replacement of special developments for standard subdivision concepts by use of the regular standard subdivisions found in Table 1.

**Relative Index:** The index to the DDC. It is called "Relative" because it shows the connection between subjects and the disciplines in which they appear. In the schedules, subjects are arranged within disciplines. In the Relative Index, subjects are listed alphabetically. Under each subject, the disciplines in which the subject is found are listed alphabetically. In the print version of the DDC, the disciplines are indented under the subject. In the electronic version, the disciplines appear as subheadings associated with the subject.

**Relative location:** The arrangement of documents according to their relationship to each other and regardless of their location on the shelves. *See also* **Fixed location.**

**Relocation:** The shifting of a topic from one number to another number that differs from the old number in respects other than length. Notes at both ends of the relocation identify the new and former numbers. *See also* **Discontinuation.**

**Retroactive citation order:** In number building, the combination of characteristics (facets) of a class starting with a number coming later in the schedule as the base number, then adding as instructed from numbers earlier in the sequence.

**Reused number:** A number with a total change in meaning from one edition to another. Usually numbers are reused only in complete revisions or when the reused number has been vacant for two consecutive editions.

**Revision:** The result of editorial work that alters the text of any class of the DDC. There are three degrees of revision: *Routine revision* is limited to updating terminology, clarifying notes, and providing modest expansions. *Extensive revision* involves a major reworking of subdivisions but leaves the main outline of the schedule intact. *Complete revision* (formerly called a phoenix) is a new development; the base number remains unchanged from the previous edition, but virtually all subdivisions are changed. Changes for complete and extensive revisions are shown through comparative and equivalence tables rather than through relocation notes in the schedule or table affected. *See also* **Comparative table; Equivalence table.**

**Revision note:** A note that introduces a complete or extensive revision.

**Routine revision:** *See* **Revision** *(Routine revision).*

**Rule of application:** The rule instructing that works about the application of one subject to a second subject or the influence of one subject on another subject are classified with the second subject.

**Rule of three:** The rule instructing that works giving equal treatment to three or more subjects that are all subdivisions of a broader subject are classified in the first higher number that includes all of them.

**Rule of zero:** The rule instructing that subdivisions beginning with zero should be avoided if there is a choice between the 0 subdivision and subdivisions beginning with 1–9 in the same position in the notation. Similarly, subdivisions beginning with 00 should be avoided when there is a choice between 00 and 0.

**Scatter note:** A class-elsewhere, see-reference, or relocation note that leads to multiple locations in the DDC. *See also* **Class-elsewhere note; Relocation; See reference.**

**Schedule reduction:** The elimination of certain provisions of a previous edition, often resulting in discontinued numbers. *See also* **Discontinuation.**

**Schedules:** (1) Listings of subjects and their subdivisions arranged in a systematic order with notation given for each subject and its subdivisions. (2) The series of DDC numbers 000–999, their headings, and notes.

**Scope note:** A note indicating that the meaning of a class number is broader or narrower than is apparent from the heading.

**Section:** The third level of subdivision in the DDC, represented by the first three digits in the notation, e.g., 641 in 641 Food and drink. *See also* **DDC Summaries; Division; Main class.**

**See-also reference:** (1) In the schedules and tables, a note leading to classes that are tangentially related to the topic and therefore might be confused with it. (2) In the Relative Index, a note leading to a synonym, broader term, or related term. (3) In the Manual, a note leading to related Manual notes.

**See-Manual reference:** A note leading from an entry in the schedules or tables to additional information about the number in the Manual.

**See reference:** A note (introduced by the word "for") that leads from the stated or implied comprehensive or interdisciplinary number for a subject to component parts of the subject in numbers other than direct subdivisions of the original number or span. *See also* **Class-elsewhere note.**

**Segmentation:** The indication of logical breaks in a number by a typographical device, e.g., slash marks or prime marks. Segmentation marks indicate the end of an abridged number or the beginning of a standard subdivision.

**Shelf mark:** *See* **Call number.**

**Standard subdivisions:** Subdivisions found in Table 1 that represent frequently recurring physical forms (dictionaries, periodicals) or approaches (history, research) applicable to any subject or discipline. They may be used with any number in the schedules and tables for topics that approximate the whole of the number unless there are instructions to the contrary. *See also* **Tables.**

**Standard-subdivisions-are-added note:** A note indicating which topics in a multiterm heading may have standard subdivisions added to them. The designated topics are considered to approximate the whole of the number. *See also* **Approximate the whole.**

**Standing room:** A term characterizing a topic without sufficient literature to have its own number, and considerably narrower in scope than the class number in which it is included. Standard subdivisions cannot be added to a topic in standing room, nor are other number-building techniques allowed. Topics listed in including notes have standing room in the class number, as do minor unnamed topics that logically fall in the same place in the DDC. To have standing room is the opposite of approximating the whole. *See also* **Approximate the whole.**

**Subdivision:** (1) A subordinate member of a class, e.g., 518 Numerical analysis is a subdivision of class 510 Mathematics, and 518.5 Numerical approximation is a subdivision of 518. *See also* **Class (3).** (2) Notation that may be added to other numbers to make a class number appropriately specific to the work being classified. *See also* **Standard Subdivisions; Tables.**

**Subdivisions-are-added note:** A note used where subdivisions are provided by add instructions indicating which topics in a multiterm heading may have subdivisions added to them. The designated topics are considered to approximate the whole of the number. *See also* **Approximate the whole.**

**Subject:** An object of study. Also called topic. It may be a person or a group of persons, thing, place, process, activity, abstraction, or any combination of these. In the DDC, subjects are arranged by disciplines. A subject is often studied in more than one discipline, e.g., marriage is studied in several disciplines such as ethics, religion, sociology, and law. *See also* **Discipline.**

**Subject catalog:** An index to the contents of a collection. If access is provided alphabetically by words, it is called an alphabetical subject catalog. If access is provided by the notation of a classification system, it is called a classified catalog. *See also* **Classified catalog.**

**Subordinate:** Describes a number or topic at a lower (narrower) level than another number or topic in the same hierarchy. *See also* **Superordinate.**

**Summary:** A listing of the chief subdivisions of a class that provides an overview of its structure. *See also* **DDC Summaries.**

**Superordinate:** Describes a number or topic at a higher (broader) level than another number or topic in the same hierarchy. *See also* **Subordinate.**

**Synthesis of notation:** *See* **Number building.**

**Table of preference:** *See* **Preference order.**

**Tables:** In the DDC, lists of notation that may be added to other numbers to make a class number appropriately specific to the work being classified. The numbers found in a table are never used alone. There are two kinds of tables: (1) The six numbered auxiliary tables (Tables 1–6) representing standard subdivisions, geographic areas, languages, ethnic groups, etc. (2) Lists of special notation found in add notes under specific numbers throughout the schedules and occasionally in Tables 1–6. These lists are called add tables. *See also* **Add note.**

**Topic:** *See* **Subject.**

**Unabridged edition:** *See* **Full edition.**

**Variant-name note:** A note listing synonyms or near synonyms for a topic in a heading when it is awkward or inappropriate to include such information in the heading.

**Word-by-word alphabetization:** Refers to the filing of entries word by word, not letter by letter. For example, New York files before Newark in word-by-word alphabetization; Newark files before New York in letter-by-letter alphabetization.

**Work:** A distinct intellectual or artistic expression.

**Work mark:** The part of a book number that consists of a letter appended to the author (or biographee) designation to show the first letter of the title (or first letter of the surname of the biographer). *See also* **Book number.**

# SELECTED
# BIBLIOGRAPHY

# SELECTED BIBLIOGRAPHY

*Abridged WebDewey*. Dublin, OH: OCLC, 2002– .

*Anglo-American Cataloguing Rules*. 2nd ed. 2002 revision. Prepared under the direction of the Joint Steering Committee for Revision of AACR, a committee of the American Library Association, the Australian Committee on Cataloguing, the British Library, the Canadian Committee on Cataloguing, Chartered Institute of Library and Information Professionals, the Library of Congress. Chicago: American Library Association, 2002.

Beall, Julienne. "Dewey for Windows." In Green, *Knowledge Organization and Change*, 396–405.

_____. "Editing the Dewey Decimal Classification Online: The Evaluation of the DDC Database." In Williamson and Hudon, *Classification Research for Knowledge Representation and Organization*, 29–37.

Boll, John J. "DDC Classification Rules: An Outline History and Comparison of Two Sets of Rules." *Cataloging & Classification Quarterly* 8, no. 2 (1987): 49–70.

Chan, Lois, Mai. *Cataloging and Classification*. 2nd ed. New York: McGraw-Hill, 1994.

_____. "Classification, Present and Future." *Cataloging & Classification Quarterly* 21, no. 2 (1995): 5–17.

_____. "Exploiting LCSH, LCC, and DDC to Retrieve Networked Resources: Issues and Challenges." In *Proceedings of the Bicentennial Conference on Bibliographic Control for the New Millennium: Confronting the Challenges of Networked Resources and the Web, Washington, D.C., November 15–17, 2000, sponsored by the Library of Congress Cataloging Directorate*, edited by Ann M. Sandberg-Fox, 159–78. Washington, DC: Library of Congress, Cataloging Distribution Service, 2001.

Cochrane, Pauline A., and Eric Johnson. "Visual Dewey: DDC in a Hypertextual Browser for the Library User." In Green, *Knowledge Organization and Change*, 95–106.

Comaromi, John P. *Book Numbers: A Historical Study and Practical Guide to Their Use*. Littleton, CO: Libraries Unlimited, 1981.

_____. "Conception and Development of the Dewey Decimal Classification." *International Classification* 3, no. 1 (1976): 11–15.

_____. "Dewey, Melvil, 1851–1931." In *ALA World Encyclopedia of Library and Information Services*, 2nd ed., 248–50. Chicago: American Library Association, 1986.

_____. *The Eighteen Editions of the Dewey Decimal Classification*. Albany, NY: Forest Press, 1976.

Comaromi, John P., and Peter J. Paulson. "The Dewey Decimal Classification Approaches the 21st Century." In *Information Communications and Technology Transfer*, edited by E. V. Smith and S. Keenan, 469–75. New York and Amsterdam: Elsevier, 1987.

Comaromi, John P., and Margaret J. Warren. *Manual on the Use of the Dewey Decimal Classification: Edition 19*. Albany, NY: Forest Press, 1982.

Dewey, Melvil. *004–006 Data Processing and Computer Science and Changes in Related Disciplines*. Prepared by Julianne Beall et al. Albany, NY: Forest Press, 1985.

_____. *Abridged Dewey Decimal Classification and Relative Index*. Edition 14. Edited by Joan S. Mitchell, Julianne Beall, Giles Martin, Winton E. Matthews, Jr., and Gregory R. New. Dublin, OH: OCLC, 2004.

_____. *A Classification and Subject Index for Cataloguing and Arranging the Books and Pamphlets of a Library*. Amherst, MA: Printed by the Case, Lockwood & Brainard Co., 1876. Reprinted as *Dewey Decimal Classification, Centennial 1876–1976,* by Forest Press Division, Lake Placid Education Foundation. Kingsport, TN: Kingsport Press, 1976.

_____. "Decimal Classification Beginnings." *Library Journal* 45 (February 15, 1920): 151–54. Reprinted in *Library Journal* 115 (June 15, 1990): 87–90.

_____. *Dewey Decimal Classification and Relative Index*. Edition 22. Edited by Joan S. Mitchell, Julianne Beall, Giles Martin, Winton E. Matthews, Jr., and Gregory R. New. 4 vols. Dublin, OH: OCLC, 2003.

_____. *Dewey Decimal Classification and Relative Index*. Edition 21. Edited by Joan S. Mitchell, Julianne Beall, Winton E. Matthews, Jr., and Gregory R. New. 4 vols. Albany, NY: OCLC Forest Press, 1996.

_____. *Dewey Decimal Classification and Relative Index*. Edition 20. Edited by John P. Comaromi, Julianne Beall, Winton E. Matthews, Jr., and Gregory R. New. 4 vols. Albany, NY: OCLC Forest Press, 1989.

*Dewey for Windows*. Dublin, OH: OCLC Forest Press, 1996–2001.

Drabenstott, Karen Markey, and others. "Analysis of a Bibliographic Database Enhanced with a Library Classification." *Library Resources & Technical Services* 34, no. 2 (April 1990): 179–98.

*Electronic Dewey*. Dublin, OH: OCLC, 1993–1994.

*Ethnologue*. 14th ed. Dallas, TX: Summer Institute of Linguistics, 2000. Also available at www.sil.org/ethnologue.

Foskett, A. C. *The Subject Approach to Information*. 5th ed. London: Library Association, 1996.

Gorman, Michael. "The Longer the Number, the Smaller the Spine, or Up and Down with Melvil and Elsie." *American Libraries* 12, no. 8 (1981): 498–99.

Green, Rebecca, ed. *Knowledge Organization and Change: Proceedings of the 4th International ISKO Conference, Washington, DC, USA, 1996.* Frankfurt/Main: INDEKS Verlag, 1996.

Hinton, Frances. [Review of the Dewey Decimal Classification]. *Library Resources & Technical Services* 10 (Summer 1966): 393–402.

Holley, Robert P., ed. *Dewey: An International Perspective: Papers from a Workshop on the Dewey Decimal Classification and DDC 20 Presented at the General Conference of the International Federation of Library Associations and Institutions (IFLA), Paris, France, 1989.* Munich: K.G. Saur, 1991.

Hyman, Richard. *Shelf Access in Libraries.* Chicago: American Library Association, 1982.

International Organization for Standardization. *ISO 999:1996, Guidelines for the Content, Organization, and Presentation of Indexes.* Geneva: ISO, 1996.

Koch, Traugott, Heike Neuroth, and Michael Day. "Renardus: Cross-browsing European Subject Gateways via a Common Classification System (DDC)." In *Subject Retrieval in a Networked Environment: Proceedings of the IFLA Satellite Meeting Held in Dublin, OH, 14–16 August 2001 and Sponsored by the IFLA Classification and Indexing Section, the IFLA Information Technology Section and OCLC,* edited by Ia C. McIlwaine, 25–33. Munich: K.G. Saur, 2003.

Lehnus, Donald J. *Book Numbers: History, Principles, and Applications.* Chicago: American Library Association, 1980.

Liu, Songqiao. "The Automatic Decomposition of DDC Synthesized Numbers." Ph.D. diss., University of California, Los Angeles, 1993.

Liu, Songqiao, and Elaine Svenonius. "DORS: DDC Online Retrieval System (Model Online Catalog Interface)." *Library Resources & Technical Services* 35 (October 1991): 359–75.

Markey, Karen, and Anh N. Demeyer. *Dewey Decimal Classification Online Project: Evaluation of a Library Schedule and Index Integrated into the Subject Searching Capabilities of an Online Catalog: Final Report to the Council on Library Resources.* Dublin, OH: OCLC Online Computer Library Center, 1986. Report No. OCLC/OPR/RR-86/1.

Merrill, W.S. *Code for Classifiers: Principles Governing the Consistent Placing of Books in a System of Classification.* Chicago: American Library Association, 1969.

Miksa, Francis. "The DDC, the Universe of Knowledge, and the Post-modern Library." In Green, *Knowledge Organization and Change,* 406–12.

Mitchell, Joan S. "DDC 21 and Beyond: The Dewey Decimal Classification Prepares for the Future." *Cataloging & Classification Quarterly* 21, no. 2 (1995): 37–47.

_____. "The Dewey Decimal Classification at 120: Edition 21 and Beyond." In Green, *Knowledge Organization and Change*, 378–85.

_____. "Flexible Structures in the Dewey Decimal Classification." *Knowledge Organization* 25, no. 4 (1998): 156–58.

_____. "Options in the Dewey Decimal Classification System: The Current Perspective." *Cataloging & Classification Quarterly* 19, no. 3/4 (1995): 89–103.

_____. "Relationships in the Dewey Decimal Classification System." In *Relationships in the Organization of Knowledge*, edited by Carol A. Bean and Rebecca Green, 211–26. Dordrecht: Kluwer Academic, 2001.

Mitchell, Joan S., and Mark A. Crook. "A Study of Libraries Using the Dewey Decimal Classification in the OCLC Online Union Catalog: Preliminary Findings." In *Annual Review of OCLC Research 1994*, 47–50. Dublin, OH: OCLC, 1995.

New, Gregory R. "Revising Life Sciences in Dewey Edition 21." In Green, *Knowledge Organization and Change*, 386–95.

Paulson, Peter J. "Dewey into the 90s." *The Bookmark* (Albany, NY) 47 (Spring 1989): 176–78. Paper presented at an ALA Workshop on DDC 20 at the 1989 ALA Conference.

*People, Places & Things: A List of Popular Library of Congress Subject Headings with Dewey Numbers*. Dublin, OH: OCLC, 2001.

Sears, Minnie Earl. *Sears List of Subject Headings*. 18th ed. Edited by Joseph Miller. New York: H.W. Wilson, 2004.

Svenonius, Elaine, Songqiao Liu, and Bhagirathi Subrahmanyam. "Automation of Chain Indexing." In Williamson and Hudon, *Classification Research for Knowledge Representation and Organization*, 351–64.

Taylor, Arlene. *Wynar's Introduction to Cataloging and Classification*. 9th ed. Englewood, CO: Libraries Unlimited, 2000.

Vizine-Goetz, Diane. "Cataloging Productivity Tools." In *Annual Review of OCLC Research 1994*, 15–20. Dublin, OH: OCLC, 1995.

_____. "The Dewey Decimal Classification as an Online Classification Tool." In Williamson and Hudon, *Classification Research for Knowledge Representation and Organization*, 373–80.

_____. "Dewey in CORC: Classification in Metadata and Pathfinders." In *CORC: New Tools and Possibilities for Cooperative Electronic Resource Description*, edited by Karen Calhoun and John H. Riemer, 67–80. Binghamton, NY: Haworth, 2001. Co-published simultaneously in *Journal of Internet Cataloging* 4, no. 1/2 (2001): 67–80.

_____. "Online Classification: Implications for Classifying and Document[-like Object] Retrieval." In Green, *Knowledge Organization and Change*, 249–53.

Waldhart, Thomas J., Joseph B. Miller, and Lois Mai Chan. "Provision of Local Assisted Access to Selected Internet Information Resources by ARL Academic Libraries." *Journal of Academic Librarianship* 26, no. 2 (2000): 100–109.

*WebDewey*. Dublin, OH: OCLC, 2000– .

Williamson, Nancy J., and Michèle Hudon, eds. *Classification Research for Knowledge Representation and Organization: Proceedings of the 5th International Study Conference on Classification Research, Toronto, Canada, 1991*. New York and Amsterdam: Elsevier, 1992.

Winkel, Lois, ed. *Subject Headings for Children: A List of Subject Headings Used by the Library of Congress with Abridged Dewey Numbers Added*. 2nd ed., numbers verified by Winton E. Matthews, Jr. 2 vols. Albany, NY: OCLC Forest Press, 1998.

Wursten, Richard B., comp. *In Celebration of Revised 780: Music in Dewey Decimal Classification Edition 20*. MLA Technical Report No. 19. Canton, MA: Music Library Association, 1990.

# INDEX

# INDEX

**Dewey Decimal Classification: Principles and Application** was designed and composed in Times New Roman and Arial typefaces by Lisa Hanifan of Lisa Hanifan/ Graphic Design, Albany, New York. The book was printed and bound by Edwards Brothers, Inc., Ann Arbor, Michigan.